CORVETTE®

FIFTY 50 YEARS

Written by Randy Leffingwell
Photographed by Randy Leffingwell and David Newhardt

MBI Publishing Company

First published in 2002 by MBI Publishing Company, Galtier Plaza, Suite 200, 380 Jackson Street, St. Paul, MN 55101-3885 USA

The information in this book is true and complete to the best of our knowledge. All recommendations are made without any guarantee on the part of the author or Publisher, who also disclaim any liability incurred in connection with the use of this data or specific details.

We recognize that some words, model names and designations, for example, mentioned herein are the property of the trademark holder. We use them for identification purposes only. This is not an official publication.

MBI Publishing Company books are also available at discounts in bulk quantity for industrial or sales-promotional use. For details write to Special Sales Manager at Motorbooks International Wholesalers & Distributors, Galtier Plaza, Suite 200, 380 Jackson Street, St. Paul, MN 55101-3885 USA.

Library of Congress Cataloging-in-Publication Data Available
ISBN 0-7603-1180-3

On the Front Cover:,
The Stingray was as aggressive as it looked. Properly equipped, the car was capable of quarter-mile times in the 13-second range. *David Newhardt*

On the Endpaper: The radical cowl-induction hood scoop looked cool—an important consideration in the muscle-car era—but more importantly it made the car faster. It increased horsepower by drawing in cool air for the engine and improved aerodynamics by venting the high-pressure area at the base of the windshield. *David Newhardt*

On the Frontispiece: Jim Jeffords, SCCA B-production national champion in both 1958 and 1959, painted his 1959 Corvette purple, a color inspired by the then-popular song "The Purple People Eater."

On the Title Page: There's no way you'd mistake this low-slung sports car as anything but a Corvette. The 2002 Z06 model shown here gave the C5 real credibility with racers.

On the Back Cover: During the 1970s, removable roof panels—known as "T-tops"—replaced the convertible top as the preferred configuration for open-air motoring. *David Newhardt*

Edited by Darwin Holmstrom

Designed by Stephanie Michaud

Printed in Hong Kong

Disclaimer Notice:
"The information contained herein is for your enjoyment and intended to be accurate. Because General Motors and its licensing representative, Equity Management Inc., have not specifically reviewed this information, they assume no responsibility or liability for any inaccuracies or omissions, nor make any warranties or representations regarding this Product."

Trademark Notice:
CHEVROLET, CHEVY, Chevrolet "Bow Tie" emblems, CORVETTE and VETTE, GRAND SPORT, STINGRAY, ZR-1, CORVETTE 50th ANNIVERSARY LIMITED EDITION are General Motors Trademarks used under license to MBI Publishing Company.

CONTENTS

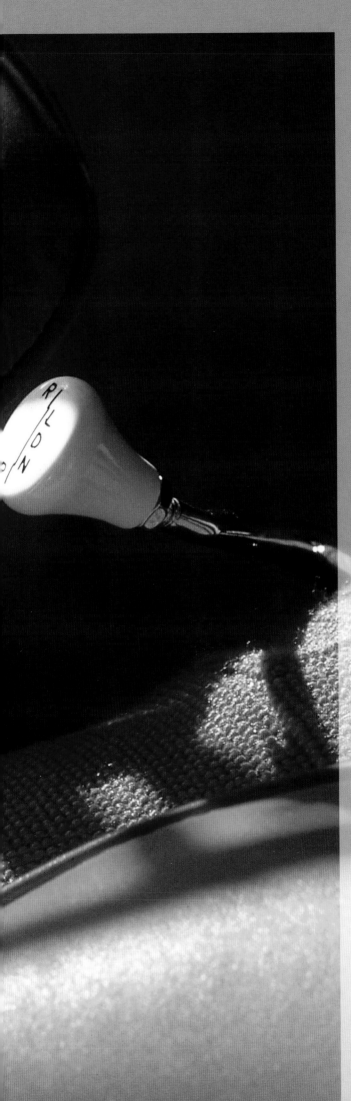

FOREWORD

Celebrations are important to everyone associated with Chevrolet. Whether it's to acknowledge a record sales month for one of our product lines, the recognition by a magazine for a vehicle's outstanding qualities, or taking of the checkered flag at one of the many hundreds of motorsports events held throughout the season, it's a reason to be proud.

It was just a year ago that our division turned 90. When the first vehicle rolled through the doors of Louis Chevrolet's small shop in 1911, little did he know that the cars and trucks that carried his name would become the cornerstone of corporate parent General Motors' success.

A multitude of product lines have worn the Chevrolet name. While a few are no longer around, many still command great respect for their perseverance and success in the ever-changing marketplace. One of the most famous Chevrolets of all—Corvette— will celebrate its 50th anniversary on June 30, 2003.

For all of those fifty years, Corvette has remained true to its two-seat sports car heritage. Carefully crafted from a precise blend of power, performance, style, and comfort, Chevrolet's flagship continues to reign as one of GM's design and technology bellwethers. A fiberglass body, 'T-top' removable roof panels, and a fiberglass-reinforced monoleaf rear spring are among many mass-production firsts introduced on Corvette.

No single vehicle in automotive history has a heritage as rich or as celebrated. Corvette has been the only American-produced performance car to consistently challenge the world's top sports cars, both in its on-track achievements and its popularity with consumers. With total sales of nearly $1.2 million, it has become not only America's favorite sports car but also a true American icon.

When the first Corvette rolled off a makeshift assembly line in Flint, Michigan, the Corvette "enthusiast" had not yet been born. Over the following decades, however, there has been a Corvette revolution as evidenced by the numerous owners' clubs in the United States and around the globe. As if further testament is required, the independently-operated National Corvette Museum in Bowling Green, Kentucky, is the only museum in the world dedicated to showcasing the history of a single vehicle line.

There is simply nothing to compare with the dedication of every man and woman who has had a part in designing, developing, manufacturing, marketing, and selling this great automotive nameplate. Nor is there any doubt that Corvette owners are the most devoted enthusiasts imaginable.

As we celebrate Corvette's golden anniversary, we must honor the glorious past yet stay focused as we cast a bright eye toward what we envision for the future. Those fortunate enough to shape that future promise that it will continue, make Chevrolet proud.

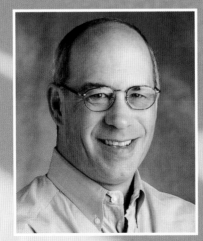

Kurt Ritter

Kurt Ritter
Chevrolet General Manager

ACKNOWLEDGMENTS

Dedication: For my son, Paul, with admiration for his taste in cars and for his decisions in life.

My sincere thanks to Peter Brock, Redmond, Washington, for providing his extraordinary photos of the C5R racing efforts. Peter has chronicled this effort from the rollout, and as designer of the legendary Cobra Daytona Coupe, brings an unmatched perspective to his racing coverage. I am further grateful to Gayle and Peter for their generous hospitality and ongoing encouragement.

I also wish to thank fellow author Mike Mueller, Atlanta, Georgia, for his help and the introductions he made to collectors in the southeast.

I am extremely grateful to John L. Stein, editor of *Corvette Quarterly*, for opening his files to me and for generously allowing me to quote from the magazine. As the journal-of-record of this fine automobile, this publication was an immeasurable help in filling many of the holes I uncovered in other histories.

While many car owners proved heroic in their help and encouragement while shooting the photos for this book, I want to single out Kenn Funk, Glendale, California, whose 1969 L88 we rolled out for multiple photo shoots. His patience never flagged. Thank you so much, Kenn.

I visited the four corners of the United States to find and photograph significant cars for this book, logging 23,000 miles by the time it was done.

Tom and Susan Armstrong, Issaquah, Washington; Sheldon Aubut, Esko, Minnesota; Laverne Berha, my best friend in Texas, Houston, Texas; Ellen Bierly and Jan Leyden, Indianapolis Motor Speedway Museum, Speedway, Indiana; John Carefoot, Cincinnati, Ohio; Otis and Bettina Chandler, Ojai, California; Steve and Debbie Earle, Buellton, California; Dave and Jan Ferguson, Quartz Hill, California; Marty Fowler, Kennett, Missouri; Henry and Rita Fuchs, Oxnard, California; Kris Gardner, Camarillo, California; Jim and Dee Gessner, Mentone, California; Steve and Keith Goldin, Homestead, Florida; Bill and Sandie Herron, Sarasota, Florida; David and Merideth Hmura, Homer Glen, Illinois; Mark Hyman, St. Louis, Missouri; Jim and Nancy Jaeger, Indian Hill, Ohio; Doug and Carol Johnson, Maryland Heights, Missouri; Roger Judski and David Judski Jr., Roger's Corvette's, Maitland, Florida; Ralph Kramer, Indianapolis, Indiana; Leslie Krause, Santa Paula, California; Bob and Cheryl Lawton, San Jose, California; Kevin Mackay, Corvette Repair, Inc., Valley Stream, New York; Larry Martin, Houston, Texas; Rich and Shar Mason, Carson City, Nevada; Chip Miller, Carlisle, Pennsylvania; Leonard and Marjorie and son Jonathan "Hoss" Nagel, Buena Park, California; John and Sally Neas, Tulsa, Oklahoma; Kent Rockwell, Orcutt, California; Glen Spielberg, Merrick, New York; Robert Taylor, Santa Barbara, California; David and Cynthia Thurber, Santa Barbara, California; Bob Tomczak, Wauconda, Illinois; Bill and Betty Tower, Plant City, Florida; Ed and Linda Van Scoy, Gilbert, Arizona; Dave Wiehle, Cortland, Illinois; Mike and Laurie Yager and Nathan Sheets, Mid-America Direct, Effingham, Illinois; Harry Yeaggy, Cincinnati, Ohio.

My deepest thanks go to Jim Gessner, Mentone, California, for his tireless efforts in unearthing fantastic cars and wonderful stories, and for his careful and detailed scrutiny of my text.

Equal gratitude goes to Ed Wittwer, Corvette Service, Inc., Carpenteria, California, for his countless introductions, his gentle manner and his limitless enthusiasm and encouragement.

At MBI Publishing Company, I want to thank my editor, Darwin Holmstrom, for his patience, direction, and wisdom, and Senior Editor Lee Klancher for years of making me a better writer and a more focused photographer.

Almost last but far from least is my friend and fellow author/photographer David Newhardt, Pasadena, California. David, a *Motor Trend* staffer, came to my rescue as the deadline approached, tirelessly filling in countless shoots for me and adding his wonderful images to this book. He and Susan were with me as the saga of this book became one of the most significant journeys of my life, and I'm forever grateful for their friendship.

Standing beside me on that same demanding journey were my dearest friends, Otis and Bettina Chandler, whose love and encouragement are indescribable sources of strength and peace to me.

Finally, to my best friend and partner, Carolyn, thank you for everything. You have helped me become the man I want to be. I love you.

—Randy Leffingwell, Santa Barbara, California

CHAPTER ONE

A NEAR INEVITABILITY

he Corvette could only have come from General Motors. This is not just because Chevrolet general manager Tom Keating, chief engineer Ed Cole, and vice president of styling Harley Earl agreed this new car would be badged as a Chevrolet. It was more involved than that. The Corvette resulted from 30 years of work by GM's greatest thinker, Alfred Pritchard Sloan. Sloan and Donaldson Brown together devised a far-sighted management strategy in the early 1920s. Brown became Sloan's co-conspirator in the years after GM's board elected Sloan president in May 1923. By then, these two men had undone the conglomerate mess that their former boss, the entrepreneurial automobile enthusiast William Crapo Durant, had left behind.

Durant was the father of General Motors. He envisioned a system in which GM owned and controlled every part and product needed to manufacture his automobiles. The term for this, *vertical integration,* was not coined yet. What Durant created was a less laudable free will among the companies he owned. By the time he walked out in December 1920, his system had devolved into a corporate free-for-all. Durant had too many automakers producing too many similar models at too near the same price with no central control.

The healthy post–World War I U.S. economy collapsed in 1920 as Europe's recovery hit full speed. The recession hit hard in the United States. The fundamental difference between Billy Durant's car company and Henry Ford's operations took giant General Motors down to second place. In the best of times, Durant's products competed with one another. As money tightened, he had no small, basic, cheap car to sell, as Ford did. Durant soon had no corporate income.

Sloan joined GM in 1916. Brown arrived at GM when Pierre S. du Pont stepped in to become GM president as part of the du Pont's *(previous pages) For half a century, the Corvette has defined the American sports car.*

Called Anniversary Red, this one-year-only color is part of the optional package Chevrolet created to celebrate half a century of its sports car. The 50th Anniversary package was available on coupes and convertibles only, and not for the Z06. 2002 General Motors Corporation. Used with permission of GM Media Archives.

Ed Cole was chief engineer at Chevy in 1952. Cole and Earl worked together to create a running prototype to present to Keating and GM president Harlow Curtice for production approval. 2002 General Motors Corporation. Used with permission of GM Media Archives.

efforts to bail GM out of its enormous troubles in 1921. With du Pont in place as the hard decision maker, Brown became GM's financial brain and Sloan became its backbone. Together, they made something rational out of the chaos.

Brown, Sloan, and du Pont monitored each company's performance individually, examining and revising GM's entire product lineup. By late 1921, they offered cars ranging from $700 Chevrolets to $6,000 Cadillacs.

A clay mock-up of the 1953 Corvette in the design studio. 2002 General Motors Corporation. Used with permission of GM Media Archives.

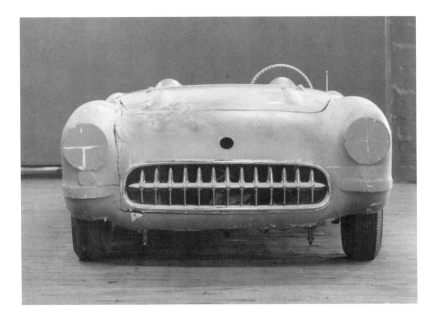

Brown established the goal of achieving the highest possible return on rate of investment, a theory that guides most successful companies today. Sloan and Brown believed the purpose of any company was to protect and enrich the investment of its owners, stockholders—in GM's case—a philosophy that would affect product decisions to this day. He and Brown accepted delayed corporate gratification, as Sloan wrote years later in his autobiography, *My Years with General Motors.* "The question is not simply one of maximizing the rate of return for a specific short period of time. Mr. Brown's thought on this was that the fundamental consideration was [to achieve] an average return over a long period of time." If ever any single product in automotive history demanded patience to achieve its return on

investment, it was Chevrolet's sports car. That was only one of several elements needed for the Corvette to succeed, however.

As Arthur Kuhn wrote in his book, *GM Passes Ford 1918–1938,* Brown and Sloan recognized that offering an automobile "exclusive in design, possessing superior engineering qualities and carrying with it a peculiar appeal to fashion afforded the opportunity for a favorable rate of return." This, as Brown wrote in his own book, *Some Reminiscences of an Industrialist,* required "ingenuity in anticipating the changing tastes of the buying public." They levered that philosophy into place and pressed forward in other ways that enabled the corporation to serve its stockholders best.

A CAR FOR EVERY PURSE

It was Sloan who, as early as 1921, had verbalized the evolving General Motors philosophy as a slogan: "A car for every purse and purpose." By 1925, Sloan and du Pont recognized a growing market in Europe for their cars, but they concluded it was wiser to buy an existing company and its products and factories than to start from scratch. GM acquired major interests in Vauxhall Automobiles in the United Kingdom and Adam Opel A. G. in Germany. At home, new customers were created when GM began financing purchases of its cars. It not only brought in first-time buyers, it benefited shareholders who realized there were new profits in interest payments. By late 1925, General Motors produced one of every five automobiles sold in the United States and kept one dollar in every three dollars of profit the auto industry reaped.

Sloan demanded his divisions communicate with each other on everything from engineering to advertising. He and other vice presidents began touring the United States and Europe to see firsthand new mechanical and engineering developments and styling trends. "I tried to keep my eyes open for any new things that applied to the automobile industry," he recalled years later. He and Donaldson Brown created a Policy Group for Social and Economic Trends that monitored the effects of these conditions on present and future plans.

Alfred Sloan was among the first of America's corporate pillars to recognize that product appearance influenced sales. Sloan described the revelation in his autobiography. The Auburn Automobile Company introduced 1924 models with fully enclosed bodies (in contrast to Ford's still open Model Ts). The new Auburns, mechanically identical to the previous year, featured "advanced styling and coloring. A sweeping belt line . . . often painted in contrasting colors [that] gave a striking impression." Sloan and Brown took note when Auburn's revenue losses from 1923 turned to gains before 1925.

(left) The second-generation Corvette featured optional big-block engines, moving Corvette to the forefront of the muscle car movement.

GM chairman Alfred Sloan hired Harley Earl in 1927 from his Hollywood family car-body business to create the "Art and Colour Section," the world's first styling department. By dictating that Earl's department restyle GM cars each year, Sloan is credited for introducing planned obsolescence. 2002 General Motors Corporation. Used with permission of GM Media Archives.

By the time the Corvette celebrated its 25th anniversary in 1978 the engine had lost some of its steam because of pollution controls, but the Corvette still provided more excitement than most cars available at that time.

Lawrence P. Fisher, general manager of Cadillac division and one of the founding brothers of Fisher Body (the corporation's body maker but still outside GM at this point), agreed with Sloan that GM would benefit by paying more attention to the cars' appearance. Cadillac still sold bare chassis to wealthy clients who wanted to be seen in personalized custom vehicles. One of Cadillac's Los Angeles dealers, Don Lee, had acquired J. W. Earl Automobile Works, a custom coach-building firm, eight years earlier. Many of Lee's customers were Hollywood stars, flashy, trend-setting people who wanted cars that reflected their screen images and, more important, were different from anyone else's.

J. W. Earl had started in 1911 making custom car and truck bodies as service vehicles and props for the emerging talking-film industry. By 1918, when it showed its first complete automobiles at the L.A. Auto Show, Earl occupied its own three-story, block-long building south of downtown Los Angeles. Earl's Stanford University–educated son, Harley, had designed not only car bodies but also airplane fuselages for the Glen L. Martin Company, one of southern California's earliest aircraft manufacturers. Airplane lines and contours were part of Harley Earl's post-Stanford education.

Fisher first visited Harley Earl in early 1925. He watched the 32-year-old designer forming scale models of cars in clay. This technique let Earl experiment with lines, shapes, and reflections of light before committing to large-scale wood mock-ups. Earl blended fender lines into running

Cadillac boss Lawrence Fisher hired Earl to create the 1927 LaSalle, the industry's first car designed by a stylist instead of an engineer.

Harley Earl initiated and ran the styling department at GM until he retired in 1959. His credits include tail fins and the original Corvette. 2002 General Motors Corporation. Used with permission of GM Media Archives.

The Corvette recaptured its lost performance when the fourth-generation car was introduced for the 1984 model year.

boards, hoods into windshields, engine compartment sheet metal into body side panels. For Fisher this was a revelation. At most American car makers, the chassis engineering division designed and delivered its frame complete with the engine, hood, radiator, running gear, suspension, wheels, tires, and fenders to each body division, which bolted on its own passenger compartment, each element conceived independently. Fisher saw Earl with shapes that appeared molded from one piece and cast from one mind.

Fisher brought Sloan photographs. They had a new entry-level Cadillac for spring 1927 called the LaSalle, part of Sloan's effort to fill holes in GM's price range. They hired Earl as a consultant to design a car as beautiful as his customs. While he was in Detroit, Fisher showed him working drawings of the 1927 Cadillacs. Fisher and Sloan now feared these would be overshadowed by Earl's LaSalle. Harley pronounced the Cadillacs drab but thought that fitting wire wheels would at least lower them, making them appear longer and more dramatic. He suggested using bright paint. Cadillac in 1924 had

offered three colors for its model range. "Hollywood Harley" recommended they offer cars in any of 500 color and interior options.

The LaSalle turned heads and brought the buyers into showrooms. Sales of the Cadillacs brought Earl back to General Motors to head Sloan's newest creation, the Art and Colour Section, starting on July 27, 1927. Answering only to Sloan, he was to direct the design of general production cars and do research and development work by creating additional special car designs.

Not until September 1940 did his promotion to vice president of a renamed styling section give him the title to match his impact. This came partially as the result of a highly visible failure in 1929. Earl designed a car for Buick, GM's most profitable division since 1918. He intended for the car body to fit down inside the chassis, but the engineering department "redesigned" it so it would mount onto its existing chassis without any additional work. Preoccupied by design assignments that followed the Buick, Earl never saw the car after its designs left his studio in late 1927.

The design would have been a gorgeous and bold leap from the previous model. With engineering's revisions, it was a disaster, quickly dubbed the "pregnant Buick." Division sales plummeted and Sloan pulled it from production after only one year. The damage was brutal; the Depression, which began in October 1929, hit Buick the hardest of any GM division, turning the once profitable nameplate into a money-losing division.

Earl escaped unscathed. Sloan reacted decisively. He tightened his authority over manufacturing and production engineers. The Buick clarified for everyone the impact of successful and awful design. It fathered another GM innovation: the annual model change. Previously, successful car builders updated their models whenever improvements were ready, generally shutting down production to instigate the changes. Sloan first observed this new effect in 1924 among weaker competitors Hudson, Dodge, and Chrysler, who, in that year's shrinking market, brought out new models with heavy promotion and experienced a healthy and enduring surge in sales. Sloan's sales department began to capitalize on this phenomenon. "Each year," he wrote in his autobiography, "we build the best car we possibly can to satisfy our customer, and then the next year we build another to make him dissatisfied." There was sound Sloan-Brown business sense to this. "The primary object of the corporation," he wrote, "was to make money, not just to make motor cars."

When Earl's 1933 Chevrolets were introduced, the public, startled by the bulging curves and uneasy proportions of the 1929 Buick, loved them. People called the cars stylish, judging the overall design unified. The success of these cars led the public to label their creators "stylists."

Over the years Chevrolet has produced several limited edition cars to celebrate the Corvette's being chosen as the official pace car for the Indianapolis 500. This is a 1998 example.

Mitchell's Sting Ray was somewhat street legal, and he used it as a daily driver to commute to work. 2002 General Motors Corporation. Used with permission of GM Media Archives.

Some within GM called Earl's department "the beauty parlor," but their opinions changed as year-end reports tallied each division's performance. Sloan was an advocate from the start, and Earl's influence grew.

"For a long while," Sloan wrote, "the Art and Colour Section occupied quarters in the General Motors Building Annex in Detroit. The focal point of the work area was the blackboard room. To this room came executives from Fisher Body and every car division. We were all window-shoppers in the Art and Colour 'sales' rooms," he continued. "Art and Colour was proposing new designs, presenting new idea sketches, selling progress. As time went by more and more of these ideas appeared to be feasible."

Earl first visited Europe for GM in 1927 with Lawrence Fisher, calling on every car manufacturer and car body maker they could get in to see. They learned that what worked in one part of the world would not be appropriate in another. Some ideas would succeed only if they were adapted and modified to match GM's assessment of what was good for America and good for GM customers.

World War II ended in Europe in May 1945 and in Japan in August. Years of hard work and good wages with few goods available for consumers had left Americans with pent-up desires, especially for products using steel or rubber, two materials critical to war efforts. When North Korea invaded South Korea on June 25, 1950, it seemed worrying but distant. Americans went to fight because it became clear that communism was the real enemy, but it was another war thousands of miles away. It need not interrupt the return to American life that many had begun anxiously.

In 1950, there were 1.5 million television sets in America. A year later there would be 15 million sets. In November 1952, Americans elected General Dwight David "Ike" Eisenhower their next president. Eisenhower represented the battle against the Red Menace, the political code name for the threat of communism taking over the world. He quickly authorized an interstate highway system, similar to the auto routes, autobahns, and autostradi of Europe. The long, smooth American roads, meant for efficient movement of U.S. armed forces, fueled a hunger for automobiles. The country was developing a middle class that had enough money to pay its bills with some left over. Leisure time became a concept and then a reality, and the automobile helped. By December 1, 1950, the United States had 2,200 drive-in theaters, double the year before. Magazines and newspapers questioned whether or not automobiles would kill movie theaters.

By the early 1950s, air conditioning, radios, and automatic transmissions were primary options that General Motors intended to fit as standard equipment on all but its lowest priced products. GM felt these were what Americans wanted most in their cars. With some 80 models in their production line-up in the early 1950s, the central office fulfilled Alfred Sloan's promise to offer a car for every purse and purpose. Earl's blackboards revealed a new car Harley hoped one of the divisions would buy, one he knew needed GM's touch. It was a sports car that he felt sure Mr. Sloan's successor, the corporation's new chairman, Charles E. Wilson, would see as "exclusive in design, possessing superior engineering qualities and carrying with it a peculiar appeal to fashion [that] afforded the opportunity for a favorable rate of return."

Corvette reintroduced the Z06 version of the Corvette in the fall of 2000. This latest Z06 is the fastest standard-production Corvette yet.

1950-1952

CHAPTER TWO

COMPETITION
CREATES A WATERSHED

ebster's New World Dictionary defines a watershed as "a ridge or stretch of land dividing the areas drained by different rivers or river systems." It also says it's "a crucial turning point affecting action, opinion, etc." Chevrolet's sports car was both of these. Several independent events, forces outside Chevrolet and General Motors, flowing like separate rivers, moved toward one single point in the early 1950s. They gathered speed, power, and mass as they tumbled toward Chevrolet's crucial turning point.

The first of these forces was organized labor. Motivated by patriotism, its members had worked hard during World War II, but by 1950 workers had grown restive. When the government lifted wartime wage and price controls, the United Auto Workers (UAW) sought pay raises. Unhappy with Chrysler's offer, they struck the number three automaker on January 24, 1950, and stayed out for 100 days. GM's President Charlie Wilson would not risk his corporation. Chevrolet had just passed Ford sales for the first time since 1927, selling more than one million cars in 1949. These had been restyled with Harley Earl's supervision under new Chevrolet studio chief Ed Glowacke. GM settled a five-year benchmark contract with autoworkers on May 23. A month later, on June 25, North Korea invaded South Korea, and a world that had seemed safe and secure for automakers and their workers began to change.

Within a year the United States had committed 2.9 million troops and Chevrolet was occupied with its largest military contract ever, manufacturing Allison J-35 turbojet engines at its Tonawanda, New York, plant. This consumed factory floor space and its labor force. In its automobile line, Chevrolet lagged behind Ford sales in convertibles and station wagons, a fact that told division general manager Thomas H. Keating that Chevrolet held little interest among younger buyers, with families and without. Yet Chevrolet, despite outselling Ford again in 1950, was tapped out from jet engine production and a slowing *(previous pages) This was the optimist's view of the future, deeply ingrained in the minds and hearts of U.S. industrialists: Americans, flush with post war self-confidence, zooming toward tomorrow in a car like none of them had seen before.*

Within months Jaguar knew it had a winner and re-engineered the car to accept a steel body, ultimately producing 12,078 examples between 1949 and 1954. They introduced a coupe in 1951 and a convertible in 1953. The car's 10-second 0–60 miles-per-hour time and 120 miles-per-hour top speed (hence its "XK-120" designation) inspired Harley Earl.

Briggs Weaver designed two identical roadsters and a coupe for Cunningham. They weighed 2,400 pounds, nearly 900 pounds less than Cunningham's previous racing models, and these new cars were slightly smaller as well.

economy. It couldn't afford to restyle its cars for 1953, although Ford would have new models in 1952. Keating approached GM's engineering policy committee (another Sloan/Brown instigation) and convinced committee members that Chevrolet's conservatism was hurting its sales. He felt its reliance on six-cylinder engines exemplified the condition, particularly when Detroit's best-kept secret was Ford's eminent overhead-valve V-8 (which would arrive for the 1954 model year). After seeing Ford's smart new 1952 models in late December 1951, Wilson agreed to help Keating turn Chevrolet around. In early January 1952, he told the Chevrolet chief he could have anything, or anyone, he needed to improve Chevrolet. Keating identified Ed Cole, the Cadillac engineer who had managed the development team responsible for Cadillac's 331-cubic-inch displacement, 210-horsepower, short-stroke high-compression, overhead-valve V-8 in 1949.

Ed Cole graduated from the GM Institute in December 1932 and promptly joined the Cadillac division as an engineer. Eighteen years later, racer Briggs Cunningham entered the 1950 Le Mans race with a Cadillac-V-8-engined Ford, the Fordillac. Then he learned from race organizers he could only race production-based cars or pure prototypes. Stymied, he contacted Cadillac's chief engineer, Cole, who suggested Cunningham run Cadillac Coupe de Villes. Cole tested Cunningham's Fordillac on the chassis dynamometer, and from what he learned, he designed a five-carburetor manifold for the GM cars. He also helped Cunningham prepare an ungainly prototype dubbed "Le Monstre." Finally, he loaned him a Cadillac engineer, Frank Burrell, who went along to the race. (The coupe finished the race in 10th place; Le Monstre came in 11th.) In early 1952, Cole was supervising Cadillac's production of the army's T-41 tank at GM's plant in Cleveland. In the spring, Wilson asked Harlow Curtice, his executive vice president, to supervise Chevrolet's turnaround. Curtice summoned Cole home immediately. Soon after Cole arrived, after his promotion to chief engineer at Chevrolet division in May 1952, he brought in chassis expert Maurice Olley. Early in his career, Olley had worked for Rolls-Royce in England and in America before joining Cadillac and Cole. Now Keating had the engineers he needed to transform Chevrolet into a younger buyer's car company. What he needed next was a product.

STEEL, THE ESSENTIAL ELEMENT

Steel was the second pivotal element in this story. It was crucial for manufacturing automobiles. It also was essential for making the tanks, ships, and shells bound for Korea. The war there made things complicated. U.S. President Harry Truman re-imposed wage and price controls on January 26, 1951, six months after the United States joined the fight in Korea and about four years after lifting the controls placed during World War II. Yet Truman's new Wage Stabilization Board authorized pay increases for steelworkers. The steel companies, believing they were unable to raise prices to cover the elevated costs, refused to pay the new rates. Intending to avert a strike, Truman seized the steel mills on April 8, 1952, using the existing employees and management to produce steel. Answering a suit by the mill owners, a lower court judge ruled Truman's seizures illegal. In response, 600,000 steelworkers walked out, dropping steel production from 300,000 tons a day to 20,000. At the end of May, a higher court transferred

By this time, Briggs had found better power and easier access to engines and accessories through Chrysler Corporation. He fitted his cars with Chrysler's 331, cubic-inch V-8s, topped with four dual-throat Weber carburetors.

the mills back to government control and workers returned. Then on June 2, the Supreme Court ruled Truman had usurped powers that belonged to Congress in a time of war. Workers went back out and remained outside for 53 days. In sympathy, Great Lakes iron-ore shippers remained in port, interrupting movement of this critical raw material. Because of the wartime need for steel, the government's National Production Authority halted all steel delivery to consumer goods producers. Workers returned on July 24, 1952, with a smaller wage increase than first approved while steel was allowed to raise its rates $4 per ton. For the auto industry, the Korean War had invaded Detroit. Only Ford Motor Company's own River Rouge plant, fed with Ford iron-ore delivered by Ford's own shipping line, ensured them steel output during the strike. For GM and others, even when the huge ore ships returned to the Great Lakes, steel producers and the auto industry had to face a threatened coal miner's strike in the fall of 1952 that would again shut down the steel-making furnaces. The seed of doubt this episode had planted among all auto makers required alternative thinking about materials.

Fiberglass was the most appealing, and this was the third element of the inevitable flow toward the Chevrolet sports car. By 1952, however, GM and the entire industry had known about this material—also called glass reinforced plastic (GRP)—for 20 years. Its uses went back even further.

Plastic itself dates back to 1868 when chemist John Wesley Hyatt produced the first cellulose nitrate compound. He called it "celluloid" and found commercial applications for it in billiard balls, dentures,

Between World War I and II, Howard "Dutch" Darrin created some of America's most memorable and stylish car bodies for luxury car builders such as Packard and Lincoln. For his "own" two-seat sports car, he carried over classic features such as the half-convertible roof with exposed landau bars. It was car styling out of another time, and it never caught on.

men's shirt collars, and side windows in automobiles; however, the sun's ultraviolet rays rapidly yellowed and dried out the material in windows.

Dr. Leo Henrik Baekelund first formed phenolformaldehyde in 1909. He named the resin he developed from his compound "Bakelite." Electrical appliance makers used it for decades to save hands from heat and isolate metal components from electric current.

Through the next 35 years, plastic development continued. While there were only two basic resin compounds offered commercially at the end of World War I, there were dozens by the outbreak of World War II. By 1929 in Germany, Daimler-Benz and Bayer Chemical had begun to mold body panels, rear decks, and fenders; however, they dropped the project after completing only a few prototypes.

Henry Ford first got interested in industrial uses for soybeans and their by-products in 1931. These included phenolformaldehyde, which Henry learned could be mixed with various wood fibers to make a strong, reinforced plastic. Ford's engineers could mold or press it into compound curves or straight, flat panels. By 1941, his staff scientists constructed an entire car body out of the soybean plastic.

By 1940, General Motors, working with Dr. R. Games Slater, produced dashboard trim and even steering wheels out of plastic. Slater was a research chemist with Owens-Corning, and in 1944 he and others experimented with fibers of fine glass woven into a matt and bonded with polyester resins. O-C marketed this substance under the trade name Fiberglas, and while it was different from GRP, the two materials became universally known as fiberglass.

Out in southern California, boat builders recognized that fiberglass yielded an easily shaped, low-maintenance hull. Bill Tritt, a boat maker in Montecito near Santa Barbara, started the Glasspar Company in 1950. He and his partners got a call from an air force major, Kenneth Brooks, who had another use in mind. He wanted to give his wife a Jeep for her personal use, but he wanted it to look better than a boxy Jeep.

Tritt took the job and completed the car body early in 1951. He named it the Boxer. It was smart looking and its light green color attracted attention. One very interested individual was the local sales engineer from U.S. Rubber. The company's Naugatuck, Connecticut, chemical division produced Vibrin, a polyester plastic that Tritt used as a key ingredient in the mix of his GRP. Naugatuck's Vibrin sales director, Dr. Earl Ebers, became a vigorous supporter of the Boxer project. He had long wanted to get into a Detroit design studio, but he'd had no luck. (Naugatuck had another compound, a cloth it also wanted to see in automobiles, called Naugahyde.)

Glasspar and Naugatuck collaborated on making four more Boxer bodies in mid-February 1952.

Darrin first experimented with fiberglass car bodies in 1946. He recognized the economy and creative flexibility it offered. By 1952, he had convinced Henry J. Kaiser to enter the sports car market, and in 1953 Kaiser introduced this two-seater. Through 1953 and 1954, he sold only 435 examples.

Darrin devised sliding doors that disappeared into unused space in the front fenders behind the front tires. It offered a less cramped interior than Jaguar's XK-120, but it was still far from spacious. Sadly, it cost nearly $5,000, as much as a Cadillac or Lincoln sedan.

In a fluke of timing, days later, *Life* magazine published a lengthy illustrated story called "Plastic Bodies for Autos" just as newspapers and trade magazines carried stories of continuing steel shortages. Ebers' phone began to ring. One call came from another southern Californian, a Chrysler and Willys dealer in Downey, south of Los Angeles, named Blanchard "Woody" Woodill. Friends had talked him into making his own sports car. He eventually bought something like 90 bodies from Glasspar. He manufactured a car he called the Wildfire, his version of the Brooks Boxer that he built on an angle-iron chassis made for him by Harold Post in Orange, California. Woodill sold his Wildfire either as a kit for about $1,200, or complete with a Willys 90-horsepower six-cylinder or Ford 135-horsepower flathead V-8 engine for about $3,200.

More significantly, Chevrolet engineering called Ebers. (GM already had some experience with fiberglass. During World War II, Cadillac scrapped the tooling for its body fenders. After the war ended, Ed Cole, who knew of the material from various wartime applications, found it was a quick way to

While its side view appropriated sweeps and curves from Jaguar, the front end was unique to Darrin, and many feel that was part of the car's downfall. The "puckered kiss" grille was not widely admired. Behind it labored a standard Kaiser 90-horsepower six-cylinder mated to a three-speed automatic that yielded only 98 miles-per-hour top speed and 0–60 miles-per-hour acceleration in 15 seconds.

make replacement fenders.) Ebers acquired the Brooks Boxer and showed it at the National Plastics Exposition in mid-March 1952. He met other Chevy engineers during the shows, and from their reactions, he decided to drive the car directly to GM's styling auditorium. Ebers and his staff showed engineers they could take a mold from a fender and produce an exact duplicate out of fiberglass.

Chevrolet engineering and GM styling quickly adopted the material for experimental car bodies and dream cars. They also used it on these prototype and show cars to replace conventional plaster of Paris–over–wood forms that previously they had covered with hand-hammered steel.

There in his own styling auditorium in March 1952, Harley Earl could see this vehicle itself, not just magazine and newspaper pictures and stories. He saw materials that were the next advance in his car design/model-making process, a substance that could make something happen, in prototype form, quickly and easily. He also saw before him a type of automobile that had been in his head for some time.

THE FOURTH ELEMENT

The fourth element was the sports car itself. While these two-seaters raised little interest among many American customers, they already had captivated America's most innovative car designers, engineers, and builders. As early as April 1944, Maurice Olley, Ed Cole's chassis design engineer at Cadillac but on loan to the British Ministry of Supply at the time, spoke to the Society of Automotive Engineers. He speculated on the types of cars consumers would see after World War II. As a veteran of automaking in the United Kingdom and the United States, he bemoaned Detroit's devotion to chrome and sheet metal excesses. He enthused over small, fun-to-drive cars, hoping to see new vehicles patterned after European models but possessing American engineering.

In 1952, U.S. buyers registered more than four million new automobiles. More than three million of these were four-door and two-door sedans, but only 11,199 of them were sports cars. Some of the difference came from Americans' need for family cars that were unavailable in the 1940s due to World War II. Still, by 1950 many young people, including Earl's own sons, Jerry and Jim, found sports cars intriguing. (The boys came by their interest hereditarily. In 1911, when Harley was 18, he entered and won a car race driving his father's sporty Mercer roadster.) Few models were available in the early 1950s, however; tiny Crosleys and curvaceous Kurtis-Krafts were built in the United States. The new Cunningham Cadillac–engined C-1 or the Anglo-American Nash-Healey was far too costly for even Jerry Earl's college student budget. England produced the sensuous Jaguar

In addition to the roadster version (bottom), Chevrolet experimented with other variations of the Corvette, such as a version with a removable hardtop (second from bottom), the fastback Corvair (third from bottom), which was shown at the 1954 Motorama show, and the Nomad version (top), which later appeared in production form using Chevrolet's full-sized sedan frame. 2002 General Motors Corporation. Used with permission of GM Media Archives.

This was the 33rd car produced, now restored to NCRS (National Corvette Restorers' Society) highest standards. While GM design chief Harley Earl supervised its appearance, he assigned Bob McLean to create its specifications, and Duane "Sparky" Bohnstedt to style its appearance.

XK-120, the spindly MG-TC, the Aston-Martins, and Triumphs. These were primarily intended for export sale in North America (nearly 60 percent of the 12,000 XK-120s produced ended up here). They sold to so few Americans, however, that the domestic makers paid little attention to them publicly.

Harley Earl noticed. As GM's vice president of styling, his budget was generous and his expenses were never challenged. His department produced automobiles for the major annual European shows, taking cars to Paris, Geneva, London, and Milan. Earl and GM officers and designers often stayed for weeks, visiting car makers and watching international races. Earl appreciated the cars he saw overseas,

and he admired the lines and the performance of the Jaguars, though he knew European sports cars might not translate directly to GM's audiences.

Earl was well acquainted with international sportsman Briggs Cunningham who had raced yachts for the America's Cup and Cadillacs at Le Mans. In June 1950, Earl watched the 24-hour race alongside Ed Cole with a guest pass from the Cunningham team. Later that year when Cunningham competed in an endurance race at Watkins Glen, New York, Earl arrived in his 20-foot-long, two-seat Buick Y-job. Cunningham, who was near to completing his prototype C-1 production road car, teased him, asking Earl why GM couldn't build a "proper" sports car, something Cunningham could race. A year later, after Cunningham ran four of his 1951 C-2R models at Le Mans, Earl arrived at Watkins Glen in his new, smaller 16 1/2-foot Buick LeSabre. This still was no sports car from General Motors. So Cunningham built his C-3, completing the first in 1953, but now using Chrysler's new hemispherical head

Harley Earl designed countless custom bodies for his father's Cadillac customers, always favoring long hood and short rear deck proportions. Earl noticed sports cars he saw from Europe copied this style and he specified the same for his new creation: the Corvette. European race cars covered their lights to protect the glass from flying stones.

Harley Earl loved to make cars look longer, lower, and wider than they really were. Bob McLean, working from Jaguar XK-120 dimensions, stretched, squashed, and pulled those dimensions to create the new Corvette. To make sure the passenger cockpit and engine fit within its 102-inch wheelbase, McLean began his design work at the rear axle and worked forward, setting dimensions as he went.

Molding the plastic body to "Sparky" Bohnstedt's bullet taillights caused fiberglass body makers terrible problems. Restorers now moan about the delicate multi piece rear bumper assemblies. Airflow over the rear stalled exhaust fumes, and early cars often discolored around the protruding pipes.

high-performance, 310-horsepower V-8s. His cars had brought attention to America's modest efforts at sports car production wherever they competed overseas during the early 1950s, but Cunningham continued to chide his friend Harley.

Several English-American hybrids appeared. A Belgian engineer of Russian parentage, Zora Arkus-Duntov, helped other racers stuff Ford, Mercury, and then Cadillac V-8s into Sydney Allard's unsophisticated English roadsters in the late 1940s. (Listing his hometown as New York, Duntov raced an Allard J2 with a Ford V-8 fitted with cylinder heads of his own design in the inaugural Palm Beach Shores road race, January 3, 1950. He helped another New Yorker, Tom Cole, prepare his Cadillac-engined Allard as well.) On the West Coast, Frank Kurtis produced 36 of his Sports model in 1949 before television super-salesman Earl "Mad Man" Muntz acquired the rights. He renamed the car the Muntz Jet and eventually built 394 of them, using Cadillac V-8s in 1949 and Lincoln engines from 1950 through 1954. Englishman Donald Healey made a deal in 1951 to use 3.8-liter, six-cylinder Nash engines in his Pininfarina-bodied coupes and roadsters. He shipped all 506 to the United States.

American industrialist Henry J. Kaiser entered the small market for compact, sporty cars with his Henry J in late 1950. He had collaborated with Joseph W. Frazer, a former Chrysler vice president of sales, to form Kaiser-Frazer. They hired two exceptional designers, Howard "Dutch" Darrin and Bill Stout. Darrin had created stunning bodies for Packards, Lincolns, and others; one of Stout's more significant projects was his own Scarabs, design-study vehicles, some of them fabricated in fiberglass.

In Milwaukee, industrial designer Brooks Stevens used the Henry J 100-inch wheelbase chassis and installed Willys 2.8-liter, in-line six-cylinder engines. He created bodywork resembling the fearsome 1930s Mercedes-Benz SSK two-seat racers. Stevens called his car the Excalibur J, and he built

True to sports cars of the era, luggage capacity in the trunk was severely limited. As Chevrolet hurried the car into production, it could only offer it in white with a red interior. Chevrolet offered two options, a heater and an AM radio, though all 300 first-year cars were produced with the options as standard equipment.

Postwar steel shortages in the United Kingdom delayed development of Jaguar's new Mk. VII sedan, but the firm had completed development of its new XK engine. Jaguar decided to build a two-seat aluminum-body roadster to show off the engine and create a demand for the new sedan. They only planned to produce 240 roadsters.

three prototypes that ran successfully in Sports Car Club of America (SCCA) D-modified class races. Stevens wanted Kaiser-Frazer to put into production a road-going version of his Excalibur, but Henry Kaiser wasn't yet convinced that America was ready for a sports car.

Dutch Darrin worked for Kaiser out of his own studio in California. On his own time with expenses coming from his own pocket, Darrin created a low, sleek two-seater hoping, like Stevens, that Kaiser would produce it. As with Stevens' car, Darrin based his roadster on the Henry J chassis, using the same Willys six. He fabricated its body out of fiberglass. In August 1952, he showed the car to Kaiser, who didn't like it until his new young wife fell in love with it. When Kaiser asked Darrin why he'd done it, the designer told him he'd heard that Chevrolet and Ford were already working on similar projects. This car, Darrin explained, would be the Kaiser-Frazer answer to the others' challenges.

WHAT THE CUSTOMER WANTS

Nearly every element was in place, each ingredient flowing steadily toward the confluence, the next turning point in Chevrolet's auto-making history. By the early 1950s, Alfred Sloan's faith in Harley Earl had moved the designer into the as-yet undefined realm of product planner. Earl used carefully controlled environments to monitor public response to his ideas.

GM had begun hosting "Industrialist's Luncheons" in the late 1930s at the Waldorf Astoria Hotel grand ballroom in New York City. It was clever psychology; GM showed the future to these men (and it was men only; their wives were not invited). By taking these influential customers into its confidence, the corporation educated them at the same time it gauged what these conservative individuals liked. When these men left the Waldorf, they knew where GM was headed. They could knowledgeably advise their clients to invest in GM. At the same time, Harley Earl and other GM officers knew better what kind of automobile these most influential—and wealthy—customers might buy for themselves.

GM's challenge to Darrin and Kaiser was a not so-well-kept secret by mid-1952. In Chevrolet studios, now directed by Clare MacKichan, designers frantically worked toward a show opening January 17 at the Waldorf Astoria. Corporate accountants had balanced the cost-per-luncheon-invitee of the earlier events against possible sales revenues. They calculated the luncheons as losses, giving no value to the information gained or goodwill spent. Executive vice president Harlow Curtice had a business background, yet he understood the Sloan/Brown theory of giving an idea time to pay off. Under his influence (he would become president of GM in February 1953 when Charlie Wilson went to Eisenhower's Pentagon as secretary of defense), the luncheons became broader and more public. Renamed *Transportation Unlimited,* these shows ran several days. Wives were definitely invited. These

programs in 1949 and 1950 met with so much success that the sales staff considered taking the show beyond New York. With strained finances and few new products to show off, however, Curtice canceled the 1951 and 1952 series. (Earl was forced to debut his LeSabre dream car at the Paris auto show in 1952.)

For 1953, Curtice approved adding Miami in February, then Chicago, Los Angeles, San Francisco, Dallas, and concluding in Kansas City in June. Looking for a more evocative title, they appropriated the term *Motorama* from a fledgling car display that had begun in Los Angeles three years earlier. For 1953, Harley Earl would introduce the Cadillac El Dorado, the Oldsmobile Fiesta, Wildfire, and Starfire, the Buick Skylark and Wildcat, the Pontiac Parisienne, and another model from Cadillac, the

Seat movement, which was limited by frame rails rising over the rear axle, cramped the car's interior, yet many fans, seduced by the sweeping exterior lines of what they argued was the most beautiful car in the world, accepted the tight fit. In England, the car sold for £ 998, slightly less than $3,500.

LeMans. Oldsmobile's Starfire and Wildfire and the Cadillac LeMans were fiberglass. Wilson and Curtice had excluded Chevrolet from the 1949 and 1950 shows, believing that a division producing cars for the masses didn't project the right image for dream cars. Tom Keating asked for a new vote for 1953.

Between 1950 and 1952, Chevrolet division sales dropped almost 40 percent, prompting Wilson's offer of anyone or anything. Keating now had Ed Cole and the board of directors' support. Now he and Cole needed something novel to excite customers, to draw them into the showrooms. Keating made it clear that the 1953 Motorama would have at least one Chevrolet. Soon after Cole got to Detroit from Cleveland in late May 1952, he and Keating went shopping at Earl's studio.

Earl drew his sports car idea from an existing pattern: Fit a unique, stylish two-seat body around a production engine and frame. He first envisioned this car in the late fall of 1951 as something GM could sell for about $1,800, close to Triumphs or MGs and about half the price of Jaguar's $3,345 XK-120. He even moved a Jaguar into the Body Development Studio so his staff had a design target. He assigned Bob McLean, a young California Institute of Technology graduate of both engineering and industrial design, to create a car. He tagged a recent hire, Duane "Sparky" Bohnstedt, to style the body for the project.

(bottom opposite) While beauty is subjective, performance is measurable, and the Jaguar XK engine yielded the fastest production automobile in the world. Its 160 horsepower provided a top speed of 120 miles per hour. A later XK-120 version, the XK-120M, offered 180 horsepower and achieved better than 130 miles per hour from its in-line six-cylinder engine.

Earl wanted to use a V-8 engine, but only Cadillac, Buick (with a 322-cubic inch displacement 188-horsepower engine), and Oldsmobile (with its 304-cubic inch displacement 165-horsepower version) produced them, and the upper division's jealously guarded their technological advances as part of their marketing advantage. He'd have to use Chevrolet's six. Earl's other objectives, including adopting the Jaguar as inspiration, set McLean's direction. Virtually every sports car of the period emulated the long hood/short rear deck parameters of the classic 1930s cars. McLean and Bohnstedt followed convention. McLean penciled in the in-line six-cylinder engine. He designed a new 102-inch wheelbase frame. To make everything fit, he began his design work at the rear axle of his chassis, drawing in the passenger/driver compartment and working forward. He set the engine well back, matching the Jaguar and allowing him to keep the car balanced. The car had nearly equal weight on the front and rear axles when it was loaded. McLean drew a 57-inch front track and 59-inch rear, some 6 inches wider at front and 9 inches wider at the rear than the Jaguar. This followed Earl's standards of making cars appear lower, longer, and wider.

Time passed rapidly. Near the end of spring, on June 2, 1952, Earl finally showed Bohnstedt's finished full-size clay model to a small group, including GM chairman Harlow Curtice, who had enjoyed a private showing earlier. For this show, Curtice brought along Tom Keating and Ed Cole.

Cole and Keating were thrilled, Cole, by some accounts, almost jumping in excitement. They made it clear to Earl that this was the car they wanted for Motorama. Earl was equally pleased. Without their enthusiasm, the sports car would have languished in the studio. No other division had expressed any interest in adopting the project. Only one feature remained to power this new car into the market place. The fifth and final element that made the sports car real was the issue of competition, not in racing, but in production.

BECOMING A SPORTS CAR ENTHUSIAST

Ford's styling chief, Franklin Q. Hershey, had worked for GM, reaching the position of Cadillac's chief of design before he was terminated in 1948 for running a side business making ashtrays. Unlike his boss at GM, Hershey didn't much care for sports cars or European cars. He loved American classics, having worked at Walter Murphy Body Company in Pasadena, California, in his first job making custom bodies for Duesenbergs, Packards, and other cars. So in late 1951 when a group of Ford designers and engineers formed the Ford Motorsports Club, Hershey passed on the invitation to join. A few months later, in early 1952, his attitude changed as Jim and Cheryl Farrell reported in their book, *Ford Design Department—Concept & Show Cars, 1932–1961.* Just after Hershey had been hired away from Packard to head Ford's styling, club member J. R. "Dick" Samsen, one of his design-

The stubby two-speed automatic transmission shift lever protruded from the carpeted tunnel between the seats. Side windows did not roll up or down but were completely removable. With windows fitted, owners had to slip their hands inside through the opening vent windows to reach the round white door knob to open the doors.

ers, asked him why Ford didn't build a sports car. Hershey told him the company knew it could not make money on a sports car. That is, until one late winter evening when a close friend and dinner guest at Hershey's home, a designer working for GM, showed his host a photograph. It was Chevrolet's new sports car, and Hershey knew immediately what he and Ford division must do. Overnight he became a sports car enthusiast, buying himself a Jaguar XK-120 and studying every other sports car available. In March 1952, he hired a GM designer, Bill Boyer, right from under Harley Earl's nose to design Ford's response to Chevrolet's new sports car. Boyer worked feverishly in a small secure studio with Dick Samsen and Allan Kornmiller and a few engineers and fabricators, basing their car, as Bob McLean had based his Chevrolet, on Jaguar's XK-120. Boyer, Samsen, and Kornmiller had a full-size clay model ready for Ford management to see in the Dearborn design studio as the doors opened on GM's Motorama in New York City's Waldorf Astoria Hotel on January 17, 1953.

THE BIRTH OF A TREND

Within weeks of Keating and Cole seeing McLean's sports car, they sensed they had been present at the birth of a trend. They had no idea Ford knew about what they were seeing. That factor would come into play a few short months later, about the time more than 125,000 sports car and performance enthusiasts gathered in southern California. At the fourth annual International Motorama, the independent show held in Los Angeles each June, a record-breaking crowd wandered through exhibition halls filled with dozens of custom and sports cars. The review in *Automotive Industries* the most

influential monitor of business and technical developments for car makers, reported that "more than $2 million worth of hot rods, custom built and European cars were on display. . . a dozen different models feature glass reinforced plastic bodies." The accompanying page of pictures showed a Glasspar coupe, a Hudson Italia, and a Ferrari-like open two-seater built on a Ford chassis with a Cadillac engine, the Fordillac. Through the summer and fall, major automakers from Packard (with its Pan American) to Ford of France (with its Comette) announced or introduced sports cars for the coming year. Ford hinted it might bring the rounded Comette to the United States to cater to the growing sports car market, and Ford and other makers promoted their own growing uses of fiberglass in prototype and show cars as well as production applications.

Chevrolet had endured a two-year-long cold spell in consumer enthusiasm. Now the climate was improving. Just as in any watershed, various streams run with an increasing sense of destiny and urgency toward the ocean. The elements here were flowing: Better-paid laborers made a growing middle class; a shortage of steel proved the potential of fiberglass; a hungry division needed to bring younger ideas to younger buyers. A fierce rival, propelled by two former employees, moved stealthily toward direct competition.

When the crowds saw GM's Motorama in New York City on January 17, 1953, they glimpsed the best idea of a powerful and influential designer whose work had almost fallen on blind eyes. The public's response in years to come finally would be judged a watershed for Chevrolet, General Motors, and the American auto industry.

1953-1955

CHAPTER THREE

A FUTURE CLASSIC STRUGGLES TO LIFE

o mislead curious corporate insiders, Keating approved disguising the sports car with the code name Project Opel since Earl's styling department did work for GM's German subsidiary. Cole ordered one car, which was completed to show standards for the 1953 Motorama event. Provided it didn't bomb, Keating agreed to start production of the car the following summer for presentation as a 1954 model.

Cole's staff worked on the performance of the standard "Blue Flame Six" to get closer to sports car proportions, and Maurice Olley began to engineer the hastily drawn chassis to meet GM production procedures. It was a challenge.

Olley had to revise the 1949 sedan-configuration front suspension to fit inside McLean's slim body. The final drive was a Hotchkiss rear end that Olley secured with four-leaf springs sloping upward at the rear and attached to the frame by tension shackles. This angle induced understeer, the plow steering that engineers liked for sedans. Olley quickened Chevrolet's regular worm-and-sector steering system to achieve a more sports car–like response. He could only use production brakes as well, but he enlarged the master cylinder and adjusted front-to-rear bias to give slightly more to the rear.

The low rearward engine placement finally forced Olley to design a new frame formed of steel boxed-section side members that he tied together with a central crossing X-member. His X-frame swooped low enough that he set the driveshaft above it, avoiding the more conventional technique that drilled holes for the shaft, weakening the torsional strength of the chassis. The new frame represented a huge expense in the car's development. Although Olley saved money using stock or mostly stock pieces elsewhere, the financially strapped division had to make other compromises.

In the end, Earl and Cole accepted Chevrolet's six-cylinder engine. Cole's colleague on the Cadillac V-8 development, Harry Barr, had joined him at Chevrolet. In stock trim in sedans, the Blue

(previous pages) In December 1953, Chevrolet moved Corvette production from its small Flint factory to a dedicated facility in St. Louis.

Although the new factory in St. Louis had the capacity to produce 10,000 cars a year, Chevrolet produced just 3,640 Corvettes for 1954, fully a third of which remained unsold at the end of the year.

Flame Six, first offered in 1941, produced 115 horsepower. Barr added mechanical valve lifters, a new aluminum intake manifold for three Carter carburetors, and a split exhaust manifold leading to separate exhaust mufflers and pipes on each side at the rear. Then, by increasing compression from the stock 7.5:1 to 8.0:1, Barr raised output to 150 horsepower. Olley examined mufflers and later wrote, "Sports car enthusiasts [agree] the exhaust should have the right note. They don't agree what this is. Some prefer 'foo-blap' while others go for 'foo-gobble.' It is impossible to please them all." Olley chose the latter.

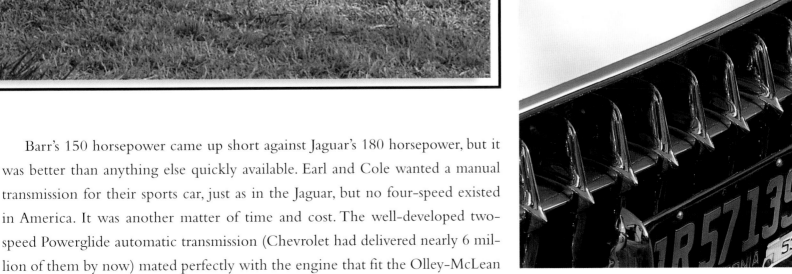

Barr's 150 horsepower came up short against Jaguar's 180 horsepower, but it was better than anything else quickly available. Earl and Cole wanted a manual transmission for their sports car, just as in the Jaguar, but no four-speed existed in America. It was another matter of time and cost. The well-developed two-speed Powerglide automatic transmission (Chevrolet had delivered nearly 6 million of them by now) mated perfectly with the engine that fit the Olley-McLean

(above) The only visible differences between a normal early production 1953 model and this supercharged car are the script badge on the nose and replacement of Chevrolet's steel wheels with 1953 Buick Skylark wire wheels. Otherwise, nothing gives away the substantial improvement in performance offered by the McCullough blower.

Some of the history of this nearly unique car is still unclear. It seems that McCullough not only fitted the supercharger to improve performance but Art Oberly also may have added the Buick Skylark wire wheels to render a more sports car–like appearance. It was not a simple conversion, and very few other cars have appeared with the wire wheels.

package. Olley defended the decision, sounding more like Alfred Sloan than Ed Cole when he presented a paper to the Society of Automotive Engineers (SAE) on January 14, 1953, three days before the world first saw the car. Americans, Olley concluded with foresight, were less willing to trade the luxury that was increasingly available in American sedans for the austerity common to sports cars.

As the end of the year approached, Keating and Earl agreed to build the Motorama show car out of fiberglass. If the car went into production, Chevrolet would make it in steel.

Appearing in brilliant white fiberglass in the Waldorf Grand ballroom, the car now bore the name *Corvette* written in a simple script across its nose. Myron Scott, Campbell-Ewald ad agency's chief photographer, came up with the name. He admired the fast naval vessels of that name that performed patrol duties during World War II as destroyer escorts in North Atlantic convoys.

After Motorama, Chevrolet and GM management felt confident about the two-seater. The enthusiastic response of New York City's 306,000 Motorama guests (and ultimately 1.7 million in all six cities) suggested they start production before 1954.

Art Oberly and Erik Kaughman added twin vacuum-pressure gauges, mounting them on a production-looking bracket. Because of the length of tubing required to move the compressed supercharged air around the engine, one gauge monitors pressure out of the supercharger and the other checks it as it enters the carburetors.

McCullough's supercharger is visible at the right front corner of the engine compartment. A flexible hose links it to the three stock Carter carburetors connected by another solid red-painted tube dubbed the "log." Because the supercharger was large, Oberly and Kaughman repositioned the factory air cleaner out of the engine compartment and into the upper rear of the right front fender, a kind of early "cold box" intake.

The new Corvette project caught some suppliers unaware. The car had been in Earl's mind for nearly two years and in Cole's imagination for six months; however, getting production approved required work beyond design and chassis engineering. Chevrolet had to find someone to make the car body.

MOLDING FIBERGLASS

On February 5, 1953, Robert Morrison was back in Detroit to see Carl Klein, a junior Chevrolet division purchasing agent. Morrison had sold Fords until the early 1950s when he and his partners inherited an ailing, undercapitalized molded glass–reinforced plastics operation. Morrison had turned things around, and by late 1952 he was producing thousands of molded fiberglass bread palettes for Wonder Bread's Continental Baking division. He spun off that business into a tray division. With 12 presses in Ashtabula, Ohio, and 10 more in a satellite operation in nearby Linesville, across the Pennsylvania state line, he was busy. He and his partners still talked about the auto industry, but they concluded that it was too big, and with their 30,000 square feet of manufacturing space, they were too small.

Yet in late fall 1952, some body engineers came to visit from General Motors' Fisher Body Fabrication and Assembly division. They carried drawings for more than 100 parts. Could Morrison's Molded Fiber Glass Company (MFG) produce them? How long might it take? What about cost? What kind of quantities?

Morrison told them MFG could do the work, but then the project seemed to die. He heard nothing for weeks. Then in mid-January a supplier sent him a telegram: "Go to the Waldorf Astoria Hotel in New York City this coming weekend," it said. "Go see the display."

Money was tight, not only for Chevrolet but also for Morrison. He didn't go. He recalled years later what he missed: "In that ballroom was Chevrolet's new fiberglass two-seat sports car. GM had planted the car with microphones, to eavesdrop on the guests they had invited in to see it and some other prototypes. They heard 'It's lovely. It's cute.' They heard people say they wished they had one."

The Corvette on one of its early trips to the fabled Brickyard, the Indianapolis Motor Speedway. 2002 General Motors Corporation. Used with permission of GM Media Archives.

McCullough's promotional literature produced in early 1954 in cooperation with the Ethyl Corporation of San Francisco reported that 0–60 miles-per-hour times dropped from 12 seconds to 9 seconds. Horsepower at the rear wheels increased from 87 with the standard three Carters, to 117, a 35-percent jump. Oberly and Kaughman ran acceleration tests at Fontana Raceway in Fontana, California, and produced high 13-second quarter-mile times.

Both 1953 and 1954 models operated on 6-volt electrical systems. Turn signals were a $16.75 option, though like all 1953 and 1954 Corvette options, both cars were built with all the options included. Wide whitewall tires—6.70x15—were another standard option.

Historians believe that fewer than two dozen McCullough supercharged engines were produced in 1953 and 1954.

(opposite) The Blue Flame Six persevered, still offering 150 horsepower (87 at the rear wheels) as it had through 1953. Sometime during the model year, Chevrolet revised camshaft lobes, increasing gross output to 155 horsepower. The Blue Flame and 150 decals were fitted only to painted valve covers. Some cars were delivered with chrome-plated covers, and these got no decals.

On Monday, January 24, Morrison heard from Chevrolet. Could some men come down to see the plant the next day? Project engineer Carl Jakust and his boss, E. J. "Jim" Premo, chief body engineer for Chevrolet division, arrived the next day. Though the Fisher Body engineers had shown plans to Morrison before, the Chevrolet body engineers took new measurements of each fiberglass press. They planned to redesign their parts to fit Morrison's machinery. Morrison told them his presses were in use; he'd buy new ones, and he offered to help redesign the parts himself so that they not only would mold well but also would be strong.

Jakust and Premo were still nervous. Did MFG have the capacity to meet Chevrolet's need? This was crucial. Chevrolet had lost the youth market to Ford. Ford's postwar cars had V-8s and had convertible tops. Chevrolet needed to get this two-seat sports car out as fast as possible. It wanted to produce 50 each day.

So on Tuesday, February 5, two weeks after Jakust and Premo's visit, Morrison drove over to Detroit to meet Klein at 9 A.M. to plan production of 12,300 sets of the 103 body parts that made the Corvette. General Motors needed delivery spread over 18 months.

Signals got crossed. Klein was gone for the day. Morrison asked to see his boss, Ed Furbacher, Chevrolet's senior purchasing agent. Furbacher was also gone for the day. Morrison felt that he'd been stood up. He headed for the elevator. When the door opened, Elmer Gormsen stepped out. Gormsen was chief purchasing agent for Chevrolet division and boss of the two missing buyers. He had met Morrison on his last visit to GM. Gormsen was direct, telling Morrison that Chevrolet had decided to build the Corvette in steel. No one in that industry had the capacity to produce 50 bodies a day, he said.

But Morrison hadn't had his say. Harold Boeschenstein, chairman of Owens-Corning, was a friend and an ardent supporter of Morrison and of MFG. Boeschenstein had personally promised help. Morrison had located a large building near Ashtabula that was immediately available.

Gormsen walked Morrison to the door, telling him vaguely that if anything changed, he'd get in touch. Morrison had an afternoon appointment with Kaiser-Frazer engineers and drove across town figuring the Chevrolet deal was dead. His afternoon stretched into evening, checking fits and finish of each piece. He took Kaiser's engineers to dinner. That long session with Kaiser was scarcely fruitful. Kaiser ordered 500 sets, but Morrison warned his people "to go easy on this, make a hundred parts and then stub your toe. Don't make any more.' I had a feeling they weren't too solid by that time," he recalled.

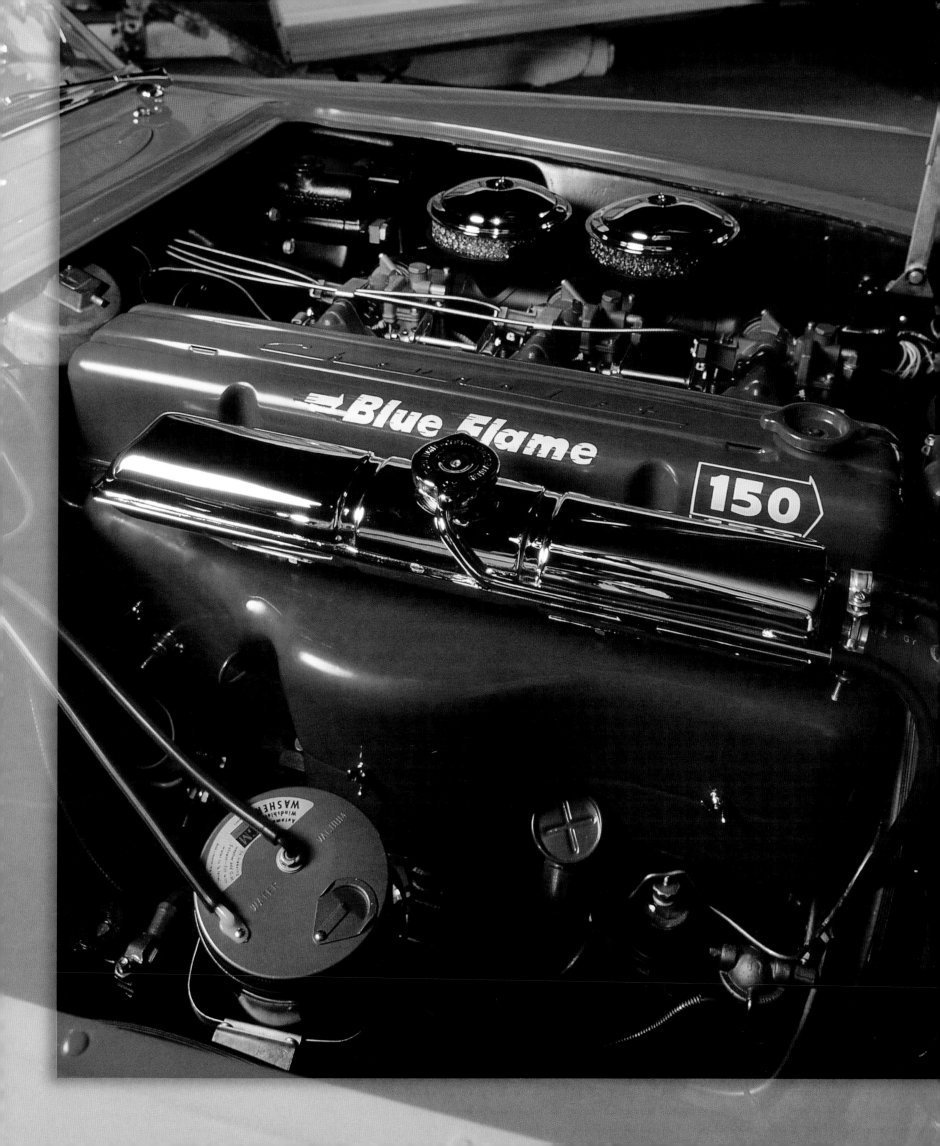

Sportsman Red, Polo White, and black exterior cars got red interiors, and all models for 1954 got beige convertible tops. (Chevrolet fitted Pennant Blue cars with beige interiors.) The cars still used only removable windows (Chevrolet provided a bag in the trunk for storage), and door opening could only be accomplished by reaching in through the pivoting front quarter window.

It had been a long, bad day. He left Detroit around 8:30 P.M., driving steadily but unhurriedly back to Ashtabula. *Why race home with bad news,* he thought.

"I got home about 1:30 the next morning. My wife got up and told me, 'There's a man calling you from Detroit. Wants you to call him no matter how late you get in.' So I called the number and it's Elmer Gormsen. He kind of laughed and said I didn't need to call him so late. But since I did, he said to go ahead and get that building. 'Because we've decided we're going to do the Corvette with a fiberglass body.'"

Robert S. Morrison was back in the automobile business. MFG had a $4 million contract. Chevrolet wanted the first of the 300 complete sets of body panels before June 1. It was a night Morrison's children would remember all their lives. His son, Robert Jr., recalled that the early morning of February 6, 1953, was the first time that he and his sister had ever tasted champagne.

On February 6, hours after Elmer Gormsen hired Robert Morrison (and as show staff prepped the prototype car for the Miami Motorama opening), Morrison and his partners left after inspecting the empty building nearby. It was an old railroad structure laced with tracks and totally unusable. Morrison called Harold Boeschenstein, and Owens-Corning came through. Then he called Gormsen to tell him MFG would be constructing a new building just for the Corvette.

When MFG got the order, the whole young fiberglass industry knew about it. Morrison only had four of his key people left after spinning off his tray-making operation. When the new 167,000-square-foot Corvette building was complete, his organization was stretched thin.

While Chevrolet introduced the Corvette at $3,733 fully equipped in 1953, it listed the base price at $3,498. For 1954, it reduced the base price to $2,774, but it did so by listing the automatic transmission, tires, and other previous standard equipment as options. This led some to believe that Chevrolet also offered a manual gearbox.

"Chevrolet was quite cooperative with man power," Morrison recalled. "And resin suppliers and Owens-Corning sent people in. Paid their expenses. Didn't cost us a penny. You'd see a salesman from one company and a salesman from another working on the same press. Competitors working alongside each other helping us get the work out." Chevrolet body engineers quickly learned from the suppliers the techniques for producing bodies.

By midyear, Chevrolet had remedied the exhaust staining problem by fitting exhaust pipe extensions. These moved the gases out into the airstream coming over the rear of the car and out away from the body. These were stainless steel.

One method was called hand lay-up. GM engineering parts fabrication department already used this slow, exact process to create Motorama Dream Cars and Earl's prototypes, including the Corvette. The "matched-metal die method" was similar to steel body production and offered many benefits. Large presses used either cast iron or plate-steel molds that were mated to each other. Morrison's 15 new hydraulic presses compressed these molds together like steel-stamping dies to form the fiberglass panels under as much as 500 tons of pressure. MFG also established a recipe for Corvette fiberglass that has changed little over time. Roughly 30 percent of the mix is glass fiber, 29 percent is aluminum silicate filler, and the remaining 41 percent is isothalic resin. In the 340-pound 1953 car body, this broke down

This was a car engineered in Harley Earl's styling department. Chevrolet's General Manager Tom Keating and others agreed it could greatly help Chevrolet regain its shrinking audience, so the car was hurried into production. Engineers took just enough time to change fanciful ideas into an automobile that could come off an assembly line and go around a corner. The 1953 and 1954 Corvettes represented a remarkable achievement. 2002 General Motors Corporation. Used with permission of GM Media Archives.

With 195 horsepower now on tap and a three-speed manual transmission available to manage it, performance and driving excitement improved greatly.

to about 136 pounds of fiberglass, 153 pounds of resin, and 51 pounds of the inert filler. This formula and the matched-metal die method provided the greatest quality and consistency of pieces, something critically important for an interchangeable parts–oriented business like auto making. In addition, matched-metal was the fastest process, and its molds offered the benefit of a production life of as many as 20,000 impressions.

Gormsen told Morrison that Chevrolet rejected steel, in the end, because tooling costs would have been four or five times higher for steel than for fiberglass. Worse, it would have taken much longer to produce steel-stamping dies than MFG needed to make its molds. Chevrolet had learned from Morrison that they could consolidate parts, which meant fewer dies. Still, Chevrolet had concerns.

"There was a sort of betting going on up in Detroit," Morrison explained, "that we wouldn't be able to make the underbody; there *was* some trouble. In early June 1953, the foreman in charge of repairing the underbodies said he needed 40 more people.

"The underbody was breaking right at the junction of the driveshaft: tube and the kick-up right before the rear axle. There were two sharp angles and no way for it to give at all. Every damned one of them was breaking."

Morrison graduated from college with a degree in economics and a minor in chemistry; he learned his engineering by doing it. MFG's Corvette presses were huge compared to the 42 x 48-inch

The motivation for this car remains a mystery. The long-established Ghia Carrozzerie in Italy operated a subsidiary in Switzerland, Ghia Aigle. What can be determined is that a buyer took delivery of a 1954 Corvette roadster for use in Europe. Sometime after delivery, he presented it to Ghia of Switzerland, who, some now say, turned it into a replica of a Ferrari 250GT coupe.

platens Fisher Body saw when it first came to Ashtabula. The underbody piece for the 1953 car was 10 feet long, 6 feet wide, and 26 inches deep from the lowest spot to the highest. Morrison saw the break and knew the cure.

" 'Get a big bucket of water and get some cloths,' I said. 'When the press opens, put the cool wet cloths right over that spot that breaks. And leave it there for a few seconds.'

"It eliminated all the breakage. Most any resin is weak when it's hot. Cooling it down with the wet cloth, we got it strong enough quickly so we could lift it out without breaking."

Ghia designed its version of the Corvette with a fixed roof, roll-up windows, reclining leather seats, and a four-speed transmission. Its curious multinational personality is reinforced by a Veliga-instrumented Ferrari dashboard.

HITTING THE STREETS

When the new Corvette hit the streets in September 1953, it landed more with a dull thud than a big splash. Its price, fully equipped and in white only, came in at $3,513, not Earl's target, $1,800. The Blue Flame Special and Powerglide transmission moved the car from 0 to 60 miles per hour in 11 seconds and gave it a top speed of 105 miles per hour. The target Jaguar XK-120 cost $268 less, hit 60 miles per hour a second quicker, and went 25 miles per hour faster. Jaguar and even the fiberglass Kaiser-Darrin, with its odd, slide-open doors, were available in a variety of colors. Corvette side windows were sunlight-yellowing plastic and tops were only black. Build quality was inconsistent. Assembly line workers struggled to get machine-made bits to fit handmade bodies. The car suffered teething problems.

Corvette's biggest gamble was simple economics: supply versus demand. Tom Keating hedged his bets when he authorized first-year production of just 300 cars. The only news of the car following its debut appeared in automotive trade journals and plastics industry reports. By September, the 1.7 million people who attended the Motoramas had nearly forgotten about it. A small story in *Automotive Industries* magazine reviewing the Motorama shows informed readers that while Chevrolet planned to sell the Corvette for around $3,000, this price represented a net loss to the division of nearly $2,000 per car. Keating's gamble was taking on serious proportions. The news intended to make the car seem like a bargain; to the business community, the Corvette sounded like a mistake. Keating needed to rekindle the momentum developed at the Motorama shows. He had to gauge customer reaction, monitor factory production glitches, and watch assembly costs. The cars

manufactured in Flint through July were still prototypes in many ways. Workers fitted hand-formed stainless steel trim and cast bronze pieces, while cars built in August had used pot metal. A. O. Smith Corporation, the outside contractor making Corvette's frames, fabricated hand-formed gussets to reinforce rear spring mounts. Technicians were revising these from one frame to the next until Cole and Olley settled on a final design.

Chevrolet held a press introduction on September 29. Fifty journalists shared eight cars, and each drove a seven-mile course at GM's Milford Proving Ground. The Flint factory delivered a few more cars before October 1. Some of these stayed within GM, going straight to engineers who used them for further development, or to executives. Dealers learned in early July that they should not accept orders promising delivery in 1953. The division then delivered another 50 cars through its highest-volume dealers to an A-list of handpicked, carefully selected, highly visible entertainers, prominent athletes, and executives from other major companies. Briggs Cunningham and his father-in-law each ordered one during the New York auto show, but when Briggs got his, he kept it only a week, judging it "not much of a car." Normal customers found that Chevrolet was circulating a few Corvettes from one dealer to the next, staying two or three days as display models. The 306,000 New Yorkers

Even if the performance may have deteriorated slightly from the heavier steel body, the car benefited from true dual exhausts. This car makes a delightful sound. Its resemblance to mid-1950s Ferraris, especially from this rear view, is uncanny if not intentional.

The evolution here would have Harley Earl either grinning or spinning in his grave. Earl's Chevrolet stylist Carl Renner produced the car for the 1954 Motorama, giving the public an advanced view of another car already approved for production. Earl based the station wagon on a production-standard Chevrolet chassis; the current owner, however, chose something much wilder.

who spoke unwittingly into the styling department's concealed microphones said if General Motors would build it, they would come. Some 20,000 went to their local dealers hoping to order cars. They never had a chance.

It got worse. Once the other 250 cars became available, there weren't another 250 celebrities, authorities, and athletes anxious to pay a high price for a crude car. Corvettes leaked water at the windshield and the top. It wasn't an inexpensive car, but it acted like one.

The car sent mixed signals. Tom Keating, sensitive to public perceptions, attempted to direct their interpretation. In a statement released after the introduction, he said, "In the Corvette, we have built

Carl Renner mated the front end of the Corvette to a station wagon chassis, adding in the distinctive round rear end profile and rocket taillights. The original car created a great deal of enthusiasm and demand that Chevrolet hoped would translate directly to sports car sales. Then, like almost all prototypes, Chevrolet ordered the original show car cut up and destroyed in July 1955. The car died but not the idea.

Chevrolet stylist Chuck Stebbins authored the vertical chrome strakes that first appeared on the Corvette Nomad. Chevrolet later carried these over onto the production BelAir Nomad station wagon introduced in 1955. Tom Armstrong, owner of this re-creation, had saved every photograph of the original he'd seen, so when opportunity knocked, he had his research done.

a sports car in the American tradition . . . to satisfy the American public's conception of beauty, comfort, convenience plus performance."

While Keating directed its exclusivity toward the country club set, it was too unsophisticated for them. On the other hand, sports car enthusiasts cried for more power and a transmission they could shift themselves. While Chevrolet, as a division, sold 1,342,480 cars in 1953, only 183 of them were Corvettes.

The Flint assembly plant, actually the former customer delivery garage on Van Slyke Avenue and Atherton, was small; its line was long enough for only six chassis. It gave engineers and manufacturing personnel the chance to get the bugs out of the system while the line in St. Louis was being converted to Corvette's permanent home. There were bugs. Start-up was slow, grueling, and exhausting. It took work crews three 16-hour days to assemble the first car, completed on June 30. Through July, they were satisfied to finish a car a day. By August, three cars a day rolled off the line.

Chevrolet got the plant running smoothly enough to open for tours, to show off not only the completely fiberglass car but also the somewhat unusual assembly system. Throughout October and November, members of the Michigan Education Association visited the plant. Their tour lasted four hours, long enough that Chevrolet fed them a box lunch. They moved through the structure on a kind of trolley. Retired teachers Jean and John Anderson remember that the pace was frantic. "The workers appeared to be under great pressure," Jean said. "They were working like crazy. We saw everything. I mean *everything*. They had what may have been the first robots in the auto industry, and these things would just pick up the engine block and turn it every which way. The tour guide stressed that the assembly line procedure at this plant brought all the parts together for various subassemblies and then all of those to final assembly." Parts came from outside the plant and outside Flint. Engines arrived from Chevrolet's Tonawanda plant, and A. O. Smith, in Granite City, Illinois, assembled the bare frames. Both body panels and tires came from eastern Ohio.

On December 24, Chevrolet ended production at Flint, having completed 301 cars. Four days later, production started in St. Louis at the old millwork building for buggies and early automobiles. Before the new year, the St. Louis factory completed its first 14 cars. Total production for 1953 ended at 315 cars, according to *Automotive Industries* in February 1954. By June, when the first magazine reviews appeared, production was up to 50 per day in St. Louis (it had reached 50 a month in Flint).

In May 1953, a month before production began, Chevrolet hired an ambitious, inventive engineer who first saw the Corvette as one of the crowd visiting New York's Motorama. Zora Arkus-Duntov

Hot Rod Enterprises (HRE), based in Auburn, Washington, had a customer who had hoped to create the replica, but he died before realizing his dream. He had acquired a 1955 Bel Air Nomad wagon along with more modern running gear—the ZR-1 LT5 V-8 and ZF six-speed transaxle—and much of its suspension. Successful businessman and long-time Corvette enthusiast Tom Armstrong adopted the concept, and HRE returned to work. It was a project of epic proportions and challenges.

came in with good credentials. He was born Zachary Arkuss on Christmas Day 1909 in Brussels. Writer George Damon Levy interviewed Duntov in 1988 for *Corvette Quarterly* and learned his story. When he was in his teens, his mother, a Russian physician, divorced her engineer husband. She later married Josef Duntov, another engineer, and "Zora," the Russian diminutive nickname for Zachary, began hyphenating his last names. Schooled in Germany, he loved cars and gained considerable racing and engineering experience throughout Europe. He helped several owners tame the handling of their early V-8-powered Allards. He joined Cole's staff when he was 44 and went straight to work for Olley. He got into the first engineering Corvette as soon as he could. Pressing it to its limit, he found, as he told Levy, "a car in which the two ends were fighting each other." While the rear end's canted springs did achieve Olley's goal of inducing understeer, the front end that Olley had made from modified sedan parts caused oversteer, from which it was difficult to recover. It was too late to help the 1953 production cars. Still, Duntov performed the first of countless surgeries he would undertake over the next 22 years.

Sales improved in 1954, aided by the start of major advertising for the car. (The first Detroit-area newspaper ad appeared in late May 1953. It announced a chance to see "America's Sensational Sports Car!" at the Michigan Motor Show in early June.) One 1954 series was image-oriented. It ran several times in the *New Yorker* magazine, each time using the tag line "First of the dream cars to come true." These emphasized Corvette's styling, handling, and unique appeal.

Corvette made its first international racing appearance entering the third annual 12 Hours of Sebring on March 7, with one car from A. E. Young, to be co-driven by Jack Morton. Before the race began Saturday afternoon, Young withdrew the car.

Engineering modified the camshaft, boosting horsepower by 5 to 155. Chevrolet added two paint colors, black and Sportsman Red, all with red interiors. Toward the end of the year, cars began to appear in Pennant Blue with beige interiors. Chevrolet changed the black top for 1953 into tan for 1954. While St. Louis had the capacity to produce 10,000 Corvettes a year, they manufactured just 3,640, and Chevrolet sold only 2,780. *Automotive Industries* magazine reported on November 15, 1953, that, anticipating a slowdown in production, Chevrolet would cut its St. Louis workforce from 2,900 to 1,400. Between 1953 and 1954 sales, Chevrolet found itself with a surplus of nearly 1,100 unsold cars on January 1, 1955.

Ed Cole reflected on the dilemma surrounding the Corvette in an interview at the time. Quoted 18 years afterward in Karl Ludvigsen's 1973 book *Corvette: America's Star-Spangled Sports Car,* Cole lamented that Chevrolet "had no real feeling for the market. Was the Corvette for the boulevard driver or the sports-car tiger? We weren't quite sure." The inability to define their customer—*Road & Track* enthusiasts or *New Yorker* sophisticates—caused Keating and Cole a great deal of soul searching. They slowed St. Louis production to 16 cars a day and quietly worried if that was still too much.

While management wrestled with the Corvette's future, Clare MacKichan's Chevrolet studio and Ed Cole's engineers pressed ahead with revisions and updates. Styling wanted to use an egg-crate grille design similar to the 1955 Bel Air, and it proposed a functional hood air scoop and several dummy louvers along the body panel behind the front wheels. They wanted to rid the rear end of

(opposite top) Ahem. This ain't no Blue Flame Six. Owners Tom and Susan Armstrong had the ZR-1 LT5 engine installed, and HRE created custom headers that fed exhaust into flat-bottom collectors, then to 3-inch tubes into the muffler. While the Motorama Nomad exhausts ran out through the rear fenders, Armstrong voted to keep the body clean, and HRE routed the exhaust straight out the back.

(opposite bottom) To achieve 1954 Nomad proportions and appearances, HRE and Armstrong sectioned 3 inches out of the car body and lowered the floor 1.5 inches to provide adequate headroom before fitting four leather-and-tweed bucket seats, the full-length console, heating, air conditioning, a sound system, and even beverage holders. Armstrong had the 1955 Nomad wagon dashboard cleaned up, and he replaced the instruments with digital readouts.

its troublesome taillight bullets. These required extensive hand-work from the beginning, because matched-metal molds had difficulty with the abruptness of the curves and the complexity of shapes projected out into space. But again there was no money. For 1955, colors could be changed; styling replaced Pennant Blue with Harvest Gold, and Sportsman Red became Gypsy Red. They could barely touch the body. Harley Earl and others began to hear that the car's future was in serious doubt.

Throughout 1954, the car still suffered from what reviewers and enthusiasts alike thought was insufficient horsepower. When Ed Cole arrived at the Chevrolet division, the engineering staff was already developing a new 231-cubic-inch displacement V-8 overhead-valve engine, a legacy that Ed Kelley, the previous chief engineer, left behind. Cole felt this needed immediate attention. He wanted to increase the V-8's displacement to 265-cubic-inch displacement, and Tom Keating agreed. It was an engine size Cole, Harry Barr, and a third engineer and racing enthusiast, Harry Burrell, had mused over while they were still at Cadillac. The 265 figure was a kind of genie-in-a-bottle displacement they felt offered them lots of room to grow and plenty of opportunity to play. According to Beverly Rae Kimes in *Chevrolet—A History from 1911,* Cole and Barr had designed that engine many times in their heads before Chevrolet offered them the opportunity to build the real thing. Keating's endorsement was all it took, and Alfred Sloan approved the project without ever seeing plans. Now Cole needed engineers, and he hired hundreds, taking his staff up to 2,900. He felt the need for this engine was urgent. His staff designed it and built a running model in 15 weeks. (Admittedly, for Cole and Barr, this design was old hat. They spent two years carefully and deliberately designing and developing Cadillac's 331.) Cole was so certain of the design that he ordered tooling and plant space before Barr and his engineers even fired the 265 for the first time.

Cole's engineers were anxious to see how it would affect the Corvette's performance, so they refitted the engineering

Even 195 horsepower and an available three0speed manual transmission,a legacy of unsold 1954 models meant the production barely reached 700 in 1955, and poor sales threatened the car with extinction.

development car, 1953 number 002, with a prototype V-8. It ran flawlessly for 25,000 miles out at Milford, convincing Keating and Cole to offer it not only with the Powerglide but eventually with a three-speed manual gearbox for 1955.

The new engine pumped life into the ailing Corvette. Performance jumped as 0–60 miles per hour times dropped three full seconds to 8.0 in the late 1955 cars fitted with the three-speed. Top speed climbed to 120 miles per hour,w and fuel economy improved from 17 to 20 miles per gallon. Chevrolet's timing was nearly miraculous. In March 1954, Ford announced its 160-horsepower, Y-block, V-8-engined Thunderbird with roll-up windows, to sell for $2,695. Production would begin in September. *Automotive Industries* reported the news: "A notable difference, however, is that it is being tooled for production in steel rather than plastic. The foregoing may be significant, since tooling cost is close to $5 million, compared to about $500,000 to tool the Corvette for plastic production. It could indicate that Ford expects to build more sports cars than Chevrolet does."

Motor Trend's Don MacDonald compared and contrasted the two, offering his perspective in the June 1955 issue: "The basic difference between the Corvette and Thunderbird is not so much the body material, but a conflicting analysis of the American market. The Corvette was patterned closely after the European concept of a competition car. Conversely, the designers of the Thunderbird aimed at and achieved a California custom flavor. This is why Corvette presently has an *almost* purist indifference to the problem of weather protection. It was easy for the come-lately Thunderbird to offer adequate coverage. . . ." MacDonald couldn't know it was cost, not "purism," that affected weather protection.

(previous pages) Of the 700 cars manufactured, production records are scarce. Historians guess that about 325 of these were Polo White, 180 were Gypsy Red, another 120 were Harvest Gold, and just 45 appeared in this Pennant Blue. The rarest color seems to be Corvette Copper, with perhaps only 15 manufactured.

Chevrolet Styling created the new designation for the optional V-8 engine by capitalizing the V in the side name badge, CheVrolet. As tire technology improved, GM and others switched to tubeless tires late in the 1954 model year. It is likely that nearly all 1955 models arrived on tubeless Firestone, Goodrich, or U.S. Royal tires.

The V-8 weighed 41 pounds less than the Blue Flame Six, improving handling as well as acceleration. Its 8.7-second 0–60 miles per hour times beat the McCullough supercharged six (though V-8 quarter-mile times were slower.) What's more, reviewer Ralph Poole in Road & Track *magazine's test recorded 2–3 miles per gallon better fuel economy than the six.*

Ironically, despite MacDonald's assessment of the Corvette's competitive nature compared to the Ford, at Sebring on March 13, 1955, a single Thunderbird entry ran unchallenged by Corvettes. Fred Scherer of Skokie, Illinois, and co-driver Don Davis started 9th and finished 37th.

By the end of 1955, Ford sold 16,155 copies of its T-bird, while Chevrolet had halted production midyear, stopping after assembling 700 Corvettes. Chevrolet sold just 675 (a few dozen of which were fitted with the manual gearbox).

These kinds of numbers sent ordinary men to the showers, defeated and humiliated. But neither Earl nor Cole, Keating nor Curtice were ordinary men. Alfred Sloan was still chairman, and it was he who had already said, "The question is not simply one of maximizing the rate of return for a specific short period of time . . . [but] the fundamental consideration was an average return over a long period of time." With the sales figures his other cars produced, he would tell his board it could afford to be patient.

In 1953, General Motors sold 45 percent of the new automobiles and trucks in the United States. Chevrolet knew it had scored a home run with its V-8. The Corvette just had not yet caught the buyer's imaginations. After this, few people held much hope that Cole's new engine and a manual gearbox alone could save the car. "By the looks of it, the Corvette is on its way out," Duntov wrote privately to Cole and Olley in mid-October 1954. But, he argued, "dropping the car now will have adverse effects internally and externally. It is admission of failure: failure of aggressive thinking in the eyes of the organization, failure to develop a saleable product in the eyes of the outside world."

It was not Duntov's passionate eloquence that saved the Corvette. It wasn't even Cole's V-8. The final decision rested in the boardroom, and GM's board still did what Alfred Sloan felt was best for the company. Sloan looked across town and saw Thunderbird's success. It furthered his belief that the Corvette was the right car for GM and Chevrolet at the time, even if they didn't yet have the car "right." The Thunderbird sharpened GM's senses. Chevrolet Research, a group Sloan had created, reported that 17 percent of American households were two-car families. Chevrolet had once again outsold Ford, 1,646,681 cars to 1,573,276. Yet Ford had found 16,155 buyers where Chevrolet had not; Sloan knew GM had to recapture those individuals. He had no idea Ford was about to help.

Most production V-8 1955 models came with the automatic transmission, now improved to near perfection. Historians estimate perhaps only 75 cars appeared with the 3-speed manual. Even fewer were delivered with speedometers reading in kilometers, not miles. Export Corvettes sported few other modifications.

1956-1958

CHAPTER FOUR

ED COLE GETS SERIOUS

y the time Tom Keating approved Corvette production for two additional years, through 1957, designers and engineers had little time to make substantial changes to draw back buyers lost to the Thunderbird. Still, when the Motorama staff unveiled the 1956 Corvette in the Waldorf, Earl's stylists and Cole's engineers had transformed the car.

Mercedes-Benz had replaced Jaguar XK-120s as their target. Mercedes' 300SL racing coupes appeared in 1952 with raked head-lights like the first Corvettes. When production SLs appeared for 1954, Mercedes' designer Paul Braiq had mounted the lights vertically in the fenders. The engineers slightly tilted the in-line six-cylinder engine to lower the hood, which Braiq gave two gentle bulges for clearance. To Chevrolet's Clare MacKichan, those bulges said "power," the image everyone wanted for the V-8. When stylist Bob Cadaret finished the front of the 1956 Corvette, it resembled the 1954 SL. (Stylists commonly plagiarized each other. Jaguar's designers admitted duplicating a 1940 BMW race car for their XK-120.)

Another design element came from home. Cadillac's 1955 Motorama LaSalle II dream car introduced a long horizontal scallop in the body side. Now gracing the Corvette, it imparted a classic ele-gance to the side view, creating visual appeal yet breaking up the panel. Cadaret scalloped the taillights into the fenders. He achieved an economy of line by removing the excesses. The Corvette got roll-up windows (with power windowlifts available), outside door handles, and an optional power system for the convertible top. These things were impossible between Motorama and production start in 1953. Windows required forming curved glass and fabricating lift mecha-nisms and support rails. Harley Earl had wanted Bohnstedt's show car to remind everyone of sunny days. Purists took MG-TCs and Jaguar XK-120 roadsters with side curtains and without complaints, so his expectations seemed less scandalous at the time.

(previous pages) It was supposed to look like the 1958 and 1959 models with four headlights and three front air intakes. Styling and engineering were nearly overwhelmed with big changes to the passenger car and pickup truck line, and they got swamped. Compounded by poor revenues from dismal 1954 sales, little time and no money meant only minor changes were possible for 1957.

For 1958, Chevrolet gave the Corvette an extra pair of headlights. The chrome strip running back from between the paired headlights was a 1958-only feature.

Mercedes-Benz developed the car in 1952 to evaluate its return to racing. After it won the 24 Hours of Le Mans and the Mexican Carrera Panamericana, American importer Max Hoffman quickly ordered 1,000. Because M-B had assembled it from production parts, like Chevrolet had done with its Corvette, it was easy to put into production starting in 1954.

Mercedes-Benz kept the car low by mounting its in-line three-liter six-cylinder engine on a slight angle. M-B had tamed fuel-injection so well that it introduced the system on this production sports car. With its four-speed transmission and the right final drive gearing, the 300SL could touch 150 miles per hour. Different gears let it accelerate to 60 miles per hour in less than eight seconds.

Tom Keating approved the 1956 styling changes in February 1955. The Motorama unveiling and production start were possible only by using fiberglass. (If the St. Louis plant used dies for steelstamping rather than for fiberglass molding, the 1956 car would have arrived closer to 1957.)

In mid-December 1953, Zora Duntov had written a memo that became a wake-up call to the Chevrolet division. He saw car enthusiast magazines filled up with stories about Ford. Would this exposure prompt readers to stay with Ford as their income grew? He believed Chevrolet could penetrate this market, but it would take time to get in. He proposed that Chevrolet produce engine and chassis performance parts and market them to the public.

"If the speed parts are carried as R.P.O. [regular production option] items for the Corvette," Duntov wrote in the memo, "they will be recognized by the hot-rodders as the very parts they were looking for to hop up the Chevy. . . . I do know that in 1954 sports car enthusiasts will get hold of

Chevrolet manufactured just six of these special versions, five in white and this one in Aztec Copper. This car also holds 35 national drag race victories and class records at El Mirage dry lake in California, where it was driven by Dean Moon. While exhaust exited through the rear bumper guards on production models, these six-cylinder cars ran it to the side just ahead of the rear wheels.

The exhaust pipes exited through the rear bumper on 1956–57 production Corvettes. Shown is a customized 1957 version.

the Corvette and whether we like it or not, will race it. [The] most frequent statement from this group is 'we will put a Cadillac [V-8] in it [for more power]. I think this is not good! Most likely they will meet with Allard trouble—that is, breaking, sooner or later, mostly sooner, everything between flywheel and road wheels. Since we cannot prevent people from racing Corvettes, maybe it is better to help them do a good job at it."

Duntov believed creating a sense of loyalty in Chevrolet buyers required faith that Chevrolet would produce what buyers wanted. He still had to prove himself before his ideas took on credibility, however.

His camshaft designs and the Ar-Dun cylinder heads he and his brother Yura had developed prior to joining Chevrolet earned them respect as creative development engineers. Duntov's work taming the handling of the 1956 production model established his chassis credentials within Chevrolet. The mark of Zora began to carry weight on his adopted car.

Corvettes came closer to realizing Duntov's handling goals since the new 265-cubic-inch displacement V-8 weighed 41 pounds less than the old Blue Flame Special. The V-8 was shorter and lower, which also helped handling. The engine with its single Carter four-barrel carburetor produced 210 horsepower; an optional second four-barrel raised

The redesigned body for 1956 eliminated Harley Earl's rocket taillights and introduced the cove styling motif that would remain through 1962. Body assembly quality improved for 1956 since the fiberglass panels now were pressed entirely by matched-metal molds, a much more precise method of panel forming. These six SR prototypes each were fitted with Halibrand magnesium alloy hubs and knock-off wheels.

output to 225 horsepower. Duntov ran a preproduction prototype 1956 Corvette up Pike's Peak in September 1955. Camouflaged as a full-sized passenger car, he set a new class record of 17 minutes, 24 seconds on the 12.5-mile climb to the top. Yet this meant little to average customers. Speed compared to other cars caught people's attention. The Jaguar XK-120 in hottest trim reached 130 miles per hour. Reports said Mercedes' coupe was capable of 146 miles per hour in standard trim. What if the engineers could coax 150 miles per hour out of the Corvette on Daytona Beach speed runs?

Cole gave Duntov clearance, and he moved to GM's Phoenix test track to determine how he could reach this speed. He needed another 30 horsepower, something possible with a wilder cam. Engineering cast several from his designs. Duntov could now run the engine to 6,300 rpm, producing enough power to reach, theoretically, 163 miles per hour.

This commitment to performance and publicizing the results was primarily the effort of one engineer, but not the one most people credit. While Zora Duntov could suggest changes or implement them, Ed Cole had the power to influence board chairman Harlow Curtice. A V-8 engine, new styling, Duntov's mountain record, and Daytona goals all were building blocks, raising the Corvette's foundation

(opposite lower right) While Chevrolet
extensively redesigned the car for 1956,
they hung on to the original dashboard
design. Gearshift knobs on the three-
speed manual were first white plastic
and later chrome except on these six
SR prototypes, which were among the
first 1956 models assembled.

The introduction of Corvette's Regular
Production Option (RPO) dual four-
barrel carburetor, RPO 469, provided
big news for 1956. Buyers felt the
improvement from 195 to 225
horsepower. These six SR models,
using RPO 449 with slightly higher-
lift camshafts (the so-called Duntov
cams), boasted 240 horsepower. SR
models featured a shorter steering
column to allow drivers more room to
move their arms while cornering.

higher and constructing a more stable structure for Cole's own aspirations for the car.

Cole had Duntov on his staff with road racing experience, and he had Mauri Rose, a three-time Indianapolis 500 winner working as coordinator with the private and dealer teams racing in NASCAR. Cole brought them to Milford Proving Grounds on December 13, 1955, to discuss racing Corvettes internationally starting in Sebring the next March. He invited his engine wizards Harry Barr and Walter Mackenzie (who became Chevrolet's racing manager-without-the-title), and other performance-oriented engineers, including Maurice "Rosey" Rosenberger, an engine and transmission problems troubleshooter, and Russell Sanders, chief of passenger-car chassis design, as well as outsiders Briggs Cunningham and John Fitch. Rose took notes that Corvette historians John Neas and Dick Robinson recently have unearthed and first published in *The Corvette Restorer,* the journal of the National Corvette Restorers' Society (NCRS). Chevrolet gave enthusiasts a sports car to race. Now Ed Cole wanted to know what Chevrolet should do so that they could win with it.

Fitch quickly offered constructive comments. Chevy needed to improve gear ratios in the three-speed transmission if no four-speeds were

Following successful speed record attempts on Daytona Beach in February, Ed Cole committed Chevrolet engineers to a four-car effort for the 12 Hours of Sebring in March 1956. John Fitch supervised the effort, run from a hangar at the airport circuit. For five weeks, from February 18 to race day March 26, engineers worked in Florida and in Michigan to prepare parts for the cars.

Chevrolet produced 3,467 convertibles throughout the model year, but it was these six that began to ensure the continued existence of the car. Unofficially dubbed the SRs, these cars, though largely stock in appearance, bore numerous modifications that made the cars race-ready for Sebring. They showed sports car enthusiasts what a Corvette—in street or race trim—could do.

possible. He worried about Corvette's oversteering tendencies and its 50/50 weight balance, though others present reminded him the Mercedes 300SL was 40 percent front/60 percent rear, and the new Aston-Martin DB3 was 50/50.

Cunningham found Corvette's steering too light and the wheel too close to his chest. He suggested revising the suspension since hard braking dropped the nose, dipping headlights uselessly low for night racing. He recommended doubling fuel capacity to run farther between pit stops.

Cole quickly committed his two 1956 engineering department development cars plus a third pre-production model to the Sebring event now barely 100 days away. (He had already okayed Duntov's effort with one of the cars for the January Daytona Beach Flying and Standing Mile speed records.) He ordered a single four-speed German ZF gearbox for evaluation and tagged Frank Burrell, his engineer

All four of the racers received 37-gallon fuel tanks, limited slip differentials, Halibrand magnesium
hubs, and knock-off wheels with Firestone Supersport 170 tires. Brakes were a challenge for racing.
Fitch and Duntov tried four systems before settling on Bendix Cerametallix linings inside
Chevrolet's heavily finned cast-iron drums.

who had aided Cunningham's Cadillacs at Le Mans, to run the project. After the Daytona runs, Burrell would get Duntov's Corvette at a rented garage in Sebring to supervise its conversion to a road-racing car.

At Daytona, the perfect mix of sand, low tides, and light winds never materialized. December slipped into early January 1956 before Duntov got a certified two-way run averaging 150.58 miles per hour. He met his goal using an engine that produced 240 horsepower from parts soon to be available over the counter. The crew went back to the official Daytona Speed Weeks in February with three cars, each engine with modified heads producing a 10.3:1 compression ratio and developing 255 horsepower. John Fitch, Duntov, and Betty Skelton, a veteran automobile and airplane racer, each had a car to run.

Ford showed up with its Thunderbirds, and competition was fierce. Officials measured times not only for top speed runs but also for standing-start mile runs. At the end of the week, suffering traction problems not solved even by running snow tires on the sand, John Fitch finished third (at 86.87 miles per hour) behind two Thunderbirds at the completion of the standing-start mile runs.

Racers don't need to know road speed, but they do need to know how fast their engine is turning, so John Fitch and his crew of Chevrolet engineers revised the sweeping speedometer to serve as an easily readable tachometer. This effort was Chevrolet's first factory attempt at road racing, and for Fitch, Duntov, and the others, every day meant new lessons learned and solutions invented.

Racing rules required crop hides fire extinguishers. With the materials of old, it was a gamble whether the fire or the chemicals from the extinguisher would kill the driver first.

Duntov averaged 147.3 miles per hour for the flying mile, beating all challengers, including the Thunderbirds.

In early January, Cole and Burrell learned that the Federation International de l'Automobile (FIA), Sebring's race-sanctioning body, required that all race car modifications had to be available to consumers for cars entered in production classes. They also needed to build at least 25 identical models for the racing version car to be classified as "production." They created a new model, the SR. Whether the initials meant "special racing" or "Sebring racer" remains uncertain, but the designation first appeared in print in a memo from Russ Sanders in engineering on January 6, 1956.

Rules allowed a small windscreen, and John Fitch, Zora Duntov, and Betty Skelton already had proven the value of this modification during their speed runs on the Daytona Beach. The curved plexiglass tipped the air up and over their drivers' helmets without pushing more air than necessary out of the way.

The Corvette SS proved its competitiveness on the sands of Daytona Beach back when racing took place on the beach itself. 2002 General Motors Corporation. Used with permission of GM Media Archives.

Engineering planned to equip the SR models with the Duntov camshaft, a semilocked differential, a 37-gallon fuel tank, seat belts, Auburn clutch, and Halibrand Spot disc brakes and quick change wheels. The memo confirmed that Walter Mackenzie would promote sales of complete cars through selected dealers.

Chevrolet was officially going racing. Well, not "officially." "It is particularly desirable to management," Walter Mackenzie wrote to Cole on February 6, "that dealers be used wherever possible as the parties who can own and enter the Corvettes in competition. This is more desirable even than outside private enterprises of any kind (at least in the initial stages of the new venture) because it must not be made to appear that such an outside firm or enterprise is merely being hired as a 'front' by Chevrolet." Industry critics already charged that car makers were obsessed with speed and horsepower without paying attention to safety improvements. The cries would get loud enough to reach GM chairman Harlow Curtice by 1957, with significant results for future racing efforts.

Meanwhile, Fitch added a fourth car to the team after Daytona ended. By late January, he and Burrell were in Sebring working on the team. Barr's engineers had no time to prep the fourth car, so Cole purchased items through Don Allen Chevrolet in Miami, Florida. Harry Burrell drove its break-in miles from the St. Louis factory back to Sebring. Back in Detroit, Duntov, Rosenberger, and Sanders were inventing and testing parts so they could catalog each one for eventual over-the-counter sales.

Halibrand's disc brakes were not ready. Fitch knew Sebring was hard on brakes, so he and Burrell settled on newly designed large drums. Burrell cut cooling ducts into the drum backing plates, fed by large air vents ducted from the front grille through inner fender wells. He also had to modify the Carter carburetors; these sloshed fuel in hard cornering, flooding the engine and slowing the car. Cole's engineers had studied the Mercedes 300SL. Fuel injection was something they wanted to bring to the Corvette. The Sebring carburetor tests strengthened their resolve.

Burrell and Fitch got one V-8 bored out to 307-cubic-inch displacement and fitted it with a prototype Rochester fuel injection and the ZF four-speed gearbox. The increased displacement shifted it to B-class while the other three cars remained in class C. Sixty cars started the race and, typically, 24 finished. Two of the Corvettes quit early. Class C car #5 quit after an hour with a broken rear axle. A second class C, #7, retired with a burnt piston after two hours. The fourth, #6, finished 15th overall, running with only top gear for hours. A virtually dealership-stock entry, #3, finished next to last. Fitch's B-class car, #1, worried him when its clutch began failing by the second lap, but his Le Mans experiences had taught him to nurse ailing race cars. He brought it in ninth overall, first in Class B. For anyone who knew racing, it was an impressive debut. The cars won respect from their competitors and the crowd.

Chevrolet's advertising agency, Campbell-Ewald, raced Corvette promotion into new territory. Agency writer and racing director Arthur "Barney" Clark prepared an ad for the April 1956 New York Auto Show program. He invited viewers to "Bring on the hay bales!" Clark pressed harder in the July issues of *Road & Track* and *Hot Rod*. The now-legendary ad

Engines for three of the four race cars started as stock RPO 449 models with the Duntov high-lift cam, modified to allow a 7,000 rpm redline. Engineers Harry Barr and Maurice Rosenberger bored out a fourth engine to 307 cubic inches to fit into Class B where the competition was less intense. It finished in 9th overall whereas this "production" C-class entry retired after just two hours with a burnt piston.

(above) Stylist Dave Wheeler created the shapes that became famous not with Jerry Earl at the wheel but with dentist Dr. Dick Thompson. Dubbed the SR-2, the car proved too much of a handful for the younger Earl at its debut at Road America's June Sprints in 1956. Thompson took over. He found it too slow and heavy to be seriously competitive.

Harley Earl loved European sports cars. Still, it annoyed him when his son Jerry purchased a Ferrari to go racing in SCCA events. Harley brought in a Sebring racer chassis and set his stylists to work building his son a better Corvette. Unfortunately, Harley's stylistic improvements to a pure production Corvette made it "modified" in SCCA's view, placing it against much tougher competition.

showed a stark black-and-white photo of Fitch's Corvette, headlights on, driving lights mounted below the grille, with co-driver Walt Hansgen running around the back of the car. It looked like a *Life* magazine photo. In the bleached white sky above the runner, Clark etched a new legend: "The Real McCoy." His text detailed "glove soft upholstery, roll-up windows, ample luggage space and a velvety ride." But then it hit: "Other people make a luxury car," Clark wrote with a none-too-subtle slam at Thunderbird, "that has much the same dimensions as this. That's not so tough. And the Europeans make some real rugged competition sports cars—and that's considerably tougher. But nobody but Chevrolet makes a luxury car that *also* is a genuine 100-proof sports car."

Cole and company performed postmortems. Brakes plagued them at Sebring. Production brakes were inadequate for even the six-cylinder engines with automatic transmissions. For competition with a 255-horsepower V-8, Burrell, Rosenberg, and Sanders had tried everything available on short notice. As Karl

Ludvigsen reported, "The only combination that proved it could stay the distance was that of Bendix Cerametallix linings inside heavily finned iron drums. . . . But [these brakes] were heavy, and they forced the Corvette to become heavier too."

Selecting the brakes was a decision with ramifications that went far beyond race day. It established ethics for future decisions in which someone balanced reduced weight against enhanced safety, comfort, or performance. Zora Duntov told Ludvigsen these brakes represented "a watershed decision that took the Corvette irrevocably in the direction of a larger, heavier car, barring any possible return to a lightweight design concept."

Before 1956 ended, Ed Cole succeeded Tom Keating as Chevrolet division general manager. Chevrolet division had produced only 3,467 Corvettes, while Ford *sold* more than 15,000 of its Thunderbirds. Harlow Curtice and his board members kept faith that Cole's efforts with the Corvette simply had not yet had enough time to prove themselves. Ford knew all along that Ed Cole and General Motors planned to keep the Corvette a sports car. So Chase Morsey, a Ford product planner, set the Thunderbird's direction, and design chief Frank Hershey concurred with Morsey's vision. Ford Thunderbird was to be a personal car, they agreed, something that buyers knew fit between a

While it first raced with the RPO 449 265-cubic-inch V-8 of the other Sebring racers, by February 1957, it was running a modified 283 cubic-inch V-8 tuned to 310 horsepower. Engineers continued to experiment with brakes, using most successfully a set of Chrysler 4 inch wide brake drums with flexible shoes that ensured a firm braking fit even if the drums went slightly out of round from overheating or wear.

sports car and a family passenger car. Chevrolet, they concluded, could keep trying with its poorly selling sports car.

THE "FUELIE" SYSTEM

Chevrolet opened its Engineering Center within GM's 25-building Technical Center in December 1956. Begun in 1949, the $125 million, 990-acre campus was located in suburban Warren, about 10 miles north of the General Motors building. One of the first projects engineers completed in their new digs was one started downtown in engineering's former home, the old, drafty bank building. Intent on improving intake/exhaust flow on the 265, engineering increased cylinder bore, yielding a 283-cubic-inch displacement engine. For 1957, Corvette offered two four-barrel carburetors with the engine, to produce 245 horsepower. A still hotter version cranked out 270 horsepower. The wildest tune developed 283 horsepower, the first GM engine to make one-horsepower-per-cubic-inch-of-displacement. It did it with Ramjet Fuel Injection, Chevrolet's production successor to Rochester's experimental system that Burrell ran on Fitch's 1956 Sebring B-class winner. While publicly announced in October 1956, cars with the "Fuelie" system didn't appear in large numbers until spring 1957 (prior to the May 1 four-speed introduction). Of the 6,338 Corvettes produced for 1957, Chevrolet made 1,040 with the Rochester Ramjet injection. They delivered just 664 cars with the four-speed gearbox. *Road & Track* recorded 0–60 miles per hour times of 5.7 seconds in a test car with a 4.11:1 rear axle.

When faced with saving weight, money was no object. Zora Duntov, who had plenty of seat time in Porsche's 550 Spyders at Le Mans, knew their Spyder seats were not only light but comfortable. He acquired two and fitted them into the SR-2.

Alfred Sloan's intention had been to restyle car bodies every other year, but this was costly and had become challenging since each division was adding new models. GM's product lead time slowed to three years. Chassis and powertrain engineers had mechanical improvements ready for the entire truck and passenger car line-up. Substantial engineering improvements and a new body were in the works for the Corvette. Ed Cole knew Chrysler and Ford had new bodies on much of their 1957 lineup; however, engineering delays held up GM's introductions.

"We were in the studio," former stylist Robert Cumberford explained, "working on the '57 Corvette. It just got behind. The regular car line had too many new things and they couldn't handle it: a new engine, gearbox, chassis, suspension, body and interior. The new pick-up truck had a hood with Corvette-style hood speed-bumps. That took body engineers away who would have made the four-headlight, three-grille 1957 Corvette. This is the car that everyone knows as the 1958." Between timing and dismal production and sales of 1954, a quick nip and tuck was all that were possible for the 1957 Corvette model year.

"Corvette was not a plum assignment anyway," Cumberford explained. "There was nothing really desirable about it at all. I got the Corvette to do the year they sold 700 cars. Chevrolet dealers didn't like them. How rich a plum can that be?"

Cumberford was assigned to Chuck Jordan's Studio 5, doing drawings for Earl for the intended 1957 Corvette. The young designer came up with ideas for a car for which he'd gotten no directions. Dave Holls, former GM director of corporate design, and automotive journalist Michael Lamm collaborated on a history of car design, *A Century of Automotive Style,* published in 1996. Holls worked for Earl from 1952 through 1958 and knew his procedures. This one was typical.

"Earl developed ways for getting the most from his designers," Holls wrote. "He rarely dictated and never gave clear, precise instruction. He purposely kept his suggestions vague . . . , and by changing

Many enthusiasts have suspected Jaguar's D-type racer inspired the SR-2 fin. Its creator, Bob Cumberford, recalled that it grew from a desire to improve vehicle stability, which is also why Jaguar used the fin.

Its production origins are apparent behind the oversize 8,000 rpm tachometer where the speedometer is visible. The machine-turned dash was a styling addition. Designer Bob Cumberford was responsible for stretching the nose 10 inches farther and adding the headrest and fin to the SR-2.

direction often and unexpectedly, Earl gave his designers the greatest possible latitude to use their imaginations." Studio etiquette dictated that designers took direction from their studio managers.

"This was common practice," Cumberford explained 40 years later. "I sat in this studio by myself drawing a Corvette the way I thought it ought to be and I would draw a Corvette the way the drawings were going on the wall. I'd been around long enough to know what Harley Earl and his design committee didn't like. Harley Earl had this high, squeaky voice. And he stuttered. Well, he really talked that way to fill time so that nobody else could talk. It was his way to keep everybody else silent. You could see he was appalled [by drawings on the walls]. This project was not to go in the direction that the wall showed." Cumberford emptied his drawer onto his table, and Earl asked him why these weren't on the wall as well. Cumberford said that while he liked his own ideas, he followed the studio direction. The next morning, Security told Cumberford to report to Chevrolet studio manager Clare MacKichan.

"You and a kid from drafting are doing the Corvette around the corner," MacKichan told him.

Every studio in the building had a name or a number. The room Cumberford and the "kid" would use was Harley Earl's temporary office before his own had been completed in styling's administration building. It was a windowless 20 x 40-foot space. Tony Lapine was the "kid from drafting," and Cumberford had a photostat made of an X and put it up on the door, christening the room Studio X.

"We had no direction from anybody. Zora would come in, and he and Tony would tell stories," Cumberford said. Lapine raced in Europe, as had Duntov, and Cumberford had designed race cars in California before taking his job at GM. The three of them shared this interest. So some tasks, especially racing related, just walked in the door.

Despite tight budgets and stressed stylists and engineers, many enthusiasts regard the 1957 models (and those from 1956) as the loveliest of the early Corvettes. Harley Earl had already anointed Bill Mitchell as his successor. Mitchell regularly spent time removing Earl's excesses from each of the cars Earl had already completed.

Floridian Webster Benner Jr. joined GM Styling in 1955, transferring in late 1956 to Chevrolet engineering. However, he hated Michigan winters, and by mid-1957 he was back in Florida. He still had friends in styling and engineering, and they helped him initiate his own ideas, including fitting ribbed aluminum into the coves and mounting 1954 Buick Skylark wire wheels all around.

Jerry Earl, Harley's sports car enthusiast son, purchased a Ferrari to compete in SCCA events in 1956. Earl didn't want his son driving something foreign. He had Chevrolet designers and engineers build his son a race car. Cumberford did the styling.

"That car was done in four or five weeks," Cumberford remembered. "They brought in a car in early May, took the body off, did molds, and sent it off. The windshield panel was the same as the Sebring car. There was no headrest on it at the beginning and the fin came later too. Other than extending the front out 10 inches to make a better aerodynamic line over the hood, there were very few changes. It was just a stock car. It had a radio."

Duntov took the car to the styling mechanical assembly shops where he supervised SR-type modifications including Sebring-type Cerametallic brakes and a few other components. At the June Sprints at Elkhart Lake, Wisconsin, Jerry Earl entered the car, the first SR-2, but national-championship contender Dick Thompson drove it. To the SCCA, however, Earl's stylized bodywork made the racer a

"modified" car. At the end of its race against much leaner machines, Thompson said it needed a lot of weight removed from it. When the car came back to Detroit, the mechanical shops removed about 300 pounds from the SR-2 without doing anything obvious.

Later Earl suggested molding a headrest into the SR's rear deck, similar to what Duntov did for the Daytona cars. But by this time, Cumberford was back doing drawings for Earl. "Then he got a wild hair about doing the SS," Cumberford said with a broad smile.

"The original idea was to provoke management. Harley Earl wanted to provoke management." The speaker here was Anatole C. Lapine, the "kid from drafting," who went on to work at Opel in Russelsheim, Germany, and later to Porsche in Stuttgart where, as design chief there, he did the 928 among other things.

"One day we found a dirty white D-type Jaguar waiting for us. 'Let's use the D-type,' Harley Earl said. 'Change the body and drop a Chevy into it. And let's go to Sebring and beat everybody!' He

Ex-Chevrolet engineer/stylist Benner, replaced the factory stock steering wheel with the wood-rimmed wheel. During the more than 20 years he owned the car, he seemingly changed its exterior color about every seven years. It was white from the factory, but by late 1967 it was blue (and he installed air conditioning). In the early 1970s, he had it painted red.

Benner drag raced this car through the first several years he owned it. He had ordered the fuel-injected 283 but couldn't get it to run well. He swapped the engine for the 270 horsepower, 283-cubic-inch version with these two four-barrel carburetors. He never went back to the fuel injection.

had a supporter in this plan, his heir-apparent, Bill Mitchell. That was the plan when Ed Cole and Harry Barr walked into the room. (Harry Barr was Chevrolet division's chief engineer by this time.)"

Lapine continued: "Harley and Bill outlined what they had in mind. Cole and Barr just stood there and smiled. Then Zora Duntov came over with Jim Premo (who had first visited Bob Morrison's fiberglass operation in Ohio and now was Barr's assistant chief engineer).

"We already knew," Lapine said, "that you couldn't change the body of a D-Jaguar by putting tin-snips to structure. It didn't matter that MistEarl didn't know this. Or that Ed Cole and Harry Barr *did*. Harley accomplished what he set out to do." Dissatisfied with the half-effort of the SR-2, Earl wanted a

full-on styling exercise to go racing. "And soon, very soon, Stan Mott, Bob Cumberford, an engineer called Del Probst and I, as the kind of draftsman of the day, started on a car that became the SS Corvette. Zora purchased a Mercedes 300SL. They took the body off and underneath was its tubular space frame." Here Bob Cumberford resumed the tale.

"Once Zora had the body off the 300SL chassis, he put the chassis up on steel stands," Cumberford said. "Then he put a Chevrolet engine, transmission, and differential beside it. He made a tube frame out of wooden dowels, copying the Mercedes around Chevrolet running gear.

"It was really not possible to get a Corvette engine to fit the space of the Jaguar engine in the D-type. You'd have to redo a lot of stuff and Zora didn't want to do that. He wanted his own car. Of course, so did Harley Earl, so the SS came out of that."

Internally, the car was referred to as the XP-64, the letters standing for Experimental Pursuit, an abbreviation Earl had adopted from the military during World War II. It represented jet fighter planes still in development stage. Ed Cole funded one car. Duntov, through creative accounting methods, got enough spare pieces fabricated to assemble a second car, a vehicle dubbed "the mule." They built

This was Corvette's first Sebring class winner, driven by Dr. Dick Thompson and Swiss racer Gaston Andre. At the end of 12 hours, they had finished 12th overall, 1st in GT class. This car and its victory codified Duntov's idea to make high performance parts available through dealers. Many racers benefited from the competitive advantages of RPO 684, a complete suspension package that also included brake ventilation.

(lower left) This was RPO 579E, Corvette's 283-cubic-inch engine with 283-horsepower output through Chevrolet's new Rochester fuel injection. It had long been a GM Engineering goal to develop one horsepower for each cubic inch of displacement. Output of this racing version was closer to 305 horsepower. It was good enough to give the car a 20-lap victory at Sebring over the nearest Mercedes-Benz 300SL.

(lower right) RPO 419 was the factory-produced auxiliary hardtop, offered for the first time in 1957 at $215.20. Oddly, with so much attention to racing and weight considerations, there was no option yet deleting carpets, door panels, passenger seats, or other nonessentials. Still, the GT class was a production-based category, and few customers would want a car with no padding and only one seat.

this test car, partially skinned in rough fiberglass, to evaluate innovations in the XP-64. The mule's engine developed much less horsepower than the aluminum-head 283-cubic inch displacement V-8 with special fuel injection that Harry Barr's engineers were preparing. What's more, while styling formed the actual race car body from magnesium sheets, the mule was thick fiberglass weighing 150 pounds more. The weight showed up new flaws in cooling and in the brakes.

Duntov and his engineers had developed a remarkable braking system. Delco-Moraine was working on disc brakes, but Duntov distrusted anything not race proven. His own front-wheel, two-leading-shoe, center-plane brakes came off a 1956 Chrysler. He put those inside 12-inch diameter, 2.5-inch-wide cast-iron face/finned aluminum drums and used them at front and rear. He devised a kind of antilock braking system using two separate Kelsey-Hayes vacuum servos; pedal pressure modulated the front brakes. He connected the second servo using a pressurized air system so it reacted to the amount of pedal pressure and front brake force. It adjusted rear braking to that pressure. Duntov wanted 70 percent front/30 percent rear brake bias. He added an in-line mercury switch actuated by the car's angle during hard braking. Closing the switch sealed off the air-pipe, effectively holding the rear brakes at the last pressure that was applied. Without this clever system, as drivers increased front braking pressure, it almost ensured rear lockup, jeopardizing directional stability. Drivers could reorient the switch during a race as weather or track conditions required. In competition, Duntov learned that the rear brake lines were too small. This caused a delay in system

response that delivered spectacular brake lockups at the worst possible moment. Duntov eventually used larger diameter tubing.

In Friday practice at Sebring, both Juan Manuel Fangio, the Argentine grand prix world champion, and English racer Stirling Moss drove the mule, turning exceptionally fast times. Chevrolet had contracted with Fangio to drive the race, but the actual car arrived late, missing Fangio's cutoff date. This released him to drive a Maserati with whom Moss also had a contract. So John Fitch, who was managing Sebring production Corvette efforts, stepped in. He reached Italian grand prix and endurance champion Piero Taruffi, who flew overnight from Rome to join him.

They qualified the mule on the front row. Race morning revealed the magnesium-bodied car in its Harley Earl–specified blue finish. It was completed to spectacular Motorama show standards. As Karl Ludvigsen reported in *Corvette: America's Star-Spangled Sports Car*, it suffered inconsistent brake balance problems and hellish cockpit heat. The magnesium panels trapped the heat that the fiberglass

Chevrolet's new general manager, Ed Cole, as quoted in the media, was overjoyed with the Sebring finish. "That was the turn of the tide. That was when the car... began to confirm our original premise: there was a demand for a product that recaptured the sport and fun of motoring."

(above) Sebring in 1956 taught Ed Cole that outright victory came not to production cars modified for the track. Outright winners were outright race cars that did not evolve from existing models but led the evolution to the next product. Ironically, it was stylist Harley Earl who was the catalyst for this progressive step.

(opposite) Harley Earl had learned to throw challenges at management in order to get his dreams turned into reality. This Corvette SS started in Earl's imagination as a D-type Jaguar with enough bodywork modifications to install a Corvette engine. He let everyone know he wanted to race it at Sebring. When Ed Cole and chief engineer Harry Barr heard, they had a better idea, and this car was the result.

While it clearly brings to mind the striking lines of Jaguar's racing D-types, its dimensions came from a Mercedes-Benz 300SL that Harley Earl imported into his styling studios. Chevrolet chief stylist Clare MacKichan devised its shape. MacKichan was the man who supervised Sparky Bohnstedt's design for the first 1953 Motorama Corvette.

insulated from the drivers. Tin snips slashed the sleek body. But there was no remedy for brake bias problems without the Duntov system perfected on the mule.

Crowds swarmed the blue SS. Fitch started the race. As he had done the year before nursing a failing clutch, he quickly found a rhythm that kept the brakes from locking while cutting lap times to within a second of Fangio's qualifying effort. Yet problems and failures continued.

Taruffi noticed the car's handling deteriorating badly. The rear tires bounced into the body or hopped frantically after each bump in the airport's concrete surface. Overheated himself, he pulled in and engineers found the car was undriveable after only 23 laps.

"The failure of the SS, the only factory appearance of Chevrolet in racing," Bob Cumberford

With some time to work, Harry Barr's engine wizards developed aluminum cylinder heads and a heavily baffled magnesium oil pan for the standard fuel-injected 283-cubic-inch V-8. Engineering created a special intake manifold ducted through a scoop on the hood. Wind, tunnel testing suggested the normal manifold and intake was slightly better. On a dynamometer, the engine developed 307 horsepower at 6,400 rpm.

With weight clearly a consideration in this new Corvette prototype, the philosophy that brought the Porsche 550 Sypder's simple bucket seats to the SR-2 dictated development of new seats for this car. The passenger side is slightly smaller than the driver's; it appears tiny due to wide-angle lens perspective.

explained, "came when a rear bushing failed after eight laps. Mounted incorrectly, it split. It broke because Harley Earl would not let them run the race car on the track because it would damage the paint."

Despite the result at Sebring, Ed Cole still saw a future in racing the SS and continuing Corvette promotion. Duntov had given him a ride in the mule. Cole promptly approved manufacture of three more cars to race at Le Mans. He let Duntov begin work on a desmodromic valve gear (without springs) for the top end of the engine. This could permit 400 horsepower at 9,000 rpm. Cole authorized constructing a 1958 and making improved SR-2 models available to private entries. Now Ed Cole's Chevrolet division was going racing, publicly.

At the top of General Motors, another perspective had coalesced. From the beginning of the American automobile industry, through acquisitions, mergers, and failures, car makers had slipped past governmental scrutiny. GM had the largest market share of automobile sales and the most at risk if Washington legislators turned their attention to the Big Three.

When a Mercedez-Benz entry crashed horrifically during the 24-hour race at Le Mans, France, in June 1955, the tragedy moved accountability onto every company president's agenda. Mercedes withdrew from racing that day; unfavorable publicity shadowed the company for years. No U.S. automaker would risk the kind of public outcry and government examination such a tragedy might inspire.

A ban on racing by the Automobile Association of America ended Chevrolet's official involvement in racing, but customers continued to race Corvettes, and GM engineers continued to develop ways to make the Corvette more competitive. 2002 General Motors Corporation. Used with permission of GM Media Archives.

Similar to Jaguar's D-type with its stabilizing wing behind the driver's head, the Corvette SS fitted a headrest that Clare MacKichan tapered to a point to manage wind resistance and hide the roll-over bar. It earned the nickname "flying football" from MacKichan's colleagues in styling.

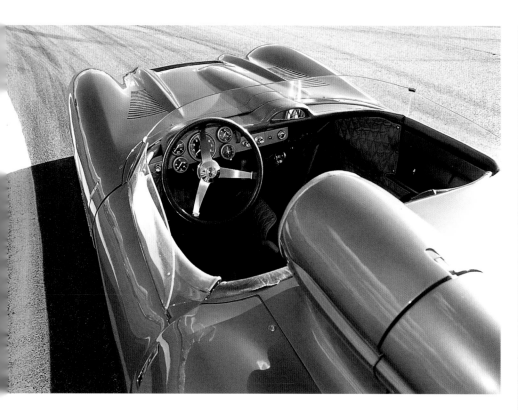

This version with its lovely sheet magnesium body never got the improvements or modifications that Duntov and his colleagues put into the heavier fiberglass mule. On race day, this car disappointed everyone. The magnesium body held the engine heat, roasting drivers John Fitch and Piero Taruffi.

Initially, Harley Earl's styling department sought approval to build four of these cars, known as XP-64 in their internal code system. The first was to be the development mule, followed by three additional Sebring entries. Time and money ran out. Still, Duntov wrote the budgets for a single car that were large enough to hide a second "mule" in them, and he did the engineering development on that fiberglass-bodied second car.

GM Chairman Harlow Curtice suggested to the Automobile Manufacturers Association (AMA) during its February 1957 board meeting that member companies "take no part in automobile racing or other competitive events involving tests of speed and that they refrain from suggesting speed in passenger car advertising or publicity." Every member ratified Curtice's proposal. It was the auto industry's equivalent of Prohibition. Factory participation never stopped; it just learned to hide better. (In fact, Chevrolet delivered 51 Corvettes in 1957 and 144 in 1958 manufactured with Regular Production Option RPO 684. This provided heavy-duty front and rear springs and shock absorbers, metallic brake linings, and heavily finned brake drums as well as fresh air ducting to rear brakes and air scoops to cool the front brakes. These last two were quickly nicknamed "elephant ears and trunks." (With their hard brake pedal pressure, they were not exactly the ideal for boulevard cruisers or grocery getters.)

"Testing and development [of the Corvette SS] would have made a big difference," Robert Cumberford concluded resignedly. "Had the car done well, Chevrolet might not have joined that AMA ban and gone racing under the table or out the back door.

"There were other designs already in the works for what became the 1958 Corvette," Cumberford continued the story. "There was one strongly influenced by the 1956 Motorama Oldsmobile Golden Rocket with the Torpedo top, probably the true source of the 1963 split window. We wanted to do the car on a 94 1/2-inch wheelbase, a car with an aluminum body and frame, aluminum V-8 in front, a full transaxle at the back. It would have given us a nice cockpit. This is what we wanted to do for the 1958 car."

Internally, the car was referred to as the XP-64, the letters standing for Experimental Pursuit, an abbreviation Earl had adopted from the military during World War II. It represented jet fighter planes still in development stage.

The transaxle was a less radical proposal than other parts of the car. Chevrolet engineering was developing a rear-mounted transmission and differential with the starter incorporated in the casing, designated Project "Q." It incorporated a full independent suspension that would have gone into production for the 1960 model year Chevrolet sedans. No one could have justified it solely for a sports car that sold barely 6,300 units in 1957, but Corvette could easily adopt it from a passenger car line selling hundreds of thousands. Lapine also worked out a retractable aluminum hardtop. Reynolds Aluminum was interested in doing the aluminum tooling in 1955.

"Tony and I were convinced that the '58 Corvette *should be* shorter, smaller, and narrower," Cumberford said. "The new aluminum 3.5-liter V-8 was much smaller. Harley Earl gave us carte blanche. No specifications. But we had to deal with Zora. He knew what was going on with hardware. It was fall of 1955, while Tony and I were in that studio. We wondered if there would even be a 1958 Corvette, the XP-94. The 1956 car wasn't out yet.

"So after hours we came up with this concept of the four-passenger Corvette. Tony, Stan Mott, and I called ourselves Automotive Research Consultants. We wrote a letter asking what readers thought about a four-passenger sports car. We sent it to John Fitch, [*Road & Track's*] John Bond, people in the SCCA, maybe 15 people. We got 15 wonderful responses, a lot of well-reasoned comments. And everybody was in favor of it. People said it evoked the Bentleys, that sports cars for racing used to be required to have four seats.

Jeffords was sponsored by Chicago's Chevrolet performance dealer, Nickey, spelled with a backwards "k" to increase its visibility. This was mostly the view other racers had of the Nickey-Jeffords car. It was a regular production option racer, ordered and delivered with Zora Duntov–sanctioned factory racing parts.

"Part of the motivation of the four-passenger car was the morality of the day. Guys didn't go out on dates by themselves with a girl. If you had a Corvette, you couldn't date. There always had to be a chaperon, or another couple, one to keep an eye on the other. Double dating was fine. A guy alone with a girl was not," Cumberford continued.

"So we got Barney Clark, who wrote the Corvette ads and who was enthusiastic about the idea, to write a description of the car as we conceived it. Big engine, so it would go as fast as European stuff. It was a chunky, high-deck, square piece of road machinery. We wrote a cover letter and took the car to Earl. He was furious. Absolutely furious.

" 'You fellahs,' he stammered, 'you got a lot of enthusiasm. My boys are just plain garden-variety boys. But you . . . We're not going to do anything with this. But as a reward for initiative, I'm going to let you design the 1961 Buick Special. . . .' "

GOING THE WRONG WAY

The Cumberford/Lapine Corvette meant the 1958 introduction had progressed to full-size clay models, but it was scrapped. Instead, the production studio did a quick face-lift on the 1956 to have it ready for production by fall 1957. Overall length grew from 168 to 177.2 inches. The car swelled 2.3 inches in width to 72.8. For sports car enthusiasts, the Corvette was going the wrong way.

It was, however, a better automobile with bumpers secured to the frame providing true accident

RPO 579D delivered to the buyer this fuel-injected 283-cubic-inch V-8 rated at 290 horsepower. What Nickey's mechanics and racing team wizards did to the car after delivery helped Jim Jeffords pilot both a 1958 and 1959 model to SCCA B-production national championships.

To anyone who followed SCCA professional racing in the late 1950s, this car and its driver will spark their memory. Jim Jeffords, an advertising executive from Milwaukee, Wisconsin, won SCCA B-production two years in a row in an RPO 684 convertible.

SCCA's production-class rules required cars to race with both seats and full carpeting as the car was delivered. It meant production class racers carried extra weight, but with 290 horsepower on tap from the factory, a few extra pounds were not critical.

protection. Acrylic lacquer replaced the nitrocellulose paints. Every instrument on the dash except the clock was relocated in front of the driver's eyes with a large 160-mile-per-hour speedometer surrounding the 6,000-rpm tachometer.

Improvements under the hood made up for added girth. Output reached 290 horsepower with the RPO 579D's Rochester fuel injection. Introduction followed General Motors' official adoption of the AMA racing ban by half a year. GM could not/would not promote racing or speed. Of course, if a customer wanted to order certain things, it only required reading the order form, and Chevrolet would never argue with its customers. One customer, Jim Jeffords, a Milwaukee advertising executive, followed the instructions at Chicago's Nickey Chevrolet. He found everything necessary except the car's exterior color. Inspired by a popular song, Jeffords painted the car a bright purple and named it *The Purple People Eater*. He won the SCCA B-production championship and under the full force of the auto industry's prohibition, Chevrolet's own carefully created RPOs heralded the birth of the muscle car in America.

CHAPTER FIVE

RUNNING IN PLACE MEANT PROGRESS AND FRUSTRATION

hat long seven-year stretch, beginning in 1956 and ending in late 1962, meant different things to different people. To customers watching the Corvette in dealer showrooms, the car moved forward in appearance slightly, following fashion as it shed fins and gathered double headlights, but it got much better mechanically, gaining muscle and agility. For Ed Cole's engineers and Harley Earl's stylists, it was a time of walking, running, and sometimes sprinting on a treadmill. Lots of work got done, but few people outside the studios ever saw it or knew of it until years later. The corporation, with its change of guard, made steady moves toward reversing progress. It was, all in all, a tough time.

Harley Earl probably would have styled Bill Mitchell into existence if the younger man didn't already exist. There would have been a Mitchell in side-elevation and then modeled into life-size clay and finally produced as another one-off, a Mitchell like a Y-Job and a LeSabre. When Earl got his Mitchell, he kept it longer than any of his personal cars.

William L. Mitchell inherited Earl's job as vice president of styling at General Motors on December 1, 1958, when he was 46. He had worked for Earl for 22 years, starting as one of his stylists. Mitchell's father had sold Buicks, and even before Earl ever touched one of those, Mitchell loved automobiles. He worked as an illustrator for the publishing and road-racing Collier family and filled his office with his own drawings of classics. The Colliers owned these kinds of cars, and they invited Mitchell into their close-knit circle of enthusiasts, where he made rapid stylized sketches of them racing. Earl saw these and hired him in 1935.

Mitchell watched his mentor work. He knew Earl had had to prove himself and the value of styling to skeptical division general

(previous pages) Normally cars painted Inca Silver appeared with white coves, though frequently second or third owners have eliminated the contrasting colors to unify the appearance, as Leonard Nagel has done with his 1959 convertible. All the colors received new names if not new formulation for the new model year.

Dual headlights arrived with chrome frames for the 1958 model, although designer Bob Cumberford had conceived them for the 1957 production year. For 1959, Chevrolet painted the headlight frames to match the body color. It was another example of eliminating frills as time went on to clean up the body design.

With sales of 9,168 for the year, 1958 marked the first time the Corvette made a profit for GM.

managers. As inheritor himself, now he had to fight his own battles against other successors who seized the opportunity of Earl's departure to regain some control. Some in GM's current management, oriented to finances, felt compelled to rein in some of styling's flamboyance and fiscal excesses, not an entirely improper idea. But Mitchell had allies, powerful division executives with "gasoline in their veins." Men such as Ed Cole understood that styling sold cars for GM, more than Ford's or Chrysler's design efforts did for them.

Mitchell tackled one perception almost immediately. He distrusted the word *styling*. He likened it to being fashionable, whereby something was "in" one day and "out" the next. He knew that industrial designers, contemporaries such as Henry Dreyfuss, Norman Belle Geddes, and Walter Dorwin Teague, argued that good design lasted forever. Soon after his promotion, Mitchell changed his department's name from *styling* to *design*.

Mitchell adopted Earl's technique of giving designers no direction with their assignment. Earl would demand a highlight line be raised or lowered as little as 1/32nd of an inch. He would trumpet displeasure across a studio if that change was not done. Mitchell's temper rivaled Earl's and he used it similarly, as punctuation, but Mitchell added a kind of volatile fickleness. He routinely flipped design concepts 180 degrees from one encounter to the next. For the 1959 Corvette, Bill Mitchell removed some of the design excesses that had marked Harley Earl's final years at GM. He took off the 1958 chrome trim strips along the trunk lid and rows of washboard-like simulated louvers on the engine hood from that model.

Chevrolet engineering carried over its 290-horsepower V-8 engine and sophisticated four-speed transmission. While the heater was still optional, hardtops and even extra-cost handling packages offered stiffer springs and heavily finned brake drums with roadworthy metallic brake linings (RPO 686). Chevrolet set the Corvette base price at $3,875. The countryclub set, ordering a boulevard cruise–ready Corvette with 245 horsepower-283, Powerglide, power top, radio, heater, sunshades, and

Bill Mitchell took over the Art and Colour Section in 1959 and made it the design center it is today. He created the Sting Ray racer, on which the Sting Ray production car was based. He used to drive his racer prototype in the streets of Detroit.

(above) The 1959 Corvette lost the decorative hood louvers of the 1958 model. Also missing were the twin chrome strips that set off the trunk contours. It was emblematic of new design chief Bill Mitchell and his growing recognition that less is sometimes more.

(bottom left) Chevrolet offered two fuel-injected versions of its 283-cubic-inch engine: the RPO 579 that provided 250 horsepower, and the wilder RPO 579D, which claimed 290-horsepower output. Curiously, Chevrolet charged the same price, $484.20, for each version, but not surprisingly, the higher performance version sold five times as many as the lesser model.

(bottom center) Inca Silver exteriors were offered with either red or black interiors, with either a black or white soft top. Chevrolet manufactured 9,670 convertibles in 1959, just 957 of which were this color. The $3,875 base price included the 230-horsepower 283-cubic-inch engine with 3-speed manual transmission.

(bottom right) Not quite half the 1959 cars produced were fitted with the four-speed manual, some 4,175 of the total. Much less popular was the Powerglide Automatic that was installed in just 1,878 of the cars manufactured. The Wonderbar AM radio was Corvette's most popular option, installed in 7,001 of the cars produced.

other minor options, paid $5,031, about what they spent for four years of their child's college tuition. Production for 1957 reached 6,339, nearly double that of 1956, and it increased to 9,168 for 1958 and 9,670 for 1959.

"BE BRAVE"

Back in 1956, GM hired another young designer, Peter Brock, out of the Los Angeles Art Center College. After his first few assignments, Mitchell transferred Brock to work with senior stylist Bob Veryzer in Bob McLean's advance design research studio. Brock joined Chuck Pohlmann, studio engineer Byron Voight, and chief modeler John Bird. Mitchell had gone to the Turin, Italy, auto show and returned to Detroit excited by several coupes he'd seen there. He announced that he wanted to do a new Corvette for production as a 1960 model. He described what he wanted and created a contest within the studios to see whose design came closest. According to Bob Veryzer's son, Robert, his father established his own theme in a two-word sign he posted in the studio: "Be Brave." Brock was daring, and Mitchell selected his concept for a car known internally as XP-84, the Q-car, to use Chevrolet's new sedan independent rear suspension and other innovations.

"I'd designed the car in coupe form, according to Mitchell's direction," Brock said. "At that point Mitchell said, 'I think we also want to do a roadster.'" Chuck Pohlmann, the other young designer in McLean's studio, and Brock became friends because they shared similar design philosophies. Pohlmann did a roadster version while Brock continued with details on his

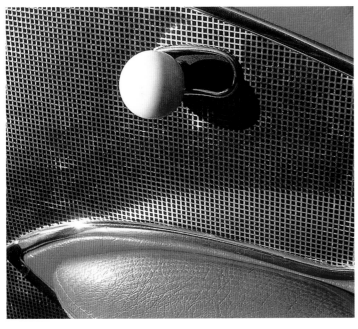

Late afternoon sunlight sculpts the hood and instrument binnacle on this excellent restoration. The twin "power bulges" first appeared on the 1956 hoods, and Chevrolet's designers openly admitted to copying those from the hood of the 1954 Mercedes-Benz 300SL.

coupe. "The two cars were nearly identical," Brock recalled, "except for the crisp horizontal line that formed the car's distinctive shape. Chuck's version, directed by Mitchell, fell away to the back. Mine forced a slight kick-up at the rear.

"Once we had the theme there were a number of versions," Brock continued. "We had one with a fully removable roof panel, like the Porsche Targa. In another, the car didn't have A pillars, just a single pillar in the center. Windscreen side glass wrapped completely around."

According to Robert Veryzer, Bob's son, who wrote about the origin of the Sting Ray in *Collectible Automobile* in June 2001, studio engineer Byron Voight and Zora Duntov together established the wheelbase and wheel track and penciled in engine placement, seat location, and other crucial dimensions while Brock and Pohlmann drew variations for Veryzer and Mitchell. Once Mitchell picked the design he liked, everything came into focus.

Chief modeler John Bird created a quarter-scale clay, then a full-sized model in coupe form. After Mitchell made his changes on it, Bird formed a roadster version of Chuck's variation. They set Brock's full-sized coupe alongside it so Mitchell, Brock, Pohlmann, McLean, and studio chief Bob Veryzer could compare details. At that point, Mitchell decided they would build only the roadster prototype because it would be easier and cheaper to do. "So they took the full-sized clay model roadster," Brock said, "and moved it out of the studio, so it wouldn't be discovered. We referred to that as the XP-96, but that car eventually became the Sting Ray race car."

"That car was built in secret," Brock continued. "With the AMA racing ban in force, there wasn't supposed to be any more sports or competition stuff at all." They set up the "hammer room," Mitchell's secret studio, "behind a tool room where design's fabrication specialists kept the hammers and tools they used to form the models. You'd go into this room and then walk around the back, through another door and the secret studio was back there. GM's high brass walking around the building wouldn't find it because, in theory, it didn't even exist."

Brock originally did the XP-84 coupe with a large single piece of glass for the rear window. The split window went in later. Mitchell imposed the hard line down the roof dividing the rear window because he admired the Bugatti-type 57SC Atlantique. He wanted the flavor of that elegant French car on the Sting Ray.

"Larry Shinoda and Chuck finished the production roadster. Larry did most of the form detailing on it, the things that Mitchell wanted on the car like the twin windscreens, hood louvers, side

The Corvette had its best year yet with the 1962 model, producing 14,531 of the convertibles. More than half of these, 8,074, went out with optional hardtops for an additional $236.75. This Roman Red was one of seven exterior colors offered.

This was the last of a lot of things for the Corvette. A major styling/design series ended with the 1962 models, and along with appearances went an engineering and mechanical heritage. Everything new was coming for 1963, but very few people outside GM knew it.

vents, and such. Really, I think all three of us, Chuck, Larry, and I, provided about equal shares in developing the final appearance of that car, but the original lines were mine. The production Sting Ray became a much larger car. But that original car was really a graceful, pretty little automobile."

Engineer Byron Voight and modeler John Bird built the Brock/Pohlmann/Shinoda XP-84 on the same 94.5-inch wheelbase that Bob Cumberford and Tony Lapine had developed for the proposed 1958 replacement. This new car used the Q-project transaxle to provide more cockpit room without a large transmission sitting between the driver and passenger. It adopted the same advanced frame and also the independent rear suspension that Cumberford and Lapine had devised.

"There were always several engineering solutions," Brock recalled, "ideas to get room in a car when it was still in the research or styling end of things. These engineering ideas, systems, could solve styling and interior problems. The real problem was cost."

Harley Earl himself came up with one engineering upgrade for the XP-84, fitting the 283-cubic-inch displacement V-8 with dry-sump lubrication. The shallow oil pan allowed Brock to drop cowl height by nearly 2 inches, allowing the entire car to sit lower. The Q-car proposal stood only 46 inches tall.

Duntov promoted aluminum not only for certain engine components such as cylinder heads but also for entire blocks, manifolds, and transmission and differential cases. Aluminum would reduce weight, thereby improving handling and fuel economy of the entire Chevrolet line. Using aluminum, a Duntov Corvette would weigh less than 2,500 pounds. While he advocated aluminum for engine and drivetrain components, however, he pushed Chevrolet to build the Corvette's body out of steel.

"There was a lot of talk," Peter Brock recalled, "that after a certain production number, it would be feasible to do it in steel. It probably would have been cheaper too. Steel would have changed the car completely, made it stiffer, lighter, and stronger."

Had Chevrolet built the car in steel, they could have formed aluminum panels on the same dies to build a lightweight GT version. They stuck with plastic for several reasons. Stamping dies for steel cost much more. Also, this retained contact with plastic companies, ensuring the earliest possibility of working with new composite materials.

"But also," Brock continued, "they could change little details like the side scoops and hood blister and all the little panels really quickly in glass, cheaper than in steel. And since the Corvette was going to have longer production runs . . ."

In December 1957, the Engineering Policy Group saw the Q-Corvette. Under Mitchell's watchful eye,

(opposite) As Mike Antonick reported in his Corvette Black Book, *for 1962, Chevrolet formed the side cove lip using fiberglass body panels, not simply accented by bright trim as before. This meant it was impossible for the factory to paint the coves different colors from the rest of the body. Ironically, this gave some customers something they'd wanted for years.*

All new and plenty exciting, Chevrolet's 250-horsepower 327-cubic-inch V-8 was the base engine. Carbureted versions cranking out 300 and 340-horsepower and a 360-horsepower fuel-injected version were also available. The most popular choice was the 340 horsepower carbureted engine, a $107.60 option. This fuelie cost $484.20, and Chevrolet produced only 1,918 of them.

This basic instrument configuration appeared first in January 1953 with the Motorama prototype, and Chevrolet got its use out of the design. Tachometers for all 1962 engines took their drive directly from the distributor (whereas in previous years only fuel-injected engines drove tachs from the distributor).

Larry Shinoda now added working hatches, and he relocated fuel caps to the left rear fender. Mitchell wanted the front fender scoops reversed, placing them at the rear of the doors. In this location, these primarily blew air onto the rear tires. Mitchell felt this accentuated the "Coke-bottle" taper he wanted for the car. Shinoda followed directions and finished a coupe and convertible, ready for presentation at the board of directors' show, the executive show-and-tell that codified or doomed production plans.

The full-size clay models and their accompanying engineering proposals for the 1958 car took the Corvette far beyond what the production 1958 model would be. Design and engineering made it equal to the most advanced, sophisticated sports—and racing—cars built anywhere in the world. Their one roadblock: one critical personnel change among the executives.

Harlow Curtice, GM chairman, retired in 1958. The GM accountant who rose to head Buick division had learned from Alfred Sloan what Harley Earl's styling could do to car sales, and he went to the top. He drove GM through the decade that saw Chevrolet division alone spend $90 million for advertising. Curtice may not have been born with "gasoline in his veins," Mitchell's measure of a man, but years of steady transfusions made him tolerant of design and engineering costs. Curtice's replacement was Frederic Donner.

Curtice wondered about car sales, respectful of Sloan and Donaldson Brown's concept of return on investment. Donner took that concept and twisted it into a Baroque art form whereby stockbrokers became even more important to GM than shareholders. Curtice had seen that interesting automobiles, produced with a pleasing appearance, sold. Donner knew that reducing costs, curbing the lavish expenditures of design and engineering, would increase dividends. Profits made GM attractive to Wall Street, not Earl's chrome and Duntov's independent rear suspensions. Experiments like the Sting Ray represented nonessentials with fiduciary downsides.

Sitting in Mitchell's Hammer Room was the car that Duntov, with prescient political savvy, knew was much too much of a reach. He retreated from his own goal and wrote to Chevrolet's chief engineer, Harry Barr. Duntov acknowledged the Q-Corvette's numerous technical advances were so expensive that current management might never allow such a car to be built. Forewarned by his perception of current corporate thinking, he suggested Chevrolet stick with the Corvette's faithful separate chassis-body assembly used from the beginning.

(above) Roman Red cars were available with black, fawn, or red interiors. This was one of just 65 cars produced with the larger 24-gallon gas tank and one of an indeterminate number built with no radio. While it never raced as far as the current owner knows, it was definitely built for speed and endurance.

Model year 1960 marked the end of the chrome teeth in the Corvette grille. This Ermine White exterior was the most popular color for that year, with 3,717 cars produced. Base price dropped $93, from $3,875 in 1959 to $3,782 for 1960.

Model year 1960 was the first year
Chevrolet produced more than 10,000
Corvettes, peaking at 10,261.

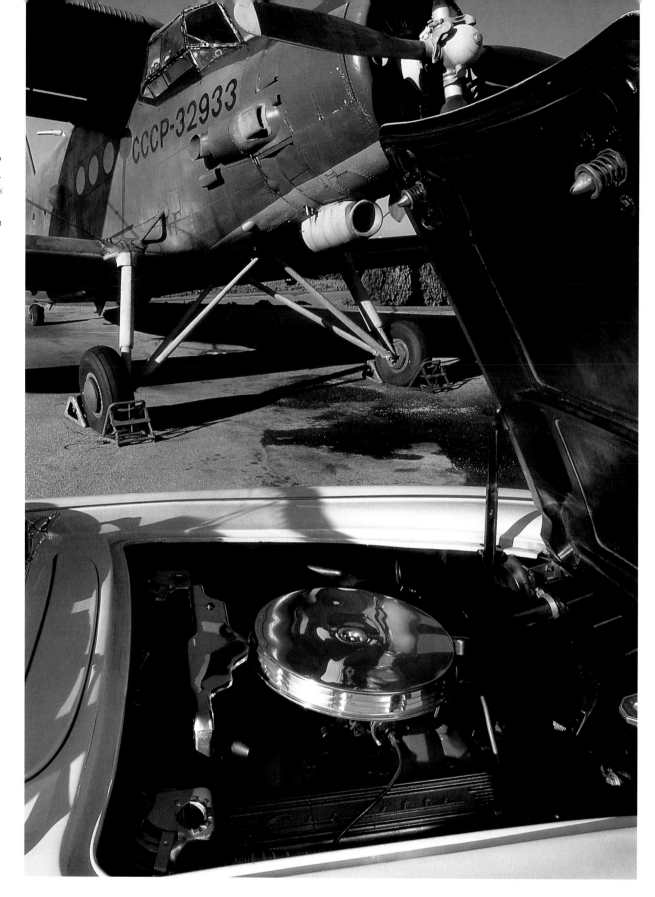

Engine options for 1960 ranged from a 230-horsepower carbureted version to a 290-horsepower fuel-injected version. The most popular power plant was this 270-horsepower carbureted model that Chevrolet installed in 2,364 cars, for a modest $182.95.

Ed Cole carried over the existing body from the 1958–59 model year for 1960, and Duntov set to work with the other engine development engineers to produce aluminum cylinder heads for the fuel-injected 283s. But production consistency difficulties made this a never-available option. Chassis engineers tamed the handling by deleting the optional heavy-duty springs while increasing the diameter of the front antisway bar and adding a rear one. The $336.60 RPO 687 was really a "PRO" (production *racing* option). It quickened the steering and fitted sintered-metallic brake linings inside new brake drums cast with large cooling fins. Base price of the car was $3,872. The top engine option was RPO 579D,

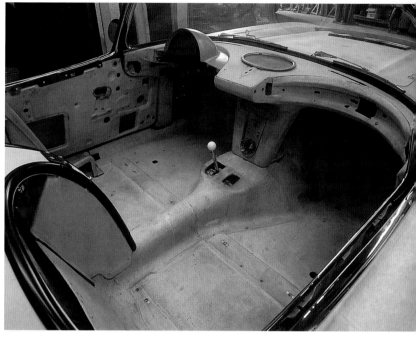

(upper left) A restoration work in progress, this significant racer was partially reassembled for a review session of its history. The car is currently being prepared for numerous vintage races and Corvette 50-year celebrations beginning in late 2002 and continuing throughout 2003.

(above) Racer John Fitch, who had headed the successful 1956 and 1957 Sebring efforts for Chevrolet, and co-driver Bob Grossman spent 24 hours in this cockpit. Production class rules required both seats and the carpet as well as the roll-bar and hardtop roof in place. Fighting off an overheating engine, they pitted according to the rules, but at each stop they packed the engine compartment with ice.

Legendary car builder/racer Briggs Cunningham entered three 1960 hardtops in the 24 Hours of Le Mans, specially prepared by Alfred Momo in New York (and with great assistance from Chevrolet's Frank Burrell and Zora Duntov). A sister car to this reached 151 miles per hour on the four-mile long Mulsanne straight, while this car finished 8th overall, 1st in its production class.

Indianapolis Chevrolet dealer Bud Gates had ordered the car with all the racing options, but only when reading the 1961 Sebring 12-hour race rules did he discover that the car needed a hardtop. At the last minute he sent a mechanic out into the new car lot at night to "borrow one." The mechanic took the first one he found, red.

Gates and co-driver Harry Heuer ran a sensible race, driving conservatively to a 22nd overall finish, good enough for 2nd in class. After the race, Bud drove the car back home to Indiana, selling it on his high-performance used-car lot 18 months later.

the 1958–59 290-horsepower 283 V-8 with the Duntov cam, solid valve lifters, 11.0:1 compression ratio, and fuel injection.

For Briggs Cunningham, the 1960 model had been a long-time coming. He entered two cars for the Sebring 12 Hours on March 26 and had New York Long Islander Alfred Momo prep his racers. Neither of them finished; car #2, with Dick Thompson and Fred Windridge co-driving, retired after an accident on the 41st lap, and the other, #1, which Cunningham shared with John Fitch, went out after a rollover accident at the Webster turn during lap 27. Four more Corvettes ran the race. Lloyd "Lucky" Casner's contribution-funded Camoradi team (the name meant Casner Motor Racing Division) entered two more Corvettes, #3 and #4, and Dallas, Texas, dealer Delmo Johnson raced with David Morgan in #5. Chuck Hall and Bill Fritts achieved the best Corvette finish, starting 6th and finishing 17th overall, first in class.

Accidents were risks of racing, and Cunningham repaired his rolled #1 car from Sebring. He entered the Sebring Corvettes and a third one (as well as a prototype E-type Jaguar) in the 24 Hours of Le Mans. Alfred Momo distrusted Duntov's prototype aluminum heads that were on the engines, so with Duntov's help, Momo got new cast-iron versions of the cylinder heads, with the larger valves and improved porting that would appear in 1961 as the production 315-horsepower engine. But Le Mans is never an easy race and Cunningham's effort was filled with drama. Bill Kimberly ran Corvette #1 off course in a thunderstorm. The car rolled and burned, but Kimberly escaped unhurt. Dick Thompson's car #2 suffered severe body damage in traffic early in the race, then lost an hour digging out of the sand during the night. It finally expired in a trail of black smoke while passing the pits on lap 207, five hours from the finish. Cunningham's Jaguar failed hours earlier that morning.

By noon, only John Fitch and Bob Grossman's #3, the Sebring rollover, was still racing. Then it started seriously overheating. Rules prohibited adding oil or water less than 24 laps, about 215 miles, from its last pit stop. They also required that all cars must complete at least four laps in the final hour. Momo told Grossman to run 15-minute laps and come in after each one. Team mechanic and GM employee Frank Burrell and Willy Frick (co-creator of the Fordillac who first introduced Cunningham to Ed Cole and Burrell) both packed the top of the engine compartment full of dry ice from Cunningham's trailer behind the pits. The fans in the main stands loved this, applauding vigorously at each ice down. When the race ended at 4 P.M., the Corvette passed the finish line in 8th place over-all. It had completed 280 laps, 2,363.5 miles, averaging 97.9 miles per hour even with ice stops, and it

(top) Gates had the car delivered to race preparer Ron Kaplan, in Chicago to complete modifications to the 315-horsepower fuel-injected 283.

(above) Ron Kaplan fitted the roll bar and the rear window tunnel for the quick-fill 37-gallon gas tank. When time came to head to Sebring, Gates' transporter broke down, so the car got thoroughly broken in while driving it to central Florida.

(continued on page 154)

Zora Duntov named it the Chevrolet Experimental Racing Vehicle. Despite GM chairman Harlow Curtice's support of the 1957 Automobile Manufacturers Association ban on racing, Duntov and his colleagues built it to meet the specifications for the 1960 Indianapolis 500. Wise engineers seeking to keep their jobs soon renamed it the Chevrolet Experimental Research Vehicle.

Press releases described it as "a research tool for Chevrolet's continuous investigations into automotive ride and handling phenomena under the most realistic conditions." It had no fenders or taillights and seated one. The "realistic" conditions certainly were not rush hour traffic on Woodward or Michigan Avenues or 12 Mile Road. It was given not a name but an acronym: CERV (Chevrolet Experimental Racing Vehicle). In view of GM chairman Frederic Donner's adamant support of the AMA 1957 racing ban, the CERV was inexplicable. It looked like a flat-out single-seat race car built to 1960 Indianapolis regulations.

After the problems Zora Duntov had experienced with the Corvette SS in early 1957, he began looking at new solutions to vehicle balance, braking effectiveness, cornering stability, power transfer to the ground, and driver comfort. He first relocated the engine behind the driver so its heat would not roast the cockpit, but the AMA ban against racing prohibited Duntov from battle testing his concepts. It wasn't until early 1959 when Duntov took the risk of starting a project to test his ideas. By now, Duntov had the nucleus of a team, with Harold Krieber and Walt Zetye who had come to work for Chevrolet back in 1946. In 1958, Zetye joined Duntov and took responsibility for the chassis development up until the mid-1970s.

The three engineers created the CERV on a 96-inch wheelbase (the Indy minimum), with front and rear track at 56 inches, the actual body width only 52 inches, and the overall length was 172 inches. It was nicknamed the "Hillclimber" because Duntov's first idea was to run it at Pike's Peak. Duntov developed an all-aluminum block 283-cubic-inch engine to power the car. This engine used a high silicon content alloy that required no cylinder liners. They cast the heads and most of the hang-on parts—water pump housing, flywheel, clutch pressure place, and starter motor case—in aluminum. A magnesium fuel-injection intake manifold provided sufficient airflow to produce 353 horsepower. They fit what was basically a stock four-speed close ratio transmission behind the engine, ahead of the final drive. This configuration required extra car length, but there was no money available for a final drive between the gearbox and flywheel. Duntov's design kept the weight between the axles, resulting in more neutral handling, one of the goals of his experiment.

For brakes, Duntov and Zetye fitted regular production-option Al-Fin large-diameter drums, the rears mounted inboard, alongside the differential.

The rudimentary antilock rear brake system from the SS reappeared, more refined, in the first CERV. Duntov improved on the rear independent suspension from the prototype Q-Corvettes to use for the CERV, while he essentially carried its front suspension over from the SS racer.

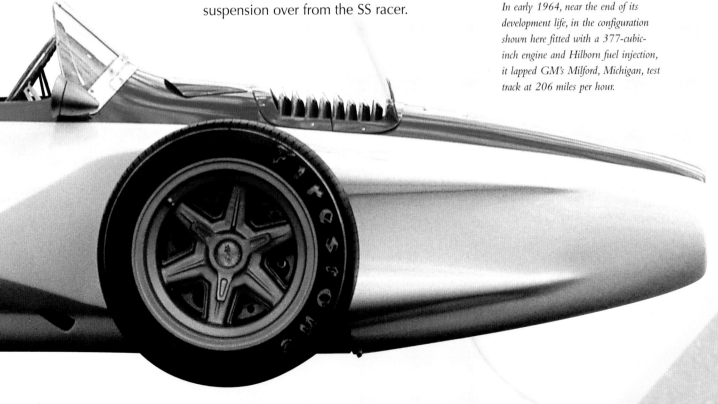

This first appeared to the public at the U.S. Grand Prix at Riverside Raceway in California in November 1960. Duntov let Stirling Moss take a few "demonstration laps" before the world's motoring press. The wheelbase of 96 inches was the Indy minimum, with overall length stretching to 172 inches. In early 1964, near the end of its development life, in the configuration shown here fitted with a 377-cubic-inch engine and Hilborn fuel injection, it lapped GM's Milford, Michigan, test track at 206 miles per hour.

The body was barely 52 inches wide and weighed just 80 pounds. Total vehicle weight without oil or gas was only 1,450 pounds. Throughout its brief life, it served as a test bed for both Firestone and Goodyear wide-tread tires for racing and street uses. Both makers admitted it was a real challenge meeting the car's potential for straight-line acceleration and its hard-cornering capabilities.

They mounted all of this on a chrome-molybdenum alloy steel tube frame, surrounded by a two-layer paper-thin fiberglass body that Tony Lapine and Larry Shinoda created in the Hammer Room. Without liquids, the completed CERV weighed only 1,450 pounds.

Other projects interrupted Duntov, Zetye, and Krieger through the spring and summer of 1960 (including Cunningham's Le Mans Corvette effort). Duntov couldn't run his first trials up Pike's Peak until September. He felt fast but bystanders who had no accurate records of others' test times exaggerated their recollections. They convinced Duntov and his colleagues they were off the pace.

Disheartened, they returned to Warren with the CERV. Firestone withdrew its support and everyone got back to work. Of course, after the event, when winning times were published, Duntov learned his CERV would have set records.

The real value of the CERV then appeared. Its formidable power-to-weight ratio—less than 5.25 pounds per horsepower—provided both Firestone and Goodyear with an excellent platform on which to test and develop the wider tires they wanted to introduce. Walter MacKenzie, former racing manager for Chevrolet who was then director of product information, renamed the CERV, Chevrolet Engineering Research Vehicle. This kept the management calm while Duntov resumed work.

In 1960, NASCAR founder Bill France challenged racers to lap Daytona speedway at 180 miles per hour, offering a $10,000 reward. Duntov had already topped 170 miles per hour at GM's Proving Grounds. He had topped 170 again at Riverside and yet again in testing at Sebring. He thought 180 miles per hour was achievable.

Back in Warren, he and his crew tried a supercharger and then twin-turbochargers. Working when time permitted through 1962, they developed the engine's reliability. Dynamometer tests measured 500 horsepower with an 8.5:1 compression ratio. Then work began with the 377-cubic-inch engines destined for other competition projects, filling most of 1963. But Duntov used one of the 377s, with Hilborn fuel injection, an extremely efficient cross-ram induction intake, and a slightly cleaner front, body nose cone. He reached his magic 180 miles per hour around GM's Milford Proving Ground 4.5-mile oval, and he kept going, finally averaging 206 miles per hour.

(right) Chevrolet division manager Ed Cole and Zora Duntov both had good experiences testing prototype Corvettes at Pike's Peak, and their goal for the CERV was similar. In early days it was even called "the Hillclimber." Its seat back is very vertical to give the driver excellent visibility, unlike more reclining Grand Prix and Indy car seating positions meant to keep drivers out of the wind.

The first engine displaced 283 cubic inches, cast from high-silicon aluminum alloy that allowed Chevrolet to run the engine without cylinder liners. Duntov also fitted the very limited aluminum cylinder heads that had been proposed as regular production options but never made it. Equipped with his high-lift cam and other intake and exhaust modifications, Duntov recorded 353 horsepower at 6,200 rpm. Later, fellow engineer Denny Davis tried a supercharger and also turbochargers on the engine, ultimately achieving nearly 500 horsepower from the aluminum 283.

For 1961, the Corvette received a new grille.

(continued from page 149)

won its class. One of Casner's Camoradi USA-entry Corvettes, driven by Lou Lilley and Fred Gamble, finished 21st overall, about 500 miles back.

In 1960, Chevrolet produced 10,261 Corvettes, cracking the break-even point for the first time in its eight-year life. After Ford had enlarged its Thunderbird to seat four, Ed Cole hoped the Corvette would absorb the two-seater enthusiasts who felt betrayed. There were very few.

A PERSONAL RACE CAR

In 1961, the taillights were changed too. The four-lights design remains a styling cue today.

Bill Mitchell was a racing enthusiast by osmosis, never having competed himself. He was enthralled by these purpose-built vehicles, however. His involvement with Sam, Miles, and Barron Collier Jr., gave him a passion for motorsports. Mitchell urged along the completion of Jerry Earl's SR-2 in 1956, and later he acquired, for $1, the 1957 SS mule chassis on which Duntov had done his brake development work for Sebring. The AMA racing ban covered corporate involvement; however, Mitchell saw no problem in his being a private race car owner. He asked designers Larry Shinoda and Ed Wayne to convert the hidden Q-Corvette XP-96 roadster theme into his own personal race car.

Mitchell and Shinoda ran it with a modified 283, similar to the 1957 SS engine, developing 280 horsepower. The first Sting Ray body was 1/8-inch thick fiberglass, nearly production heft, reinforced with aluminum. Dick Thompson premiered the bright red racer at Marlboro Raceway in Maryland in mid-April 1959. Despite a repeat of Sebring's 1957 race with unreliable brakes, too much unrestrained power, and no limited-slip differential, Thompson still managed to finish fourth in the first appearance.

Aerodynamics was an "engineering solution," in those days, like Harley Earl's dry sump. "The Sting Ray was terrible aerodynamically," Peter Brock remembered. "When Thompson first drove the car, the front wheels came off the ground at 140 miles per hour. The lift on the hood was like an airplane wing."

Mitchell's team manager was Dean Bedford, a GM engineer who also supervised the engineering development of the road car. He partially solved the front lift problem by shimming up the rear springs, creating a nose-down "hot rod rake." This eliminated some, but not all, of the problem. Then the thick body panels cracked from stress. After Road America, Bedford formed a new nose and tail section of three-layer fiberglass silk reinforced with balsa wood. These thinner panels gave the nose and tail such flexibility that it deformed but popped back when hit. Thompson said they literally waved at high speed; however, it saved 75 pounds over the original body. Throughout the season, one problem after another vexed Mitchell, Bedford, sometimes-mechanic Shinoda, and driver Thompson. Thompson even rolled the car on a downhill stretch racing at Meadowdale International Raceway in suburban Chicago. Mitchell's deep pockets were not bottomless. He handled each problem according to the budget he had available, and somehow the Sting Ray showed up at the next event. Tony

Lapine even slipped in to co-drive a 500-miler at Road America. Through the season, because the car's slippery shape allowed higher speeds than production Corvettes could achieve and came close to production car weight (2,360 pounds without driver), it used up brakes relentlessly. In the winter of 1959 and 1960, Bedford completely overhauled the braking system, throwing out the Kelsey-Hayes system and installing a single Hydrovac booster that Bendix had modified to allow better pedal modulation. But Mitchell once again ruled out disc brakes, the obvious solution, because of costs.

During the 1960 season, the car reappeared in silver with the simpler braking system and a paper-thin fiberglass skin that pulled body weight down to 2,000 pounds. With so many other problems to control, Mitchell, Bedford, and Thompson agreed to a modest tune, 280 horsepower at the flywheel, for reliability. With a 3.70:1 rear end, Thompson could see 155 miles per hour on tracks like Bridgehampton on Long Island, New York, and Meadowdale in northwest suburban Chicago. Thompson put it to good use, thrilling spectators and chasing—but rarely beating—Augie Pabst in his Chevrolet-engined Scarab. Still, long before the last race of the season, Thompson won the C-modified class championship through his consistent, careful driving.

Mitchell retired the car after the 1960 season. It had cost him a fortune, yet it established the Sting Ray as *the* racing Corvette. He returned it to design for a complete renovation, where it got new paint and, finally, a Corvette badge. It went on the GM show tour, exhibited first at the Chicago automobile show in mid-February 1961. After a year on display platforms, Mitchell took it back to use as his fair-weather commuter car, eventually installing Dunlop disk brakes and a 427-cubic-inch displacement engine.

THE STING RAY

Months passed. Calendar year 1960 became 1961. Harry Barr's engineers were at work on an enlarged 283, and externally the Corvette changed enough for customers to fall once again into Alfred Sloan's trap of satisfaction one year and dissatisfaction the next.

"Gene, go down to the basement, you're going to be working with one of the guys on the sports car." That was the late Gene Garfinkle's introduction to what would become the Sting Ray production design project. He was another product of the

Black and Wylie qualified the car second fastest, but it was last to leave the grid when the green flag dropped. Wylie admitted he'd flooded the engine trying to get moving. It just wouldn't start. No matter; 12 hours later they finished 1st in class, 18th overall.

Chevrolet factory support of outside professional racers was extensive in these days. Factory engineers would show up at major events "on vacation" from their drawing boards or fabrication shops at the new tech center in Warren. With the design engineers in the pits, problems got solved at racing speeds.

Art Center, plucked from California before graduation. He was working in the Buick production studio when one of Mitchell's people came in and sent him to the Corvette.

"Ed Wayne and I ended up doing all the drawings," he went on. "We had Chuck Pohlmann's Sting Ray roadster there to work with as a reference. We were just doing the lofting [elevation] drawings. The production car is actually on a shorter wheelbase and its body sections were a little steeper.

"The coupe had its split rear window. Mitchell certainly loved the Bugatti but, remember, there was also the Scaglione-designed Bertone Alfa Romeo design study B.A.T. cars. The B.A.T. 5, the 7, and 8 had split back windows too. We even did a folding hardtop for the car. But in order to go through the complication of folding it up to fit into the trunk where all the suspension was, the cost was just way out of line for what they wanted to do.

Laughlin had three mechanically complete chassis delivered to Scaglietti in Modena, Italy, in late 1959. Scaglietti proposed to modify an existing aluminum coupe body to fit the Corvette chassis, a challenge with Corvette's four-inch wider wheel track. Still, when it was finished, the aluminum car weighed 400 pounds less than the complete Corvette in fiberglass.

"They brought in the Sting Ray racing car, and we had the original drawings up on the wall. Mitchell was in there three or four times a day with Ken Pickering and Harry Ellsworth, his personal secretaries.

" 'Nah, I don't want to do that,' Mitchell would say 'Can't you do that? Can't you move that over there?'

"That's how they worked. And you'd be down there for five weeks and then sent somewhere else. You'd never know what happened to the car you'd worked on. Never see it again. Until one day you'd be walking somewhere else in the building and see a full-size model of it being wheeled down a hall."

Mitchell followed Earl's precedent of producing show cars and design study vehicles meant to introduce the public to ideas that he and his design staff were looking at for future production, but he was restless. He loved power and speed as much as he loved distinctive style. Unlike many Earl Motorama studies, Mitchell's dreams ran.

While his Sting Ray raced, Mitchell had prepared the XP-700, a road-going showpiece, built in 1958. He had taken Cumberford's ideas such as the extended nose and grille from Jerry Earl's SR-2 and pushed them further. The nose of the XP-700 was three-dimensional. The rear end hinted strongly at shapes for the 1961 production car. Its removable hard top was a transparent plastic bubble, parted in the middle by a metal strip with air vents down the back and a rearview mirror perched outside on top.

Scaglietti's three coupes had nearly identical lines. He fitted each car with Borrani wire wheels. To make clear the car's lineage, he installed the "chrome teeth" grille into each car, though over time at least one of the owners removed the Corvette grille.

(opposite) Unlike some less successful European attempts at rebodying Corvettes, these Scaglietti cars stop nearly every observer in their tracks. The lines of the car seem most Italian in their sensuousness.

Laughlin specified all three 1959 chassis with the 290-horsepower fuel-injected 283-cubic-inch V-8. The Laughlin and Shelby cars used four-speed manual transmissions. The Jim Hall car came through with an automatic. Hall wanted to see how an automatic would work in racing conditions.

When the 1961 car reached the dealers, enthusiasts saw a frontend slightly changed from the 1960 car, but the rear end was a successful transfer from Mitchell's XP-700, becoming the next hint, the suggestion of what would be the Corvette in 1963.

Mechanical changes were subtle. Engineering replaced the heavy copper-core radiators with aluminum versions that were half the weight yet provided 10 percent greater capacity, improving weight balance and cooling. These had first appeared midyear in 1960 but were available only for 270-horsepower and fuel-injected cars. Two-thirds of the 1961 buyers ordered the close-ratio four-speed transmission, while about one-fifth still wanted the three-speed manual; slightly more than 10 percent chose the two-speed Powerglide automatic.

In all, Chevrolet produced 10,939 of the 1961 models. The top performance engine was now the 315-horsepower 283-cubic-inch displacement V-8 with Rochester fuel injection. Base price was $3,934, and more than half the buyers ordered the optional removable hardtop, RPO 419, at $236.75.

Private racers campaigned Corvettes around the United States, competing first, and rather successfully, with a five-car Sebring effort. Delmo Johnson, a Chevy dealer in Dallas, entered three of these, and the other two came from Don Yenko in Cannonsburg, Pennsylvania. At the end of the 12-hour event, Johnson and co-driver Dale Morgan finished 11th overall, the best finish to date for a stock model.

Corvette mechanicals had evolved to the point in 1961 where the performance was reliable, its racing pedigree was established, and the car had earned respect. It had reached the stage in its life where outsiders wondered if a Corvette by any other name might smell so sweet, work so well, look so good, or race so successfully.

Fort Worth, Texas, entrepreneur Gary B. Laughlin drilled oil, processed petroleum, and owned Chevy dealerships. For pleasure, he raced a Ferrari 750 Monza in SCCA events, where he met and formed an idea with two other Texan racing buddies, Carroll Shelby and Jim Hall. Hall and Shelby wanted a true GT-version of the Corvette, lighter and possibly lovelier. Laughlin, tired of his huge Ferrari repair bills, offered to finance the project, and Shelby offered to engineer it. Together they'd race them. They hoped to make enough cars to qualify for SCCA's B-production class and planned to sell some to their competitors. Memos flew early in 1959 from Fort Worth to Warren, to Modena,

(previous) Every hand-built car body is slightly different, a benefit to owners of rare luxury sports cars because it guarantees individuality and exclusivity.

Building the Scaglietti coupes required shutting down the St. Louis production line to manufacture complete chassis without bodies. It was the shutdown time that killed the project; its costs were too great for either Laughlin or Chevrolet to tolerate.

Scaglietti provided leather-covered racing seats in the otherwise simple interior.

Italy. Sergio Scaglietti, car-body fabricator for Enzo Ferrari, agreed to revise an existing fastback aluminum coupe to fit the Corvette chassis for Laughlin. Three 1959 mechanically complete, bare chassis arrived at Scaglietti.

Laughlin's oil operations took him to Europe regularly, and he always visited Modena. The car got closer to what he wanted, though Scaglietti had trouble stretching his body to fit Corvette's four-inch wider track. With a Spartan interior, the new aluminum coupes weighed 400 pounds less than the fiberglass production cars.

They completed their first one, painted silver, in early 1961, on a chassis with a 1960 engine, the 290-horsepower 283-cubic-inch displacement V-8 with Rochester fuel injection, the close-ratio four-speed transmission, and Positraction. Scaglietti refitted the Corvette teeth into the front air intake. His spare interior contained two thin competition seats facing a crackle-finish instrument panel. The only identification was a hood medallion and two fender badges with the symbol of Scaglietti & C., Modena. The second prototype was done more luxuriously with an automatic transmission. This car was intended for Hall, who had begun experimenting with racing automatic transmissions. It and the third car, another four-speed transmission version, bore Corvette crossed flags on the nose and egg-crate grilles.

Some 20 years later, Zora Duntov remembered the project only from memos he saw at its beginning and end. He recalled questions about the time the regular production line had to shut down to produce cars without bodies. These interruptions were too costly when weighed against the increasing demand for production cars. Shelby recalled Laughlin saying the project was dead. Whether it was GM's faithful adherence to the AMA ban or corporate concern over controlling the Corvette (lest someone else build something that might successfully compete against it), neither one could say. Laughlin, after driving his car briefly, soured on the idea; it was a handful of ill-mannered handling and horsepower. He sold his first car for about $9,200 to a business acquaintance in Chicago. Hall barely used his car and had sold his by 1964. Carroll Shelby sold his soon after delivery, but he had not soured on the idea of running an American V-8 in a smaller European car body. He took that idea and went shopping elsewhere.

This was the last styling year for exhausts vented through the rear bumpers and taillights faired into the fender curves. The rear-end design would change completely for 1961.

While Laughlin worked with Scaglietti, Wisconsin industrial designer Gordon Kelly began a redesign project with Carrozzeria Vignale on his 1960 Corvette. Kelly worked with Brooks Stevens Associates designing Studebaker Hawks. He produced a one-eighth-scale clay model of a Corvette body and showed it to Bill Mitchell. Mitchell offered Gordon a car if he'd find a builder who would display it at the Paris Auto Show in October 1961. Vignale agreed. Kelly's lines, stubbier but more aggressive than Scaglietti's coupes, were striking behind an oversized oval egg-crate grille. The Kelly/Vignale-bodied car

(above) The 3.8-liter, in-line six-cylinder engine had become nearly a perfect power plant after years of racing and production development in the preceding XK series. With dual overhead camshafts and three side-draft carburetors, the engine produced 265 horsepower.

(left) The sleekly shaped body of Jaguar's new XKE was the product of Malcolm Sayer, who described himself as an aerodynamicist. Sayer drew his designs full-size on long paper rolls, calculating the effects of various shapes as he created them.

appeared in auto shows for a year before Kelly finally got to drive the car and test its fuel-injected 283, the RPO 687 brakes and suspension option, four-speed transmission, and Positraction differential.

CHANGES AT THE TOP

Chevrolet management changed at the top again in 1961. Semon E. "Bunkie" Knudsen was promoted from Pontiac division to head GM's biggest seller. (His father, William, had done something similar 30 years earlier.) Bunkie liked racing and understood what the AMA hoped to deny: "speed" promoted sales. He ushered out a great amount of parts, support, advice, and even money through a back door at Pontiac and into the hands of stock car and drag racers. Knudsen's actions and Pontiac's successes led to Ford's public repudiation of the AMA ban in 1962.

Knudsen arrived at Chevrolet just in time to enjoy the success of Ed Cole's hard work with Duntov, Mitchell, and their staffs. The 1962 Corvette introduced another legendary powerplant. Harry Barr's engi-

The aluminum insert in the middle of the dashboard lasted only through the first-series cars. It reflected stray light too easily into the driver's eyes. The symmetry of the gauges, however, was very pleasing.

neers started with the 283-cubic-inch displacement V-8 and increased the bore to 4.00 inches and the stroke to 3.25, to reach 327–cubic-inch displacement. The meekest engine produced 250 horsepower, while the solid lifter, Duntov-cam, fuel-injected engine developed 360 horsepower. The most powerful optional engine still cost $484.20, the same price since 1958. A car ready to prepare for racing ran $5,243, while a civilized back-road tourer with every comfort option sold for $5,014 in 1962.

The body retained the heavy steel-and-aluminum reinforcement first used in mid-1957 around the cowl and doors. This still provided stiffness and body integrity. Even with all the improvements, the body weighed nearly the same as in 1953 because engineering had identified and deleted unnecessary fiberglass layers in some panels.

A NEW CHALLENGE

Corvette designers and engineers labored on. They tackled the few lingering criticisms, their work improving the perceptions that sports car enthusiasts held about Corvettes. Inside GM, they knew great things were in store. Yet Chevrolet's only remaining competitor—Jaguar—did not rest either. The English firm accepted that the V-8 was necessary for most American buyers; however, a dual-overhead camshaft on top of a proven in-line six-cylinder engine would turn heads on their side of the Atlantic Ocean. Packaging it in a stunning body form would help even more.

Jaguar introduced its new 1962 XK-E in the spring of 1961 at the New York Auto Show, 18 months before Bunkie Knudsen could show the new Sting Ray. Jaguar's slender cars, both coupe and roadster, threw down a new challenge to Corvette. As Briggs Cunningham had predicted, the United States had become the world's largest market for sports cars. Jaguar sold most of its cars on this side of the Atlantic. Its new body on its new chassis, with independent rear suspension and four-wheel disc brakes, would sell for $4,915.

For Knudsen, Mitchell, Barr, and dozens of engineers and designers, the Jaguar XK-E meant a little more running in place, hurrying to get the last of the work perfect before everybody in the world could see what they'd been working on for seven years.

The fastback design offered similar cargo potential to the Sting Ray coupe. Unlike the Corvette's rear deck lid, the Jaguar's opened. Oddly, the big rear door opened from the side. Introduced in 1961 at $5,595, it reached nearly $6,000 by the time the Sting Ray appeared.

1963-1967

CHAPTER SIX

THE BIRTH OF A MODERN CLASSIC

he 1963 Sting Ray etched Bill Mitchell's influence and power into GM's corporate granite. Its rear-end design was startling. Peter Brock's coupe, finished by Mitchell's lieutenant, Larry Shinoda, paid homage to the classic sporting "Boat-tail" roadsters from the 1930s. By now, Mitchell's power nearly rivaled that of Harley Earl. When Zora Duntov complained that the stylish center spine hindered rearward vision, Mitchell retorted, "If you take that off, you might as well forget the whole thing." Corvette was making money, and because Earl's department had created it, the car belonged to design, not to engineering. Mitchell had the highest authority, and he made it clear that engineering's input was accepted when it did not interfere. This stopped Duntov. If there was no spine, there might be no independent rear suspension, no disc brakes.

Yet the engineering inputs had made the new car as impressive mechanically as it was visually. The car benefited from the Q-Corvette project, from Mitchell's Sting Ray race car, and from Zora's pet project, the CERV I.

Engineering settled on a 98-inch wheelbase for the production Sting Ray, called the XP-720 internally. This was 4 inches shorter than the previous car's old XK-120 dimension of 102 inches, and it improved maneuverability and handling. Using a new ladder-type frame with five crossmembers to replace the original car's X-frame, engineers dropped the center of gravity nearly 2.3 inches because this new frame let them place passengers inside the frame rails rather than on top of them as before. Engineering ran its designs through computer analysis to predetermine the necessary steel wall thicknesses and structural placement, then intentionally built their test frames too rigidly to determine what was proper not only for routine buyers but also for serious racers. The convertible frame was 10 percent and the coupe 90 percent stiffer than the 1962 car.

(previous pages) This was the view that caused the greatest attention and controversy. Observers either hated the center spine that divided the rear window or they loved it. Zora Duntov hated it, claiming it seriously obstructed rear vision. But by 1963, Design Chief Bill Mitchell had so much corporate influence that he easily defeated the powerful engineer.

Success has many parents, and more than a few Chevrolet designers claim the origin of this Sting Ray's appearance. Even its inspiration is unclear because Bill Mitchell knew European classics; everyone from France's Bugatti to Italy's Alfa Romeo had done cars with raised center spines and divided rear windows.

Engineering knew it had only so much to spend to improve the car. The frame took some, but Duntov especially wanted to use the new rear axle with fully independent rear suspension (IRS). They could devise one from the Q-sedans and Q-Corvette prototype. Engineering had done the development work years before, writing off the costs against other budgets, but GM Chairman Donner killed the production passenger car, so there was no big series project to pay for it. Whenever Duntov stated his need for an IRS, the newly important bean counters challenged him on its cost. He already knew the car business was a numbers game. He prevailed by constantly telling his inquisitors the new car with IRS would sell 30,000 units, despite clear logic suggesting most drivers would never recognize the difference.

The system that Duntov, Harold Krieger, Walter Zetye, and the Corvette engineering staff devised also adopted technology from the CERV I. It incorporated twin half shafts that emerged from a frame-mounted differential, connected (and suspended) by a transversely mounted nine-leaf spring bolted to the back of the differential housing. This system, common on race cars, used the driveshafts as part of the suspension system, saving money over more intricate European systems and a great amount of weight over the 1962 solid tube rear axle. They used a transverse spring, the only application for such a system in a U.S. automobile since the 1937 Cord front suspension. It was necessary because there was no room beneath the body for rear coil springs that also would have increased overall and unsprung weight.

Chevrolet offered its 327-cubic-inch V-8 in four power levels, from a base 250-horsepower version to a potent 360-horsepower fuel-injected version. The most popular engine was this 340-horsepower L76, which powered 8,033 Corvettes in 1963.

Krieger, Zeyte, and Duntov carried over the front suspension with subtle changes using mostly passenger car production parts that had appeared in new configurations on the CERV I. A faster steering ratio, 2.9 turns lock-to-lock instead of 3.4, capped their labors to improve road feel, steering response, and ride comfort. The Sting Ray also introduced hydraulically assisted steering, available on all but the two most powerful engine options.

Engineering's development dollars were nearly gone, so they carried over the 11-inch diameter cast-iron drum brakes all around. Buyers could order optional sintered-metallic linings and finned aluminum brake drums that provided greater fade resistance and better cooling. Corvette offered power-assisted brakes as well.

Once all this new technology was gathered together, engineering built development mules. Zetye, Duntov, and Krieger used these as daily transport, living with their work and making constant

Regardless of its authorship, the 1963 split-window coupe is one of automobile history's most striking shapes. Yet this sensuous body hides significant engineering advances, including disc brakes and a ride-improving, road-hugging independent rear suspension.

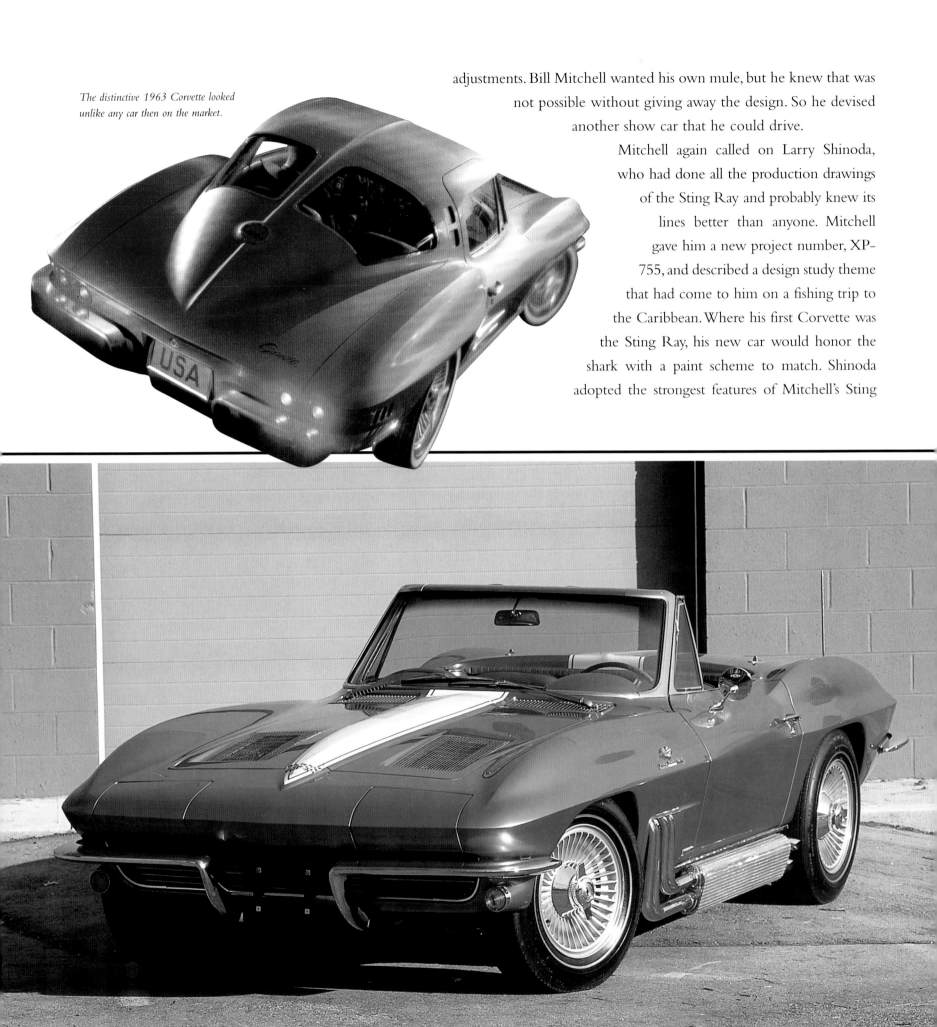

*The distinctive 1963 Corvette looked
unlike any car then on the market.*

adjustments. Bill Mitchell wanted his own mule, but he knew that was not possible without giving away the design. So he devised another show car that he could drive.

Mitchell again called on Larry Shinoda, who had done all the production drawings of the Sting Ray and probably knew its lines better than anyone. Mitchell gave him a new project number, XP-755, and described a design study theme that had come to him on a fishing trip to the Caribbean. Where his first Corvette was the Sting Ray, his new car would honor the shark with a paint scheme to match. Shinoda adopted the strongest features of Mitchell's Sting

Ray racer and of the upcoming production car, exaggerating some of them. He included the double-bubble glass top from Mitchell's first show car, the XP-700.

Alfred Sloan's first specification for Harley Earl's Art and Colour Section gave stylists a mechanical assembly area. The new Warren Tech Center had a better facility where Earl's and later Bill Mitchell's auto creations became mobile. Leonard McLay had kept Earl's supercharged Buick LeSabre running. Over time he tamed a great number of temperamental engines. He and his crew supercharged a 327 for Mitchell's new car. (Over its 10-year life, the Shark's engine compartment "tested" power steering pumps, power brake boosters, and a 427-cubic-inch displacement Mark IV engine.) Mitchell first showed it at the New York Auto Show in April 1962.

A DUAL-PURPOSE SPORTS CAR

Only Mitchell's car sported a supercharged engine; production models used the 327-cubic-inch displacement engine just as customers had seen it in 1962, mated to three- and four-speed manual transmissions as well as the Powerglide automatic. Corvette engineers offset the engine 1 inch to the right in the frame to increase driver foot well space, though naturally this trimmed passenger foot room.

Designers created a new instrument panel and gauge cluster that gave the tachometer and speedometer equal importance. The steering column offered 3 inches of length adjustment (albeit a job only accomplished in the engine compartment with a wrench). Behind the seats in the coupe, designers and engineers created a large luggage storage area, although both engineering and design exhausted their budgets before completing a working trunk lid. The only access to the luggage was from inside, lifted over the seats.

(opposite) Bill Mitchell enjoyed teasing the public as much as Harley Earl did, and this New York and Chicago auto show model continued the tradition. While it was basically a 1963 Sting Ray convertible, it picked the exterior exhaust headers and side pipes from the 1961 SP-755 Shark show car.

It was, of course, the Sting Ray body that seized viewers' attention. Frederick Donner's board approved the full-size clay coupe body in April 1960 and the interior, done in a studio separate from those doing the body, in November. Mitchell, mad about his coupe, reluctantly created a convertible in the fall only after being told to do so. Once the board committed to building the new car in fiberglass, engineering and design collaborated to make the new body stronger, tighter, and quieter. They doubled the reinforcing steel within the fiberglass panels from 1962's body, yet they thinned the panels enough to get the body weight below the previous model. Design ran 3/8th-scale models of both coupe and convertible bodies through the California Institute of Technology wind tunnels before showing them to Donner. This helped them devise the rotating housing to tame the windresistance that quad headlights generated. The wrap-over, limousine-style doors not only launched a new design trend but greatly improved entry and exit. Shinoda drew in working vents on the hood and behind the doors. The design and development sums were gone, however; there was nothing left to make that air ventilation plumbing work.

Ever since the effects of Curtice's AMA racing and performance ban rippled throughout GM, Zora Duntov cautiously commented that private customers would race Corvettes whether GM approved or not. As plans advanced for Sting Ray production, he continued to suggest it was in Chevrolet's best interest to carry on parts development to benefit racers. His sense was correct, especially when Ford's Total Performance program in 1962 effectively returned them to racing. Duntov had made sure Corvette racers were ready.

Zora and his cohorts created RPO Z06. This Special Performance Equipment package included a vacuum brake booster, a dual master cylinder, sintered-metallic brake linings within power-assisted Al-Fin drums cooled by front air scoops and vented backing plates, a 20-percent larger diameter front

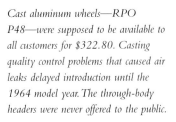

Cast aluminum wheels—RPO P48—were supposed to be available to all customers for $322.80. Casting quality control problems that caused air leaks delayed introduction until the 1964 model year. The through-body headers were never offered to the public.

Once this car finished its show life, retired Styling Chief Harley Earl used it for a while. Eventually, Chevrolet Styling produced a second show car body like it. They built it for Chairman Frederick Donner to placate him after Design and Engineering's efforts to circumvent the racing ban. Mitchell painted Donner's car Candy-Apple Red.

(bottom center) The auto show car used a real wood-rimmed steering wheel, not the optional plastic wood version that 130 Sting Ray buyers ordered with RPO N34 for a mere $16.20. The two-toned seats repeated the white racing stripe motif of the car's body.

(bottom right) Mitchell's design department engineers started with the 360-horsepower L84 fuel-injected 327 and modified it to develop closer to 375 horsepower. The car they produced for Harlow Curtice used the 340-horsepower carbureted L76 engine.

antiroll bar, larger diameter shocks, and springs nearly twice as stiff as standard. Initially, the package fit a 36.5-gallon gas tank instead of the new 20-gallon container. This package, which also included the 360-horsepower 327-cubic-inch displacement engine, M-21 close-ratio four-speed transmission, Positraction, and cast-aluminum knock-off wheels, cost the buyer an extra $1,818.45 over the base coupe price of $4,257. Initially, buyers could order the package only for coupes (because the over-size tank could not fit in the convertible). It was a pricey race-ready package; deleting the heater and defroster saved $100, but the total tipped in at $5,975.45. Later in the model year, Chevrolet discovered problems with air leaking through the porous aluminum castings. The knock-off wheels and the extra-large gas tank were deleted from the Z06 package (although the tank was available on any coupe separately), and its price was revised down to $1,293.95. At that point, Chevrolet offered it for the convertible as well. Chevrolet produced 199 of these Z06s.

Production began at St. Louis just as Bill Mitchell introduced his Shark in New York. Crews working inside the plant but outside the regular production line manufactured about 25 pilot 1963 models, getting kinks out of a system involving entirely new body pieces. They completed these cars by late June and quickly parceled them out, some going to enthusiast magazines so they could publish their stories the same time dealers unveiled the new car. (Chevrolet priced the new convertible at $4,037, one dollar less than the 1962 model had been.)

"The 1963 Corvette," *Road & Track's* publisher John Bond wrote, "has come a long way in 10 years—from a stylist's plaything to a full-blown, out-and-out dual-purpose sports car."

In *Car & Driver's* April 1963 report, technical editor Jan Norbye wrote that "the key to the personality of the [1963] Corvette lies neither in the power available nor in the revised styling, but in the chassis. Up to now the Corvette has been struggling to rise above a large number of stock components, notably in the suspension where their presence created all kinds of problems that required extensive modifications for any competition use beyond normal road rallies. The new all-independent suspension has completely transformed the Corvette. . . ."

Jim Wright, *Motor Trend's* technical editor, led off his May 1963 reexamination with a three-quarter rear view of the car sliding through dirt and a headline in letters one inch tall: "For the first time in its 10-year history, the Corvette String Ray is . . ." and then the text jumped to the next page, where it continued, ". . . in such demand that the factory has had to put on a second shift." He reminded readers of his past observations.

"The factory has never made any big profits on the Corvette but . . . Chevy brass was more than satisfied as long as it carried its performance image and prestige over to the bread-and-butter lines. We also ventured an opinion that as long as the factory kept building the car on this basis, it would be a great automobile, but if they ever put in on a straight dollar-profit basis, the Corvette would probably be ruined."

Chevrolet issued a press release late in the fall announcing double shifts at St. Louis. Their production goal for the 1963 model was 16,000 units. When the counting was done, they had sold 10,594 coupes and 10,919 convertibles, a total of 21,513 cars, It hadn't quite achieved the numbers Duntov predicted would flock to the independent rear suspension, but it far exceeded Chevrolet's own estimations, and it beat 1962 by nearly 50 percent.

A topside view of the split-window design that makes the 1963 coupe so distinctive.

Four versions of the 327-cubic-inch small-block V-8 engine were available in 1964, including a 300-horsepower version.

In racing, Duntov's Z06 coupes proved formidable in their first outing, the *Los Angeles Times* Three-Hour Invitational Race at Riverside, California, in October 1962. Bob Bondurant, Dave MacDonald, and Jerry Grant drove the three cars, a silver, a white, and a blue coupe, out from the St. Louis factory to break them in while another car was trucked out earlier. Duntov supervised their preparation for the A-production race. From the start, this event quickly became a contest between MacDonald in his Z06 and one of Carroll Shelby's new cars. After Chevrolet declined to sell him cars without bodies, Shelby took his idea to Ford. Upon hearing of Chevrolet's reaction, Ford gave Shelby all the engines and help he could use. Shelby stuffed Ford's 260 V-8s and then 289s into the English AC Ace and renamed the car after a predatory snake. Bill Krause raced the Cobra hard. Both MacDonald's Z06 and Krause's Cobra broke after the first hour, and two more Corvettes retired by the end of the second; but the fourth Corvette, entered by Mickey Thompson and driven by Doug Hooper, won the race. Thompson was pleased, but Duntov knew Shelby. Whatever failed on the Cobra was something Shelby would find and fix. Duntov had no budget for that. Next time the Cobra could win, and soon it would dominate.

Shelby's Cobra had won the A-production championship by June, yet Duntov remained philosophical. While he was disappointed, he knew that under current GM management the Cobra was insignificant. It won where it didn't matter to Donner, and Shelby didn't race in the contest Donner cared most about, the one for the pocketbooks of thousands of customers who never raced cars.

MUSCLE CAR IMITATORS

After the first year of production, Bill Mitchell sacrificed his split rear window. In preparing the body for 1963 production, body engineers had to make the spine much wider than Mitchell intended. For 1964, the car dropped the nonfunctional hood grilles but left their indentations. Styling made the left roof vent functional (but not the right). To improve handling without sacrificing ride quality, engineering replaced the front coil springs with a progressive rate version and revised shock valving to address problems on the 1963 cars. Engines got stronger with the addition of Holley 4150 carburetors, and peak power of the solid-lifter engine rose from 340 horsepower to 365 horsepower. Engineering provided a new intake manifold for the fuel-injected version, increasing output to 375 horsepower. During 1963 production, Chevrolet also replaced the Borg-Warner gearboxes with four speeds produced at GM's Muncie, Indiana, transmission plant. In the coupe, a small fan circulated air in the rear, addressing the greenhouse effect of sweltering heat under the large back windows. In all the

In 1965, the final year for fuel-injected Corvettes, Chevrolet offered a big-block 396-cubic-inch V-8 in a Corvette for the first time.

As early as 1956, Chevrolet offered optional racing car parts hidden in the order form if the buyer was diligent and perceptive. With the 1963 model year, the option was complete. Called the Z06, the $1,818.45 package included everything from improved cooling, suspension, and brakes to stronger engine and drivetrain components.

bodies, more insulation and revised body and transmission mounts quieted the complaints about too much interior mechanical and road noise. Duntov the European fought to create a true European sports car, but Duntov the pragmatist recognized that the real nature of the American grand-touring customer kept crying for attention.

Another group within GM, hungry for Corvette's performance image, found a new direction. Muscle cars, born in the 1950s at Chrysler as big cars with powerful Hemi-head engines, spawned imitators who were quick studies. Pontiac division general manager Elliott M. "Pete" Estes, its former chief engineer, launched the Tempest LeMans and GTO options in 1963 and 1964. These were compact cars stuffed with 389-cubic-inch displacement "tri-power" engines fueled by three two-barrel carburetors. These small cars were cheap to build and therefore inexpensive to purchase. Because they were not thoroughly re-engineered, their ability to handle the extra power was always in doubt, but they cost thousands less than a fully optioned Corvette. Yet they went just as quickly at the stoplight-to-stoplight drag races, the so-called American grand prix, that took place on every Saturday night on any main street. Worse for Corvette, they offered the still politically correct benefit of room for two couples on a double date. These big engines began pulling the Corvette away from Duntov's goals for the car. Yet Chevrolet's general manager, Bunkie Knudsen, fresh from Pontiac himself, felt the sports car could not be entirely left out of this new definition of sporting cars. Big engines were inevitable.

For 1964, total production reached another record, 22,229 cars, broken down into 8,304 coupes and nearly twice as many convertibles, 13,925. Chevrolet held the 1963 prices, keeping the coupe at $4,252 and the convertible at $4,037. The racers' package, now assembled from a variety of RPOs, not one alone, would set the buyer back a total of $6,526.40, a price that included the 375-horsepower "fuelie," four-speed, aluminum wheels, sintered brakes, Positraction, the F40 special front and rear suspension, and a few other necessities. (By comparison, a 389-cubic-inch displacement dual-quad, fully performance-optioned Pontiac GTO coupe cost less than $3,800.) Breaking up the Z06 option also led to some very interesting one-off cars, those created by customers with very specific needs, includ-

No radio, no heater, no clock, no air conditioning but a 36-gallon fuel tank nestled in behind the seats marked this race car as all business. Four-speed transmissions were manufactured by Borg-Warner until midyear when Muncie took over. All Z06 cars got early Muncie four-speeds.

ing such cars as a 300-horsepower, air-conditioned, automatic coupe fitted with the large fuel tank, ordered by a salesman who worked the American southwest during the summer months.

GOING TO DISC BRAKES

Design did more with an eraser than with pencils for 1965, eliminating hood and roof vents while opening the former "speedlines" behind the front tires to make real working vents. Years of battling over their cost and arguing their benefit paid off when engineering was able to provide four-wheel disc brakes at no extra cost (although for reasons few people understand, some 316 individuals ordered cars with drum brakes for which they received a $64.50 credit). Engineering had achieved near disc-brake performance from its sintered-metallic Al-Fin drum brakes, yet critics and journalists alike complained that the Corvette simply was not yet a sports car without discs.

Chevrolet engineering insisted brake performance had to be measurably better than its drums, particularly by providing superior "braking feel." GM's board refused to approve the expense of developing a power boost solely for the Corvette, and this became a requirement of the systems brought in from outside. Chevrolet engineers worked with Delco-Moraine to devise a new approach. In their system, pads barely touched the disc at all times. This provided instant pedal response and alleviated an early problem: When the rotors got wet, they were less effective than drums. Designing the caliper so the pads floated against the rotor swept it clean of moisture and road grit. Engineering selected ventilated, 1.25-inch-thick rotors for production, a full quarter-inch thicker than those used on the Grand Sport racers that evolved from the Z06 cars. Engineering adopted another racing idea and used the

There was only one engine available for the Z06—the L84 327-cubic-inch engine with Rochester fuel injection. With factory exhaust manifolds, required to run the cars in SCCA's production classes, Chevrolet rated the engine at 360 horsepower.

(opposite) Chevrolet produced 199 Z06 models, yet careful study of Mike Antonick's Corvette Black Book *suggests that fewer than this number were intended to race. Chevrolet delivered only 124 cars without radios and just 63 with the 36-gallon fuel tank. Admittedly, only those planning outings at Sebring and Daytona benefited from the big tanks; for shorter club races the extra capacity would be wasted.*

By the time Gulf Oil's Grady Davis picked up his Z06 to campaign at Sebring and Daytona, Zora Duntov had already begun working on Sting Ray prototype racers called Grand Sports. As a result, Grand Sport bits and pieces such as larger rear brakes, air cooling ducts, and front hood wind deflectors were available to Z06 competitors.

dual master cylinder similar to what it did with the Z06 package in 1963, fitting it as standard equipment on all disc–brake equipped cars, ahead of expected federal safety standards. It was a mid-1965 engine introduction that made these new brakes more valuable, however.

BANNING THE RACING BAN

GM's pursuit of performance resumed publicly within months of Ford Motor Company's announcement in mid-June 1962 that it would no longer adhere to the AMA racing ban. Once the first manufacturer broke ranks officially, no engineering department would be last, no matter what their board chairman felt. New engines and running gear appeared quickly, confirming that engineers had never

stopped tinkering. Chevrolet first revealed its 427-cubic-inch displacement V-8 big, block "mystery" motor, at the Daytona 500-mile stock car race in January 1963.

Chevrolet's 427 came from less than successful roots. Back in 1958, Chevrolet introduced its W-engine, the 348-cubic-inch displacement V-8. Engineers quickly found ways to increase its capacity to 409, but this block was large and heavy. It had many of the characteristics that Zora Duntov and others felt were exactly wrong for the Corvette.

When Jim Premo succeeded Harry Barr as Chevrolet's chief engineer, he found vigorous supporters in Bunkie Knudsen and Zora Duntov. Everyone knew Corvettes would get the larger engines; however, Duntov's high-performance engine group had been working, with Knudsen's blessings, on its own solution to that inevitability.

Richard Keinath had developed heads for a completely new engine dubbed the Mark II, heads that led to an odd configuration of intake and exhaust valves. These allowed much better breathing, but the seemingly random angles of the valve

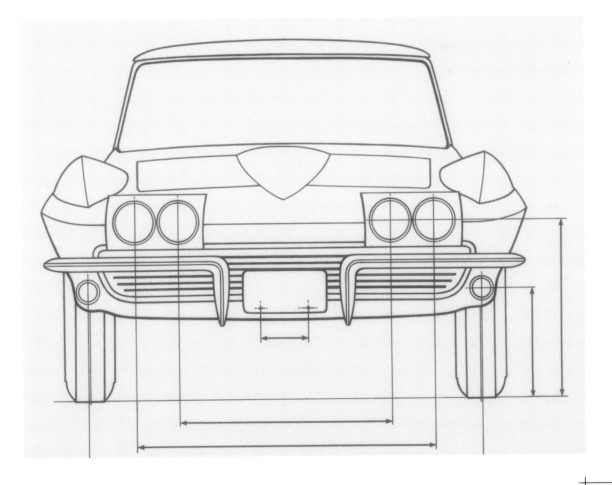

There were two most significant developments for 1965. First was the new big block 396-cubic-inch engine. The other was that Chevrolet installed disc brakes on all four wheels, rather than just up front. Another subtle distinction improved airflow and engine cooling when engineering and design made the three louvers functional behind the front wheels.

To combat roasting heat inside the Sting Ray's storage area, Chevrolet installed a three-speed fan that pulled air in through the functional louvers behind the driver's door. The outside vents on the passenger side were not functional.

(above left) All 1,897 of the Tuxedo
Black Sting Rays had a choice of black,
red, silver, or white interiors. Of nearly
22,000 1964 coupes and convertibles
produced, 19,034 had the optional
$188.30 four-speed transmission.

(above right) Chevrolet offered the
carbureted 327 in three power levels
starting with the 250-horsepower base
(which about 3,500 buyers selected).
Nearly half—10,471—of Corvette
customers ordered this $53.80 300-
horsepower, L75 version, while 7,171
ordered the 365-horsepower L76
configuration. Chevrolet sold 1,345
copies of the fuel-injected 375-
horsepower L84 engine.

Even without the split rear window,
the Corvette remained one of the most
stylish cars available.

stems quickly earned the nickname "porcupine heads." Engineering had developed the Mark II engine for stock car racing and had one completed and running by the end of 1962. Chevrolet first ran it at the Daytona 500 in 1963 and established a mystique as the "mystery engine."

California racer Mickey Thompson got a Mark II late that year and stuffed it into a Corvette that Bill Krause drove to third place overall in the February 1963 Daytona three-hour sports car races prior to the 24-hour international event. Donner heard about it, and while outside racing wasn't factory participation, his attention killed any chance of regular factory production of these engines beyond the few already assembled.

That is, they were ruled out until end-of-year sales figures spoke to Donner. When the numbers from all divisions made it clear that big engines were selling better than small ones, the manufacture of a street version of the Mark II was authorized. Because the federal government and the auto insurance industry paid more attention to car makers, especially after GM's troubles with its overly cost-controlled Corvair handling, GM management had held down the product planners' and engineers' tendencies to produce larger and more powerful engines. A board policy limited intermediate-size cars, Chevrolet's Chevelle, Pontiac's Tempest, and the like, those most suited to muscle car performance, to engine displacements below 400-cubic-inch displacement. With that in mind, the engine developers produced the Mark IV with 4.09-inch bore and 3.76-inch stroke for total capacity of 396-cubic-inch displacement.

For 1965, Chevrolet introduced this powerhouse engine, the L78, with 425 horsepower on tap. The rating was conservative, as a number of enthusiasts discovered when they simply had their engines blueprinted. Available as an option for only $292.70, some 2,157 Corvette buyers exercised the option. The price included a visual cue, a new hood that swelled in the center in a "power bulge"

While Bill Mitchell won the 1963 skirmish against Zora Duntov, magazine criticism aided Duntov in his battle against the rear split window. The most notable difference between 1963 and 1964 was the solid back glass. Aluminum alloy knock-off wheels reached regular production.

to accommodate the engine's bulk. Option N14 was even more visible. This new $134.50 package put exhaust pipes along the side of the car as they had been on countless Bill Mitchell show cars. Only 759 buyers had the nerve to announce so clearly to local police what they intended.

For 1966, the muscle power wars turned serious. By the end of 1965, Chevrolet division had a new chief executive, "Pete" Estes, fresh from Pontiac division where he and fellow collaborator John DeLorean had intensified—if not invented—muscle cars. Estes followed a similar route as Ed Cole. Both had been division chief engineers prior to their promotions. Both liked products.

Engineering stretched the Mark IV closer to its full potential by increasing bore to 4.25 inches, raising displacement to 427 cubic inches. Chevrolet offered it in two versions, an L36 with 390 horsepower using a single four-barrel carburetor, high-performance camshaft, hydraulic lifters, and 10.25:1 compression ratio to help accomplish this output. They quoted the mechanical valve lifter–equipped, higher-output L72 for 1966 production at 425 horsepower. Soon everyone knew that was an extremely conservative rating. The engine transformed the Corvette. Runs from 0–60 miles per hour took a scant 4.8 seconds, and the car hit 100 miles per hour only 11.2 seconds after leaving the line.

Beginning in 1966, option codes became mantras for performance junkies. Young men, many just eligible for the draft with a 1A classification, preferred to know L72 (427-cubic-inch displacement, 425 horsepower), M-22 (four-speed, close-ratio, heavy duty), C48 (heater/defroster delete), G81

(continued on page 202)

(top left) Disc brakes, now standard all around, were included in the base coupe and convertible prices. Yet not everyone was convinced of the improvement they represented. Some 316 Corvette buyers exercised RPO J61 refitting drum brakes instead and saved some $64.50.

(left) Chevrolet began producing the Mark IV "porcupine head" 396-cubic-inch engines in January 1965, and the first cars reached showrooms in April. The L78, available for $292.70, developed 425 horsepower at 6400 rpm and a massive 415 foot pound of torque at 4000 rpm. Chevrolet produced 2,157 L78-powered Corvettes the first year.

(right) The side-mounted exhaust system—RPO N14—improved engine breathing somewhat for the $134.50 price that buyers paid. Just 759 customers opted for the system. Positraction was much more popular, with 19,965 of the 23,562 buyers selecting that $43.05 option.

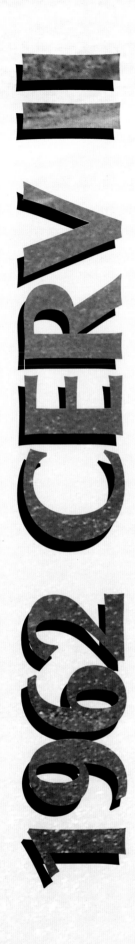

1962 CERV II

Duntov's champion, Bunkie Knudsen, had approved the CERV II in early 1962 as a follow-up project to the CERV I on the basis that it would perpetuate the valuable engineering lineage that Duntov and his colleagues had begun with the Corvette SS and CERV I. In fact, as Karl Ludvigsen explained in *Corvette: America's Star-Spangled Sports Car,* "Duntov hoped to reawaken the Corvette SS concept of a separate and parallel line of experimental/racing Corvettes."

This new vehicle was to use an alloy tube frame with a 92-inch wheelbase. The 1,800-pound sports racer would be powered by a new 244 cubic-inch engine to meet 1962 FIA regulations for 1963 prototype race cars' 4.0-liter maximum engine displacement. There was the possibility of using Mark II 427-cubic-inch engines in this car, and with 550 horsepower on hand, other opportunities arose.

All-wheel drive was one such opportunity. Knudsen and Duntov believed in using racing and competition as a means to improve and promote regular production vehicles. They understood that racing forced fast engineering solutions to problems, short cutting normal development times from months to days between one race and the next.

(above left) Duntov experimented with both magnesium and aluminum castings for the prototype 240-cubic-inch (4-liter) engine block. He also had a three-valve head to make better use of the Hilborn fuel-injection system first introduced on CERV I. With everything attached, the engine weighed just 382 pounds, yet it produced nearly 400 horsepower at 7,000 rpm. Duntov gave the car all–wheel drive and created a unique three-speed semi-automatic transmission.

(above right) One odd feature of the transmission system was that drivers started it in gear and moved off without first shifting. Changing from low to reverse requires shutting off the engine, because Duntov's experiment used neither input torque-converters nor hydraulic couplings. Internal multi-disc clutches and brake bands transmitted power.

(below) Crackling exhaust sounds bark from the four equal-length pipes on each side of Zora Duntov's prototype 4-liter/240 cubic-inch aluminum V-8 behind the driver's and passenger's seats of CERV II. Its mid-engine layout and short wheelbase put 58 percent of the vehicle weight on the rear tires.

Its thin-wall aircraft steel tubing truss frame weighed just 70 pounds. Draped with a paper-thin body of fiberglass adding only another 192 pounds, the entire package, minus oil, cooling water, and fuel, tipped the scales at just 1,378 pounds. Fully loaded with driver, it still came in just under 1,800 pounds.

Duntov worked on the all-wheel-drive CERV with Frank Winchell, Chevrolet's head of Research and Development. As Bill Mitchell had his locked styling studios, so Winchell had secret engineering labs. He was responsible for the Corvair rear-engine development. He didn't care much for racing but he loved solving problems. While they considered a four-speed manual transmission, the solution he and Duntov created for an all-wheel-drive CERV II was dual torque-converters: one front and one rear. They incorporated quick gear change capability to accommodate different track speeds. Winchell did away with the usual hydraulic coupling, using internal multi-disc clutches and brake bands to start the engine and get the car moving through its three manually selected forward gears. The paper-thin aircraft sheet-steel unit-construction tubular chassis used the engine as a stressed member. The basic structure was surrounded by a tubular substructure to carry the other loads.

Word of the CERV II slipped out and got to Donner, who suspected that Knudsen might aim to go racing again. The corporation slapped Knudsen's wrists and closed down CERV II, which already had completed wind tunnel testing as both a coupe and roadster. Chevrolet racing in internationally sanctioned events against the likes of Ferrari would not happen. At least not in the prototype category, not in anything so radically, noticeably different as a tiny, mid-engine, sports racer.

This immediately set Duntov and Knudsen to wondering about a plan B, something not quite so obvious to Donner, something that would appear much more like a regular production product. Perhaps they would involve Mitchell and even call it one of those deep sea creature names the design chief favored.

Front and rear differentials ran at slightly different final drive ratios to ensure proper power delivery. Under hard acceleration, the less heavily weighted front tires spun faster than the rears. The multi-disc clutch and automatic transmissions later proved indomitable when Texan Jim Hall adapted them to his sports racing Chaparrals. His earliest racers even resembled the CERV II.

(continued from page 196)

(Positraction), N14 (side exhaust) or N11 (off-road exhaust system), F41 (special front/rear suspension), or J56 (special heavy-duty brakes) than to think about Southeast Asia. Always there in the shadows, on the six o'clock news, in NBC-TV's "Vietnam Weekly Review" and CBS' "Vietnam Perspective," and in *Life* magazine, was the war. The baby-boomer generation, children born after World War II into the greatest period of prosperity since the mid-1920s, had trouble accepting that their time was becoming the worst of times. It was far more enjoyable to read in *Car Craft, Hot Rod,* and *Road & Track* at year-end that Chevrolet's Corvette had another banner year, selling 9,958 coupes and 17,762 convertibles, a total of 27,720 cars.

For Corvette, 1967 turned out to be the best Sting Ray yet, because delays in production engineering held up a replacement once again. Mild design updates had to do, but under the hood, the changes were far more substantial.

New code numbers entered Corvette order books: L71, the 427-cubic-inch displacement V-8 with a trio of progressively linked two-barrel carburetors, produced 435 horsepower. Some 3,754 buyers paid $437.10 and went this route. Savvy buyers got an option on the optional engine by checking L89, which fitted aluminum cylinder heads on the L71, although only 16 of these were delivered at an additional $368.65 over the engine cost. One code became legendary: L88. This was 427-cubic-inch displacement with 12.5:1 compression. Chevrolet engineering knew what it had. Hoping to keep speed-hungry trust fund–endowed youngsters from buying something far beyond their abilities, it discouraged unknowing

(lower left) It could be promoted as a weight-saving improvement. The RPO L89 aluminum cylinder heads fitted onto the L71 427 cast-iron block, cutting 75 pounds off the front end, taking engine weight down to within 40 pounds of a fully equipped 327. A Car and Driver road test saw 13.6-second quarter-mile times, at 105 miles per hour. The lighter weight improved handling as well.

(lower right) Nothing inside this coupe betrays the stunning potential of Chevrolet's most potent package to date. Just 16 buyers ordered the aluminum heads, an unproven $368.65 option on an engine already developing 435 horsepower. Even the wild L88 option costing $947.90 was more popular, with 20 produced.

buyers by quoting 430 horsepower, five less than the lesser L-71, yet doubling its price to $947.90. Topped by a single Holley sucking 850 cubic-feet of air per minute and capable of running on 103-octane fuel, the true output of this engine was closer to 560 horsepower. Buyers could get the car only with the transistorized ignition, Positraction, F41 suspension, and J50 power brakes. Ordering the engine automatically deleted the heater and radio "to cut down on weight and discourage the car's use on the street," according to a release at introduction. Only 20 individuals paid for it, many of them seeing it for what it was: a flat-out racing engine with a regular production option code.

The first of the engines appeared in late 1966, slipping out the back door to select competitors. Chevrolet's director of promotions, Vince Piggins, was more accurately the division's director of racing. Characterized as someone with deep pockets but also with "high pockets," Piggins was generous with information and advice but less willing to use his resources to provide freebies. To help customers capable of paying their way, he created an ordering system, the Central Office Purchase Order (COPO), to take advantage of what he knew Duntov and others were doing in their back rooms. Piggins released a 1966 coupe body with the L88 and other "production options" to Roger Penske, a friend known to Duntov and Chevrolet from his Grand Sport efforts. Penske and Sunoco Oil had entered the car in the 24 Hours of Daytona in February 1966.

Dick Guldstrand picked up the car at St. Louis in mid-January and drove it to Penske's Newton Square garage in Pennsylvania to supervise additional preparations, though there was not enough

(lower left) No matter how many years it has been since its introduction, the Sting Ray coupe's boat-tail body still strikes automobile-design enthusiasts as a thing of beauty.

(lower right) While badges and louvers either disappeared or became totally functional, one new design flourish appeared. Chevrolet's 427 cubic-inch big-block engines now fit under a non-functional scoop set off with contrasting color paint.

time to paint the red coupe Sunoco's blue. Guldstrand teamed Ben Moore and George Wintersteen to drive the race.

During the night, Wintersteen crashed in the car, heavily damaging the front end and losing the headlights. Guldstrand improvised and Penske's pit crew "racer taped" two flashlights onto the fenders. Guldstrand spent most of the night following the taillights of one of the Ferrari team cars. Incredibly, he broke the GT class distance record and the first production L88 finished the 24 hours in 12th place overall, first in class.

A month later in Sebring, Penske's car, now blue, finished 9th overall, tying Corvette's best ever at the airport circuit and once again winning its class.

By June, Piggins had commandeered a 1967 "pilot" preproduction car, and he helped California dealer Peyton Cramer obtain the first 1967 L88 coupe to take to Le Mans. Cramer, who owned Dana Chevrolet, knew racing; he had been Carroll Shelby's general manager at Shelby American. While L88 weighed 300 pounds more than the closest competitor in GT

(opposite top) The hood scoop and its contrasting color made a strong visual impression for the 1967 models. Beneath this hood, the 427-cubic-inch RPO L71 engine fed by three two-barrel Holley carburetors developed 435 horsepower.

(left) Hot Rod magazine writer Eric Dahlquist tested an L71 tri-power 427 and recorded quarter-mile times of 13.8 seconds at 108 miles per hour for a convertible with four-speed manual transmission. While air conditioning and the automatic transmission might have cost an extra second or two, it still was an impressive

(opposite bottom) While 3,754 buyers ordered the L71 engine, some 2,324 purchased the automatic transmission and 3,788 customers selected air conditioning, there is no way of knowing if anyone other than this owner combined the three. This combination offered highway cruising comfort and romping, stomping performance in the same car.

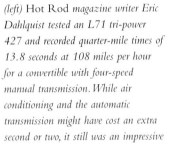

(left) Chevrolet's factory air conditioning was efficient, and the Ermine White exterior and white interior added to the impression of frosty coolness on even the warmest day. In many ways, this automobile hints at what Corvette's designers and product planners saw for the future: combining performance and luxury.

class, Dick Guldstrand, now Cramer's high-performance manager, and Bob Bondurant, by this time Dana's regular driver in its SCCA and Can-Am entries still clocked 171.5 miles per hour on the Mulsanne Straight, 22 miles per hour faster than the nearest GT Ferrari. Sadly, the blistering pace took its toll and the L88 expired after 11 hours, leaving the slower Ferrari to win GT.

While Chevrolets had raced on NASCAR ovals, road courses, drag strips, and across the salt flats at Bonneville in Utah, by the time the Sting Ray appeared, the division had adopted an unofficial and unspoken snobbery. It held that Corvettes belonged on road courses, while Impalas, Chevelles, or Camaros could drag race or go fender-to-fender around the ovals. Corvettes already had a reputation among drag racers for being expensive to buy and race and fragile to operate because they broke down regularly. But racers such as Bo Laws and Dick Moroso had another view. They said, "That car 'hooks' like nobody's business." Despite its drawbacks, and because of the efforts of outside aftermarket parts

One of Bill Mitchell's strongest influences was the
proliferation of blues in the color palette for the
Corvette. Chevrolet offered three separate variations.
The most popular were Marina Blue (3,840
produced), Lynndale Blue (1,381), and Elkhart
Blue (1,096.) There were even several colors
available for the big-block hood scoop.

Charlie Snyder from Astoria, New York, ordered an L71-equipped convertible with the hardtop to run in AHRA local and regional races. Snyder took the car directly to Motion Performance after picking it up from Baldwin Chevrolet in February 1967. Very quickly Charlie began winning races, and he made a name for himself and the car, routinely running 11.5 seconds at 124 miles per hour.

suppliers and speed shops that cooperated with local dealers, a few drag racers made their place in history racing Sting Rays.

On Long Island, New York, Baldwin Chevrolet and Joel Rosen's Motion Performance had a working relationship with Vince Piggins, who helped get them parts and engines just as he did with other dealers. Rosen, barely older than his customers, created 427-engined "Stage III" muscle Chevrolets. When he heard from Piggins that the L88 would be available in a box in midsummer 1967, he ordered two through Baldwin's parts manager John Mahler. Rosen and Mahler knew at least one likely customer.

Charlie Snyder was born and raised in nearby Astoria, and the 20-year-old loved racing. In early February 1967, he took delivery of a Marlboro Maroon hardtop convertible with the 425-horse-power 427-cubic-inch displacement engine. To protect himself from outrageous insurance rates in car theft–prone Queens, he titled the car in his mother's name, Grace Snyder. He drove the car straight to Rosen for tuning and modification. Over the next several months, "Astoria Chas," as he became known, drove to the track, raced, and won, regularly turning 11.5-second times at 124 miles per hour. He also ran after midnights on the connecting highways in Queens where crowds lined the roadway three deep to see racing under the streetlights Friday and Saturday nights. Rosen's increased power

An incoming mortar round killed 19-year-old Charlie Snyder within a month of his arriving in Vietnam. His mother and sister put the car in a garage until a year later when Motion Performance owner Joel Rosen and Baldwin parts manager John Mahler asked if they could continue to race the car in Charlie's name.

The side pipes looked stylish but drivers and passengers soon learned to step well away from the car when getting in or out. The RPO N14 Side Mount Exhaust System sold for $131.65, and of 22,940 cars produced in 1967, 4,209 buyers liked the look.

A few modifications to the car made it a full-scale Baldwin-Motion Phase III. With John Mahler at the wheel, the Ko-Motion, as Charlie had named it, rocketed into the record books in 1969 with an 11.04 second/129 miles-per-hour run made "in memory of Astoria Chas." A day later, Mahler ran a 10.74, and together with Rosen, they returned it to Charlie's mother and rolled it back into her garage where it remained for 30 more years.

and torque eventually twisted the chassis. Snyder ordered a replacement and the car sat for a month in a service bay at Baldwin. Rosen's two L88s were on the same truckload with Snyder's chassis, and he wasted no time securing one of the two (the other went to a neighborhood Camaro). To handle the new power, Baldwin's mechanics gusset-welded the chassis. Over the next few weeks, Snyder raced regularly and won repeatedly in the car he named "Ko-Motion."

Snyder got drafted in the winter of 1967. In the spring of 1968, on leave after basic training, he returned to Queens, repainted the graphics on his car, and raced several more times. Then the army sent him to Vietnam. One month after arriving, he died of injuries from an exploding mortar round. Back home, his Corvette sat in Grace's garage throughout the 1968 summer season while his family grieved the loss of their only son.

John Mahler and Joel Rosen thought about the car often. After a year passed, they approached Grace Snyder. They wanted to race it, they said. They would pay all its expenses, running it "in memory of

After a spring and summer of hard running, Charlie had to replace the chassis, which had twisted from the torque. Later, his factory original 427-cubic-inch 435 horsepower L71 engine expired. Snyder learned through Joel Rosen that L88 engines with aluminum heads would be available in crates. Snyder took one of the first two Rosen got, likely to be the first L88s in private hands.

Astoria Chas." They reminded her it had been Charlie's dream to set an AHRA record. After some hesitation, she agreed. Mahler and Rosen prepped the car through the winter and resumed racing in the spring of 1969 with Bill Foster, a local pro, often driving for them. The car made headlines, turning 11.04 seconds at 129 miles per hour and winning the A/Corvette World Record in Charlie Snyder's name. After taking the title, Mahler and Rosen performed one final modification, changing heads and fitting an 850-cfm Holley carburetor. With this set up, Mahler pulled a 10.74 at National Speedway in Queens one Saturday night, registering the accomplishment in Charlie's name. The next afternoon, with its time whitewashed in shoe polish on the window and its trophies stuffed in the foot wells, Rosen and Mahler trailered the car to Charlie's sister Sharon's home. They pushed it into her garage and covered it. It remained there for 30 years, one of a handful of Corvette drag racing legends.

1963-1967

CHAPTER SEVEN

GREAT PROJECTS ARE OFTEN THE VICTIMS OF CORPORATE AND INTERNATIONAL POLITICS

I n March 1962, Ford announced its return to racing as part of its "Total Performance" program. It blamed GM for side-stepping the AMA ban for years, though Ford's own NASCAR wins put Ford in no position to cast stones. GM Chairman Frederic Donner was embarrassed. He reiterated General Motors' intentions to honor GM's 1957 commitment.

Bunkie Knudsen had become Zora Duntov's corporate godfather. Knudsen, the new division general manager, liked seeing his cars in the spotlight. He knew that in October 1962, a Corvette Z06 had beaten Carroll Shelby's new Cobra at Riverside Raceway in California. But Duntov's description of Shelby's car made its potential clear to Knudsen. He encouraged Duntov to be discrete, above all, but to think as ambitiously as Ford and Shelby.

Duntov understood that the FIA's recent rule changes that made Grand Touring cars eligible in the World Championship for manufacturers was a subtly worded invitation to U.S. manufacturers. Yet he also recognized that entering his mid-engine CERV II four-wheel-drive coupe in Le Mans in 1964 was not discrete. He knew what it took to win the French race outright having won his class there in a Porsche 550 Spyder.

Duntov considered a "lightweight" 1,800-pound Corvette. He would need 600 horsepower to propel the car with its aerodynamic disadvantages. He and chassis engineer Walt Zetye fabricated an aluminum frame from two large-diameter parallel tubes joined at the back end by three transverse tubes and at the front by a massive 6-inch-diameter crossmember. Using aluminum saved 94 pounds over steel, and Zetye and Duntov transferred onto this car the IRS Zetye devised for the CERV that would later appear on the production Sting Ray. They cast an aluminum differential case and fitted a Dana-limited slip to replace the GM Positraction. They shortened the

(previous pages) In early 1965, Notre Dame University engineering student Tony De Lorenzo had volunteered to help classmates find interesting cars for a campus auto show. Tony called his father, who worked at GM at the time, and asked him if there was anything interesting in design or engineering that they could send. Dad visited Duntov and Mitchell. The unpainted #002 Grand Sport roadster got a coat of "Mitchell blue" and was sent to the show.

Chevrolet dealer Dick Doane first raced chassis #003, using a nearly stock 327-cubic-inch 360 horsepower cast iron engine. At the Road America 500 in September 1963, Doane blew up the engine after 92 laps. The car returned to Chevrolet to prepare it for Nassau Speed Weeks. For Nassau, the car got a quick fill gas cap and wider fenders to house 11-inch Halibrand wheels and Goodyear tires for John Mecom's racing effort.

The Z06s raced as production cars, so Duntov's idea was to produce Grand Sports that, properly developed, would compete against the world's finest prototypes. Chairman Frederick Donner upheld the 1957 AMA racing ban and cancelled the project just as it became visible.

body slightly, from 175.3 inches to 172.8, and lightened it considerably by using paper-thin fiberglass carefully laid over an aluminum substructure. Overall height grew 2 inches because the seats rested on top of, not inside of, the two major longitudinal frame members. Ground clearance, however, dropped from 7.4 to 4.3 inches. Because the race car weighed nearly 1,000 pounds less than the production car, Duntov decided to try four Girling disc brakes.

FIA racing regulations for 1963 placed no limits on engine displacement, another subtle invitation to the Americans. Engineering's 427 Mark II "mystery motor" could produce the power Duntov wanted, but it weighed too much. Boring out an all-aluminum 327-cubic-inch displacement block to within a couple of thousandths of its life might meet the same ends through different means. A 4.00-inch stroke as well as 4.00-inch bore would give him a lightweight 402-cubic-inch displacement engine. Zora and Yura Duntov, his brother, had devised the Ardun head, a hemispherical-combustion chamber, for flathead Ford V-8s in the 1940s. For the aluminum 402, they created twin-plug Hemi-heads, assembled the engine and tested it, and then discarded it as too far stressed. Back at the drawing board, they reconsidered stroke at 3.75 inches. This required less intrusive modifications to accommodate the spinning crankshaft. This engine measured 377-cubic-inch displacement. Duntov even produced three prototype dual-overhead cam versions, which produced an estimated 550 horsepower. This was less than his target of 600 horsepower, but it was more than any other option they had tried.

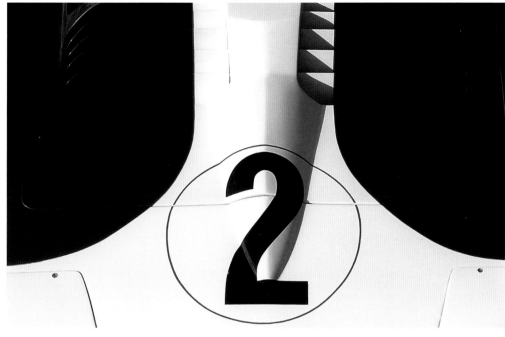

In advance of the December 1963 Nassau Speed Week races, Texas oil heir John Mecom got involved with Chevrolet's racing. Mecom hired drivers Roger Penske, A. J. Foyt, and Augie Pabst. For Chevrolet, this newcomer represented the perfect unrecognized foil to challenge Carroll Shelby's Ford-powered and well-supported Cobras.

(below) Throughout the summer of 1963, Duntov developed his aluminum-block 377-cubic-inch V-8. He installed these with four 58mm side-draft Weber carburetors into each of Mecom's "private" Grand Sports, #003 (shown here), #004, and #005. (Number 001 and 002 remained with Chevrolet.) The engine developed 485 horsepower at 6,000 rpm, but its tall induction system required a higher hood. Then in March 1965, Duntov created a 427 that would literally lift the front tires off the ground in all four gears.

Duntov took this first car, known by now as the Grand Sport (GS), to Sebring in mid-December 1962. Equipped with a race-prepared 327-cubic-inch displacement engine, he used it for shakedown runs and tire testing with Firestone and Mickey Thompson. The GS outshined Thompson's purely production-based car, but the Girling brakes proved inadequate. Actually, the Grand Sport shined a little too brightly. As they replaced the Girling rotors with new 1-inch-thick factory-produced ventilated discs, word came down from the corporation. Chevrolet was not Ford; these efforts had become too visible behind Donner's back.

Chevrolet had already filed specification papers with the FIA in Paris two weeks before Donner's edict hit Duntov's operation, forcefully halting the program. To qualify for the "Grand Touring" Group III category, the FIA required 100 identical cars constructed before June 1, 1963 (with Le Mans running June 15 and 16). Duntov had intended to produce 125 "production" cars for sale to customers to meet the FIA homologation (legalization) requirement. Later, 1,000 street-legal production cars would follow for public sale. Engineering had spoken with outside vendors about manufacturing the customer-racing cars and the street cars as well. Knudsen, however, had authorized building only 25 cars total, and just 40 of those special 377-cubic-inch displacement Hemi engines. It was clear now that Donner would never allow manufacture of 25 lightweight Corvettes. In fact, the five prototypes that Duntov already had underway were to be "scrapped, sold or used as testing and evaluation vehicles." But they would not race.

In a heartbeat, the Grand Sport project was over.

This was the most common view competitors got at Sebring in March 1964. John Cannon and A. J. Foyt shared the drive in the car marked as #2. With the car inadequately prepared, A. J. Foyt started in 62nd position. But in what has become Sebring—and Foyt—legend, A. J. passed 50 cars on the first lap! They finished 2nd in class behind teammates Penske, Jim Hall, and Hap Sharp.

Dick Doane, a Dundee, Illinois, car dealer and racer, and Grady O. Davis, vice president of Gulf Oil and an enthusiastic driver and car owner, were the beneficiaries of Donner's edict. Duntov sent out one of the completed cars to each of them, on loan, with instructions to keep their activities "low key" and not cause Chevrolet any embarrassment. Each car was white, and Duntov equipped them with production stock 360-horsepower 327-cubic-inch displacement fuel-injected engines.

Because Duntov had built only five, these cars did not qualify for production racing classes, but instead they had to go up against modified sports racers like Jim Hall's Chaparrals and Lance

Reventlow's Scarabs. This class elevation, however, allowed Doane and Davis to build real racing engines. The privately held Grand Sports went through teething troubles but eventually came to hold their own.

Grady Davis put Dr. Dick Thompson in his car. After a shaky start, Thompson and Davis had the car sorted so well that by early June it consistently finished in fifth or better overall. Through July and August, Davis' crew reworked and improved their "modified" Corvette, and when it reemerged in late August at the Watkins Glen Nationals, it was closer to Duntov's original vision. Somehow, when the SCCA totaled the points, Thompson finished fourth for the year in the C-modified category.

This frustrated Chevrolet engineers and Bunkie Knudsen, who recognized how close they were with the car. Carroll Shelby and his drivers steadily teased them. The byword around Chevrolet had been "discretely," but now through Chevrolet's back corridors, another word was whispered in a few ears: escalate.

Texas oil heir John Mecom Jr. had begun running a Cooper-engined sports racer, the Xerex Special. He had acquired the car, its builder, Roy

Unlike the production models, the air vents behind the front wheels were functional to help eliminate engine heat and underhood air pressure.

Gane, and its driver, Roger Penske, and throughout the 1963 seasons he added Augie Pabst and A. J. Foyt to his stable. The team was highly regarded, thoroughly professional, and extremely successful. Because Mecom was a newcomer, he owed allegiance to no one yet, making him the perfect team owner for Chevrolet's whispered plans.

Duntov arranged to ship Mecom several engines to install in a variety of sports racers. He called back Doane's and Davis' Grand Sports. He pulled a third car from the storage garages and set to work, preparing cars for Nassau Speed Week scheduled for early December 1963. He had Knudsen's unwritten but enthusiastic blessing.

New body modifications accommodated 11-inch-wide Halibrand wheels, necessary to fit the Mickey Thompson–inspired new wide Goodyear low-profile racing tires. Duntov's staff improved ventilation to engine and driver by liberally perforating the car nose, hood, sides, and rear. They dropped in the 377-cubic-inch displacement, all-aluminum block, aluminum-headed engines originally developed for the car with their four twin-throat Weber side-draft carburetors. Duntov's dynamometers saw 485 horsepower.

Duntov had the three Corvettes, chassis 003, 004, and 005, painted in Mecom Racing's Cadillac blue and shipped to Nassau, timed to arrive on November 30, the day before their first race. Coincidentally, several Chevrolet engineers arrived, all vacationing at the same time. Along with the Grand Sports, Mecom sent his three mid-engined Chevrolet-powered sports racers, a Lola GT, a Cooper-Monaco, and a Scarab. With this stable, piloted by some of racing's best drivers, Duntov believed that if the Corvette lightweights themselves did not win, at least a Chevrolet engine was likely to come home in first.

The Corvettes won the five-lap qualifying race, but Mecom's Lola took the 99-mile Tourist Trophy on December 1. The Grand Sports' final drives, not broken in before the races, couldn't handle the torque of the 485-horsepower engines or the pounding of the old airport course. Another Chevrolet engineer suddenly was overcome with the need for a Caribbean vacation. He flew down with carefully seasoned rear axles in his baggage.

The second weekend's 112-mile Governors Cup was a better show. A. J. Foyt won in Mecom's Chevy-engined Scarab, and the Grand Sports finished third (Roger Penske), fourth (Augie Pabst), and sixth (Dick Thompson), beating Shelby's best placed Cobra by two places. The next day's finale, the 252-Mile Nassau Trophy, ended with Dick Thompson in fourth, a Cobra in seventh, and new Mecom-inductee John Cannon in eighth. But this longer race pointed out once again the foul aerodynamics of the cars. Air pressure built up under the hoods and continually blew the fasteners. Each driver endured several pit stops to cut in new vent holes and apply racer tape to the panels.

The outside-mounted oil cooler sits under its own shroud behind the rear window. Vents everywhere funnel cool air to rear brakes and the differential.

When GM Chairman Frederick Donner shut
down the Grand Sport program, he issued
orders to destroy Chevrolet engineering's two
remaining cars: #001 and #002. Yet friends
of the project hid the cars until 1966 when
Roger Penske learned they were available. He
bought #001, recommending this car, #002,
to his long-time friend George Wintersteen.

The current owner resisted the temptation to restore the car to the racing livery used by George Wintersteen at East Coast racetracks throughout 1966. Instead, he restored the car to its first appearance at Notre Dame.

Somehow Nassau escaped Frederic Donner's sharp eyes, at least temporarily. The Grand Sport operation returned to Warren for further improvements and modifications before the 1964 season openers at Daytona and Sebring. Each race presented specific problems. Engineers fitted a new Rochester fuel-injection system to even out the engine power curve, and they installed a pneumatic air-jacking system to speed pit stop tire changes, changes that would benefit the Mecom team at both venues.

Daytona was a track where maximum speed was beneficial, as it would be at Le Mans and a few other circuits in the world. Duntov knew the Sting Ray body was a brick punching a big hole through the air. A sports-racer body like Mecom's other cars, or like his originally planned CERV II, would have been ideal. But those would introduce all new development problems. Instead, he decided to cut down the big brick, knowing that he'd pick up speed.

Duntov removed the roofs from two coupes, chassis 001 and 002. Engineers replaced the tall windshields with low windscreens and incorporated roll bars into lower fiberglass fairings. But spies were loose in the back halls at GM engineering, and shortly before the Daytona Continental 2,000-kilometer race in mid-February, Bunkie Knudsen's bosses called him in for a chat. A press release stated that Chevrolet was not associated with John Mecom Racing, ever. Donner applied effective leverage over Knudsen, and the general manager registered the threat as another permanent blotch on his record. More clearly than ever he saw little future at General Motors.

Quickly, Chevrolet sold the three coupes, two to Mecom and the third, chassis 005, to Jim Hall. Duntov had the two roadsters wrapped under covers and buried in storage in Warren. The three coupes began an odyssey of owners, races, and modifications that has filled other entire books, most notably Lowell Paddock's and Dave Friedman's 1989 history, *Corvette Grand Sport*. The cars campaigned privately, valiantly, and with some success for another three seasons, beating the best that Ford of Dearborn, Venice, and England could throw at them.

In late winter 1966, Roger Penske retired from driving but remained active as a team owner. He acquired the two remaining roadsters from Chevrolet, selling one quickly to friend George Wintersteen. Prior to Sebring in 1966, Penske put a 427-cubic-inch displacement Mark IV engine into 002, and during practice his crew bolted on aluminum heads, a first for the Mark IV and an indication that creative thinking was not dead within Chevrolet, only in hiding. Both roadsters and the coupes soldiered gamely on through the 1966 season, thrilling fans and inspiring loyalists.

TO RACE OR NOT TO RACE

In late 1962, as Chevy gave birth to the Grand Sports, Peter Brock moved back to the West Coast, joining Shelby's organization, where he watched Chevrolet and GM's board futzing and fidgeting from the long view in Venice, California. Decades later, he wrote about racing in Shelby's most intriguing car, the Cobra Daytona coupe, which Brock designed: "This dilemma [to race or not to race] split the board of directors. In the GM boardroom the battle lines were redrawn: bean counters versus engineers and marketing experts."

Neither group, Brock observed, seemed capable of convincing the other that they were right. Both sides did agree that Shelby's Cobras were too strong and only a new Chevrolet racer could meet

In their wildest versions, these "Lightweights," as Roger Penske and Dick Guldstrand called them, weighed in at just over 2,000 pounds and ran with "detuned" race engines developing 500 horsepower. This car would "go down the straights looking like a speedboat," as driver Wintersteen recalled.

Wintersteen had to cut a notch in the front cross member to shoehorn in the big L71-block 427-cubic-inch engine.

Ford's challenge. It was clear to everyone that any solution would be costly. Could they afford to meet the challenge? Well, yes, but was it worth it?

It created a conundrum. Could Chevrolet even sell Duntov's planned 125 racers at a reported $9,200 each? Further confusing things was the value of public visibility in Europe versus America. Ford, for example, had a vested interest in competing in Europe. The blue oval logo appeared on cars built in Germany and the United Kingdom. Chevrolet had no presence in Europe; in fact, at times GM had de-emphasized its ownership of Vauxhall in the United Kingdom and Opel in Germany. For Chevrolet to produce race cars that might win major races in Europe would necessitate an expensive advertising campaign just to explain to Europeans what it meant and why they should care. GM didn't plan to sell production Corvettes there, and the car wasn't well-regarded compared to other European sports cars.

Donner would not consider risking public embarrassment by circumventing the AMA ban with a racing effort in Europe. The fabulously expensive prospect of producing so few cars made Donner's accountant's blood boil. It had only been during his rule that Corvette had begun to pay for itself. He understood that little projects like this served to keep his engineers excited and loyal, and he turned a blind eye on things as long as they didn't cast the wrong light onto an observant public. Yet the Grand Sports simply could not be. The corporation, he believed, should not spend the money.

Then, in a master stroke of public relations good fortune, Donner turned a purely economic decision into a safety conscious issue. He was still smarting from the secret, seamy Ralph Nader investigations and from congressional subcommittee questions on Corvair safety. He had blurted out that GM had spent less than 1 percent of its net profit on safety-related research. It was an awful moment. The Grand Sport was the perfect project, then, for him to shut down. In the newspapers, it would read as purity of motive: Donner was upholding the June 6, 1957, AMA speed and racing ban even if no one else did so. In the eyes of the wary public, he had begun to redeem himself and General Motors. In the eyes of Wall Street stockbrokers, individuals who were far more important to Donner, he had exercised fiscal responsibility.

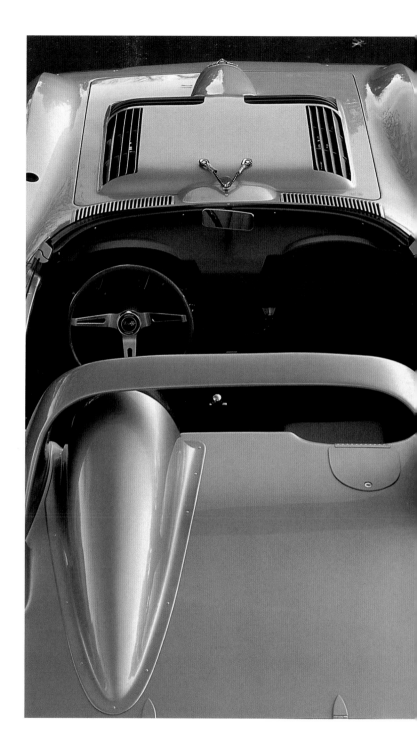

It was pure and simple, with a 200 miles per hour speedometer. The driver's seat adjusted while the passenger's was bolted in place. Because these cars raced in C-Modified class, they never had a chance to prove their potential, always outrun by pure sports racers with similar power but even less weight. Since there were only five Grand Sports, they became instant legends.

1968-1982

OFFICIAL PACE CAR
62nd ANNUAL INDIANAPOLIS 500 MILE RACE

MAY 28, 1978

CHAPTER EIGHT

THROUGH THE MIDYEARS, CORVETTES SACRIFICE MUSCLE TO LUXURY

ven before the St. Louis production plant started its preassembly runs of the 1963 Sting Rays, Bill Mitchell told his designers to think about the next Corvette. The Sting Ray was to remain in production only through 1965, possibly carried over into 1966, and so it was not too early to begin.

He set Larry Shinoda on a flight of fancy, a wild excursion with an open-wheeled single-seater not unlike Duntov's CERV I. It drew technical inspiration from Frank Winchell, Chevrolet Engineering Center's R&D chief. Winchell had developed the production Corvairs and the Monza GT and SS prototypes in 1962 and 1963. Mitchell called his new car the X-15, a project named after the Air Force's black rocket plane. Shinoda worked with John Schinella and a small group of designers and modelers in another one of those invisible, locked studios. While few people ever saw the car, it became the reality check at the far end of the spectrum from down-to-earth production products all the way to pie-in-the-sky daydreams. From it, Mitchell refined and defined what he wanted in his next personal car and in the next Corvette.

Shinoda's design, known internally as the XP-830, actually filled in at the last minute as a future Corvette when earlier plans failed. Duntov's work on the CERV II had led to suggestions that the next generation Corvette, perhaps now delayed until the 1967 model year, could be a mid-engined two-seater, reflecting the racing technology that Duntov believed Corvette customers wanted and deserved. Winchell's group had promoted the idea of a true lightweight (2,650-pound) rear-engined car, using the 327-cubic-inch displacement V-8. Its 70 percent rear weight bias rendered the car's handling frightening. Duntov's idea was mid-engined, with *(previous pages) This represented the most complete redesign since the 1968 Corvette. Chevrolet produced 6,502 of these Indy 500 pace car replicas. At $13,653, it was the first Corvette to sell for more than $10,000.*

The sculpture artists in Bill Mitchell's design studios created another striking hood for the small block. While vents on this hood were not functional, they still introduced cold air at the windshield's lowest pressure point.

While the wheelbase remained the same, the exterior was dramatically redesigned. It was so successful that Chevrolet General Manager Pete Estes ordered the St Louis factory to work a third shift to meet the demand.

the Mark IV 427, but had more neutral handling. Yet because the Corvette had always been built out of parts produced for other Chevrolet models and no pieces existed to build such a car as Winchell, Duntov, and Mitchell imagined, it was impossible. The costs to develop such pieces, even to a wealthy corporation such as General Motors ruled by an accountant like Donner, were prohibitive when balanced against the volume of Corvette sales and the likelihood those expenses might never be repaid. Design exercises produced cars with shapes as striking as Lamborghini's mid-engine Miura. But while European exotic-car buyers might accept a price tag above $20,000, GM management was sure

Corvette buyers were not ready for that. It was purely economic considerations, plus Donner's publicized indignation at the exploits of the Grand Sport and CERV I, that doomed the ambitious mid-engine next generation.

It took time and effort to make a Corvair chassis handle Corvette engines. When engineering eliminated that possibility, they and Mitchell's designers found themselves fighting an unforgiving timetable. In something like a forced-march pace, the two sides worked to bring a new car into existence.

Shinoda's creation for Mitchell became known as Mako Shark II. He renamed the earlier 1961 Shark show car, the XP-755, as the Mako Shark I, to give consistency and longevity to styling exercises that would become the new car. Chevrolet premiered the Mako II at the New York International Auto Show in April 1965. By October, design was able to ship a running, functional model, powered by a Mark IV 427-cubic-inch displacement V-8, to the Paris Salon. Throughout the rest of 1965, the two prototypes, created for something like $3 million, toured North America and Europe. They created a near frenzy of publicity and speculation based on Chevrolet's past performance. Magazines pronounced themselves certain that viewers were seeing the next Corvette when they looked at Mitchell's Mako II.

Chevrolet discontinued the two-speed Powerglide automatic transmission and introduced the new three-speed Turbo-Hydra-Matic M40 transmission. On base engine models such as this, it was a $226.45 option, and of 28,566 cars produced, 5,063 left the factory with the new automatic.

While they evolved from Larry Shinoda's Shark and Mako Shark II show cars done for Design Chief Bill Mitchell, the new production models tamed the stylistic excesses that made the show cars exciting. The new street cars just took people's breath away.

The Mako Shark II was the concept that led to the introduction of the 1968 body style. 2002 General Motors Corporation. Used with permission of GM Media Archives.

Meanwhile, in Washington, D.C., and Sacramento, California, lawmakers proposed rules and wrote regulations that would greatly affect the products of Detroit and its suburbs for nearly 20 years. As early as 1955, California began monitoring exhaust emissions. (This inspired Zora Duntov to perfect a cleaner burning fuel-injected engine. Its improved performance was a happy by-product.) For model year 1962, California required all cars sold new in the state to have positive crankcase ventilation (PCV) systems. By 1965, Congress had begun looking at legislation that would formulate acceptable levels of auto exhaust gas emissions. California mandated smog pumps on all 1966 models. These same regulations would go into effect nationwide with the 1968 model year. In 1966, the Traffic Safety Act began setting front, rear, and side-impact and visibility standards for cars sold in the United States. It also established procedures requiring manufacturers to recall vehicles on which

mechanical and safety flaws appeared. California introduced its own auto emissions standards, stricter than the rest of the country, to become mandatory with 1969 models sold in that state.

At the same time, the Chevrolet studios worked to revise the Mako Shark II into something that could be produced. They built it on the Sting Ray chassis, carrying over virtually everything mechanical from the production cars. By November 1965, Hank Haga's Production Studio had produced full-sized clay models very close to what the finished car would look like. Haga's designers replaced the Mako II boat-tail rear window with a scoop-like treatment derived from Duntov's mid-engine prototype and two of Haga's favorites, Ferrari's angular 1964 250 GTO and Porsche's 904 GTS. But as soon as engineering tested these prototypes in their wind tunnel, Corvette's perpetual aerodynamics problems reappeared. The new shark nose proved even more air-worthy than the previous Sting Ray had been. A duck-tail lip at the rear helped hold that end down, but that lifted the nose up further. Duntov fitted a small chin spoiler across the front, well below the small grille and slender fenders. It helped some.

Design carried over the tall front fender bulges from the Mako Shark II. Once again Duntov found himself fighting against Mitchell. The design chief's preferences ran counter to engineering's practicality and driver visibility. Duntov sought support

The Mako Shark II had a fastback boat tail rear end reminiscent of the first generation Sting Ray, while the production car used a small backlight under a targa-type rear roof. 2002 General Motors Corporation. Used with permission of GM Media Archives.

To improve weight balance, engineering moved the battery from the already-tightly packed engine compartment to another compartment behind the two seats.

Most L88s also arrived with other options, including Muncie's "rock crusher" M22 four-speed close-ratio transmission, J56 heavy-duty brakes, and the F41 heavy-duty front and rear suspension. These were often necessary to get the phenomenal horsepower to the ground without waste.

from Pete Estes, Chevrolet's new general manager, who came to the division from Pontiac in 1965. Like Ed Cole, Estes, who replaced Knudsen, had been a division chief engineer before his promotion to Chevrolet. Estes disliked the sight lines over the wheel humps and sent the car back to the drawing boards. Work piled up in the engineering and design departments already overburdened with the brand new Camaro, Chevrolet's response to Ford's Mustang and Pontiac's GTO. It was Chevy's entry into the nationwide muscle car wars. Chevrolet knew it had to introduce this car in 1967. Product planners could count sales lost to Pontiac and Ford every hour. Everyone involved with the Corvette agreed to hold over the Sting Ray replacement until 1968.

Under supervision from Chevrolet chief stylist David Holls, Larry Shinoda now collaborated with production studio chief Hank Haga and his staff to reduce those excesses of Shinoda's Mako Shark II that had continued onto the prototype. Mitchell had Haga's staff resurrect a removable roof panel idea that had appeared in the small experimental studios off and on since the late 1950s. By the time Mitchell approved the Corvette final clays, Porsche had introduced its 1967 model 911 Targa with a completely removable roof center section and rear window. Chevrolet design wanted to do

The badge and the sticker command attention. Anything less than 103 octane put the engine at risk, and running pump regular was an invitation to an expensive rebuild. The car thrived on Sunoco 260 and other barely disguised racing fuels of the period.

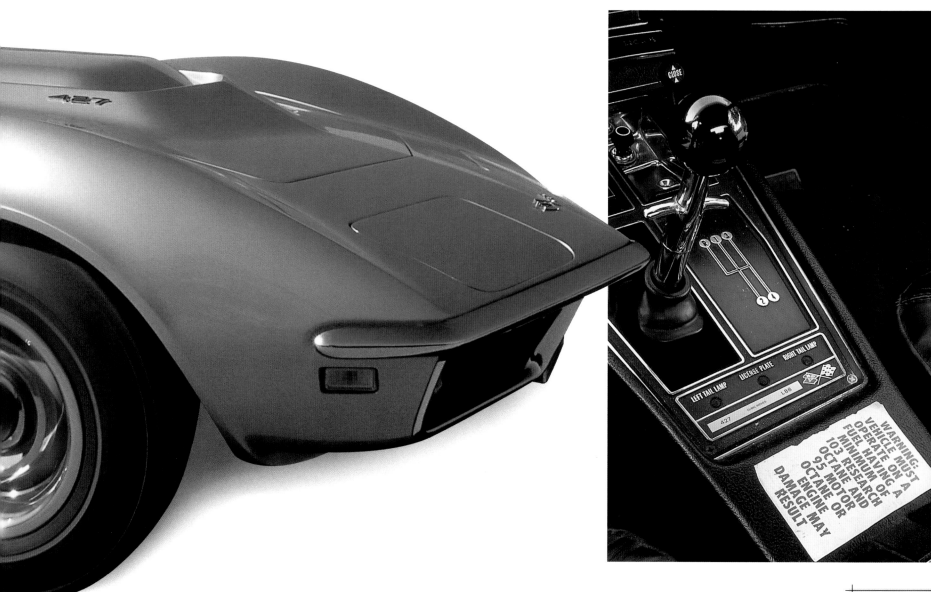

that but learned from Targa designer Butzi Porsche that the 911 was not stiff enough to support a completely open car. Its rollbar added the necessary stiffness to the steel-bodied Porsche. The Corvette's fiberglass body and steel frame were nowhere near stiff enough to accommodate an open roof. Incorporating a center beam that tied the windshield to the rear section, Chevrolet design adapted an innovation from outside industrial designer Gordon Buerhig, the T-roof.

Mitchell moved Shinoda's hidden headlights and windshield wipers from the Mako II to the production prototype, causing new problems and delays. The headlights, when closed, hung down into the airstream used for engine cooling. Yet the retractable headlights had become part of the iconography of Corvette. They would stay. Developing the vacuum plumbing to operate lights and wiper covers powerful enough to punch through snow or ice took time. Through late 1966 and early 1967, there were other problems to solve.

One of those concerns was engine cooling. Duntov had taken time off in the spring of 1967 to recover from a serious illness. Somehow engineering forgot to complete engine cooling tests. He returned to work three weeks before the press introduction for all the 1968 models, which he was to supervise. Public relations had specified that the press-preview Corvette be a heat-absorbing dark blue, powered by the Mark IV 427 big block. Duntov nearly panicked when he learned that engine cooling had been forgotten. In a typical racer's response to a problem, he lengthened the front chin spoiler and then sliced two large scoops into the bottom bodywork just ahead of the spoiler to channel more air in for engine cooling. The journalists never noticed and the combination worked well, going

Racers never divulge horsepower figures to the public until years after the car has retired. But educated guesses ran to around 580 horsepower from the English-prepared L88. It was good enough for 8th overall at Daytona and 4th overall at Sebring. At Le Mans, drivers Dave Heinz and Bob Johnson routinely saw 212 miles per hour along Mulsanne, finishing 15th overall, 1st in the over-five-liter class.

through immediately as a last-minute design change. Still, through the 1968 model year, cooling was barely sufficient for big-block engines with air-conditioning. (What's more, air-conditioning was a popular accessory. Buyers learned that inside the pinched cockpit, the newly introduced flow-through Astro-Ventilation system was completely inadequate.)

This was the laundry list of challenges that styling and engineering faced to get the Corvette completed—it would no longer be called the Sting Ray—for 1967. When Donner delayed the launch another year, it benefited the other engineers faced with meeting U.S. emissions and safety standards.

Soon after introducing the 1968 model to the press, Chevrolet reorganized its division management, disbanding Corvette engineering. Duntov was shuffled into special assignments as a roving jack-of-all-trades. Others were not so lucky, relocated to Chevrolet passenger car responsibilities.

Then the magazine reviews of regular production Corvettes began to appear. Most notable was *Car & Driver,* known for its biting wit. Editor Steve Smith didn't even bother with humor, writing in the December 1967 issue about his plans to road test the 1968 Corvette he had just driven out to Watkins Glen. "But we won't," he wrote. "The car was unfit for a road test. No amount of envious gawking by the spectators could make up for the disappointment we felt at the car's shocking lack of quality control. With less than 2,000 miles on it, the Corvette was falling apart." With a few strokes of the typewriter keys, Smith succeeded in restoring Corvette engineering. Duntov and his group were reassembled, and Duntov was named chief engineer of the Corvette. The new group worked tirelessly, but it often seemed an uphill battle with few thanks offered to also-rans.

The St. Louis factory had produced just three L88s in time for the 1968 Daytona 24 Hours. Actor James Garner bought them and prepped them in California. Those and two others that were not created in St. Louis but from over-the-counter engines installed by the racers all lost to a 1967 L88 coupe entered by Sunray DX. In February, Sunray got its first factory L88 hardtop. Don Yenko prepared that car and freshened up the other two put-together cars for Sebring. At the end of the race on March

(opposite) Goodyear, anxious to try for the most prestigious of endurance races, began investigating ways to enter. Goodyear had sponsored Enzo Ferrari's Grand Prix and Sports Car racing efforts for years, and Ferrari's North American Racing Team, run by Luigi Chinetti, also raced on Goodyears. So Goodyear's international competition director Leo Mehl approached Ferrari's U.S. team.

(lower center) Called Le Mans Blue, Chevrolet named most of its colors after racing circuits for 1969. Others included Monza Red, Riverside Gold, Daytona Yellow, Monaco Orange, and Can-Am (named for the series) White. The "coke bottle" tapered shape of the car appears most clearly in the convertibles.

(lower right) The L71 engine, with its 427 cubic inches and 435 horsepower operated through three Holley two-barrel carburetors. This induction system provided remarkable fuel economy for cruising (the linkage operated only one of the carburetors) until acceleration was needed. Then the engine could easily melt the tires.

23, Hap Sharp and Dave Morgan, after qualifying third, won GT class in Sunray's factory-built L88, finishing sixth overall. Two Camaros and a Mustang finished ahead of them.

By year-end, in the sweetest of ironies, *Car & Driver* readers voted the 1968 Corvette the "Best All-Around Car in the World," beating out the hyper-exotic, mid-engined $21,900 Lamborghini P400 Miura with its transversely mounted V-12 as the car they wanted most.

THE MANTA RAY

Bill Mitchell, ever in search of a more provocative commuter car, began to get antsy once his Mako Shark II-based production model appeared in showrooms. Advanced design studio artists reinvented Mitchell's car, creating something that looked as though modeling clay had been pulled, stretched, and extruded like taffy into a new sea creature. Mitchell called it the Manta Ray. By 1969, the elongated Mako Shark/Manta Ray was out on the show circuit, stopping viewers in their tracks, hinting at things to come in the future from Bill Mitchell's multimillion dollar playground.

Among racing efforts, one of the best known was that of Floridian Or Costanza, who got his yellow prototype L88 lightweight (one of just four built) in January 1969. Costanza's engine came with the new open chamber cylinder heads and an unusual dual disc clutch. While the public could buy the heads in June, Costanza's clutch was the only known example. Both Costanza and fellow competitor Doug Bergen of Ohio, who took delivery of a black roadster, got them through a Vince Piggins creation, the Buyer's Key Pass Program. This program allowed known racers to get special products far ahead of the general public. While Costanza didn't finish at Sebring, Bergen came in second in GT class behind Tony DeLorenzo, the son of GM's vice-president of public relations, in another L88 sponsored by fiberglass-maker Owens-Corning. In Europe, Henri Greder ran his Corvette constantly, finishing second in the Tour de France, qualifying fastest in the 1,000-kilometer race at Nurburgring and setting the fastest racing laps at Le Mans.

A two-month-long autoworkers strike created a backlog of public orders for the 1969 model, named the Stingray as one word, not two. New division gen-

It is a deceptively subtle package at a time when manufacturers often emblazoned their "muscle cars" with wild, often outrageous graphics. This most potent of muscle cars, with more than 500 horsepower under the hood in stock trim, could easily be mistaken for Corvette's most popular 427-cubic-inch 390-horsepower package with the popular side-mounted exhausts.

eral manager John DeLorean, another Pontiac graduate promoted to Chevrolet in February 1969, set back the new model introduction to February 1970 (which partially explained the very high sales number for the 16-month 1969 model year). The corresponding eight-month 1970 season, however, recorded only 17,316 sales: 10,668 coupes versus 6,648 convertibles.

Chevrolet announced late in the 1969 model year an engine option that did not appear until 1970. This small-block, solid-lifter-equipped, LT1 350-cubic inch displacement engine came much closer to Zora Duntov's own hopes for the car. He had never favored the big-block Mark IV engines. Even the aluminum ZL1 was too heavy for his liking, unbalancing a car he had worked so hard to get into shape. Yet every optional engine advanced the high-performance motivation of the muscle car era. When Frederic Donner retired as GM's president and chairman, the board selected former Chevrolet chief Ed Cole, and overnight performance was welcomed. In fact, the concept had become such a battle cry that even the LT1, with its lighter weight but inferior output to the outrageous 427s, could find a slot on an option list. However, product planners, marketing personnel, and advertising executives were aware of public sentiment and a rise in insurance premiums. The LT1 probably produced 370 horsepower, but like the L88s of the previous years, its output was down-rated to keep the safety-conscious less mindful of Chevrolet's products.

At the other end of this spectrum, engine builders stretched out the Mark IV further, increasing stroke from 3.76 to 4.00 inches to 454-cubic-inch displacement. New designations appeared, the LS5 being a 454 with hydraulic valve-lifters that, at a loaf, rated 390 horsepower. An all-aluminum LS7 was listed but never offered; its price hinted at about $3,000 while rating a conservative 460 horsepower. Racers' minds reeled at what an unrestrained LS7 might actually produce. Surely it would exceed 600 horsepower.

To address the embarrassing quality-control problems, DeLorean sent every single Corvette through a water bath with an inspector riding inside looking for something like six dozen possible leaks. After that they ran the car over a two-mile "Belgian Road," exaggerated cobblestone and potholed surfaces, followed by a short stint on a vibration table that flexed and torqued every car repeatedly. DeLorean allowed no failures to leave the plant.

Once Ed Cole arrived in the chairman's suite, his perspective changed slightly. He remained unquestionably a friend of performance, but his concerns assumed broader views and encompassed a greater variety of legitimate voices. On the one hand, the financial climate outside his doors was fairly healthy, if inflationary. America was in a wartime economy, supporting the conflict in Vietnam. The gross national product was up 7 percent, inflation up 5.7 percent, and unemployment at a decade-low 3.5 percent. The average U.S. salary was slightly more than $7,500, enough, by popular rules of thumb, to purchase or finance any product sold in any GM line.

(lower left) It was an astonishingly expensive option. The all-aluminum block L88, RPO ZL1, added $4,718.35 to the base coupe price of $4,781. So few people understood its potential that only two were built for customers, though a white convertible floated around Chevrolet engineering as Zora Duntov's development mule. In all, Chevrolet produced 154 of the engines.

(lower right) With its hood up, the cowl induction system's plumbing comes into focus. The low-pressure area at the base of the windshield draws air into the rear of the hood, sucking it forward to the low-restriction air cleaner in the hood. The foam circle around the carburetor air intake seals the system.

Cole's other concerns lay outside the financial world and outside Detroit. The nation was growing less hospitable toward the automobile. Insurance, premium rates for an unmarried 20-year-old male driving his own high-performance car to work or school reached $1,000 a year in 1968 and nearly $2,000 in 1970. Massachusetts introduced the country's first no-fault automobile insurance. On Earth Day, April 22, 1970, a nationally televised teach-in painted a grim picture of the world's environmental pollution, indicting the automobile as the chief perpetrator.

Cole, who loved and had already saved the Corvette in the mid-1950s, set out again to ensure its continued existence. He began eliminating low sales-volume options. He ordered engineers to rework all GM engines to run on low-lead 91-octane fuel. He told engineering, marketing, advertising, and public relations to use Society of Automotive Engineers (SAE) net measurement standards for engine horse-power output, numbers substantially lower than the gross-horsepower ratings previously published.

The hunkered-down stance improved
weight transfer during takeoff. Joel
Rosen, who owned Motion Performance,
built perhaps 12 of these Phase III
monsters with the help of nearby
Baldwin Chevrolet and parts manager
John Mahler.

Neither Baldwin nor Motion did much
with the interior. The single four-barrel
950 cfm Holley hiding below the Mr.
Gasket air cleaner helped pump 500
horsepower out of the original L71
engine.

The result was a slight improvement in auto insurers' regard for GM. The LT1 dropped its already conservative numbers to a 330 gross horsepower/275 horsepower net rating while the LS5 454 dropped to 365 gross/285 horsepower net. The LS7 never appeared, but an aluminum-head 454 called the LS6, rated at 425 horsepower gross/325 horsepower net, appeared and provided 0–60 miles per hour times of 5.3 seconds. (The LT1 followed quickly behind at 6.0 seconds, and it offered far better ride and handling.) Throughout Duntov's career as Corvette's chief engineer, the compromise between ride and handling had vexed him. He was in charge of building a production car with a top speed of more than 140 miles per hour in a country where that was illegal everywhere except in one state. Yet to Duntov's mind, if any Corvette owner should need to drive at 140 miles per hour, for whatever reason, the car should do so in safety. The dichotomy of Corvette buyers, some who bought the car simply for its looks in front of the country club or nightclub, and others who wanted its 140 miles per hour capability, would frustrate him into his final days with Chevrolet.

Cole wanted to keep racers as Chevy customers. Corvette introduced the ZR1 and ZR2 packages similar to the earlier Z06 options. No radio, power steering, power windows, or air-conditioning was possible with either of these. The ZR2 used the LS6 454-cubic-inch displacement 425-horsepower engine, and only 12 hardy racers bought one. The ZR1 was an even rarer breed, based on the LT1; only eight buyers shared Duntov's vision of what the Stingray could be as a competitor in SCCA's B-Production classes. Yet again it was the L88 that proved to be the racer's final choice. Jerry Thompson and John Mahler won GT (at sixth overall) in Owens-Corning–sponsored cars at

Throughout model year 1973, production couldn't keep up with demand and dealers had to turn away 8,200 orders. So for 1974, Chevrolet General Manager F. James MacDonald ordered the St. Louis plant to increase output from eight cars an hour to nine.

The transition of body shape was complete with the 1974 model. Front and rear crash absorbing bumpers made the car look as if it had a one piece body though, as always, it was composed of multiple panels of several materials.

Urethane, crash-resistant materials reached the rear end of the Corvette for 1974. The body-colored membrane covered an aluminum "bumper" fixed onto two telescoping shock absorber-like mounts.

Daytona. At Sebring, Tony DeLorenzo and Dick Lang won GT class with a new distance record, while finishing tenth overall. Production car sales crept back up for 1971, totaling 14,680 coupes and 7,121 convertibles—21,801 in all.

CLEAN AIR STANDARDS

The real impact of the new U.S. clean air standards was clear in the 1972 model year. Cole's cleanup had its effect as well; the LS6, which had sold only 188 copies in 1971, disappeared. (The legendary Muncie heavy-duty M22, close-ratio, four-speed gearbox, known as the "rock crusher" because of its durability and the gear whine, remained available through 1972 but only as part of the ZR1 package.) The only 454-cubic inch displacement engine left was rerated down to 270-horsepower SAE (of which 3,913 sold) and the solid-lifter LT1, listed at 255 horsepower, sold 1,741 copies while the ZR1 package saw its last year on the options lists with only 20 copies delivered.

In late 1971, Or Costanzo sold his yellow L88 to Toye and Dana English, father and son racers, who nicknamed it "Scrappy" because they were constantly scraping off materials to lighten the car. Just before Daytona in February

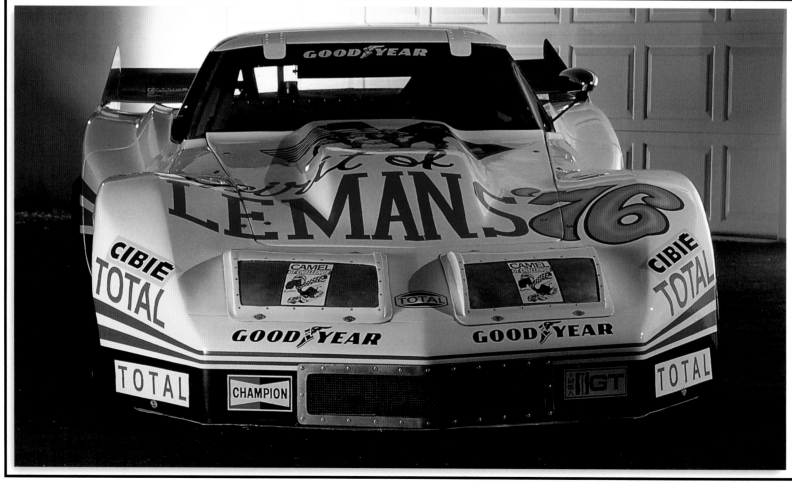

1972, Goodyear Tire approached them, asking them to run on special unmarked tires. Knowing they'd be competing against B. F. Goodrich–sponsored John Greenwood, who'd taken to painting his cars in an American flag stars-and-stripes scheme, the English team painted its car in rebel flag colors. When Dave Heinz and Bob Johnson (the Ohioan) won GT class, finishing eighth overall, Goodyear took out an ad in the *Wall Street Journal* announcing their first victory on racing radial tires. They went on to win GT class again (fourth overall) at Sebring, further thrilling Goodyear.

By early April, Goodyear realized it had a chance at the triple crown of endurance, Daytona, Sebring, and Le Mans. But invitations had already gone out (racers don't "enter" Le Mans; the organizers, L'Automobile Club de l'Ouest, the Automobile Club of the West, invites recognized competitors). Leo Mehl, Goodyear's racing director, had a long business and personal relationship with Enzo Ferrari and Ferrari's U.S. importer, Luigi Chinetti, who operated Ferrari's North American Racing Team (NART). Mehl had personally arranged tires at the last minute for their 275LM in 1963 that went on to take first overall. He knew Chinetti had six cars entered and he called in a favor.

"We want to run a Corvette in one of your spots on our new tires," he said. Chinetti balked. Mehl

These cars were Corvette in inspiration. Greenwood had Protofab build him extensively modified steel tube frames to mount the Corvette suspensions, engines, and drivetrains. He designed his own coil-over shock, twin A-arm rear suspensions to accommodate enormously wide 17 x 15-inch wheels and 28.0 x 17-15 Goodyear racing tires.

Florida's John Greenwood built two legends for endurance racing in 1976. One, the Spirit of Sebring, won that race outright. This car, the Spirit of Le Mans, qualified on the pole and ran well ahead of the pack until its engine failed.

Starting with the all-aluminum ZL1 L88 engine, Greenwood worked his magic, and rumors report he and Dick Smothers had better than 850 horsepower available. He and Smothers routinely saw 210 and 211 miles per hour on the Mulsanne Straight at Le Mans. Greenwood designed his own cross-ram magnesium intake manifolds.

suggested that a call to Enzo informing him that Goodyear had just withdrawn its sponsorship because Chinetti had refused to cooperate with a small favor might not be so well received. Chinetti backed down.

Dave Heinz and Bob Johnson started fourth in the English's four-year-old, once-wrecked former street car. They routinely saw 212 miles per hour along the Mulsanne Straight on their Goodyear radials. When the checkered flag fell, their Ferrari-red NART badge-bedecked L88 had covered 2,414.9 miles, averaging 100.6 miles per hour, good enough to finish fifteenth overall, first in the over five-liter class.

In all, Chevrolet sold 28,004 Corvettes in 1972, with 20,496 coupes delivered against 6,508 convertibles. It was a nice position for a new general manager to inherit, and that's what Jim McDonald found on October 1, 1972. Another Pontiac graduate, he knew the value of building a car in great demand. He increased production, but only slightly, understanding the drawbacks of too great supply.

Ironically, as the car began its 21st season, a pendulum had begun to swing back toward the Corvette's roots. Some of this change came on Duntov, Winchell, Mitchell, McDonald, and Estes by federal regulations, rules that required Corvette to forsake its recent high-performance identity if it was to survive.

To satisfy its own standards for 1973, design revised front fender side vents and eliminated the cowl flap that too often left owners without working windshield wipers. Chevrolet discontinued the removable back window, carried over since its introduction in 1968. Engineering fitted radial-ply tires. The cast-aluminum lightweight wheels engineering planned for delivery were never available due to quality problems. Chevy carried over the 454-cubic-inch displacement engine but revised it to provide an additional 5 horsepower, now rated at 275 and renamed the LS4. The small-block, hydraulic-lifter L82 offered 250 horsepower from the 350-cubic-inch displacement cast-iron engine; however, Duntov's chassis engineer Walt Zetye and body engineer Bob Vogelei changed body and engine mounts and applied more sound insulation throughout the body, stiffening the car while decreasing road and mechanical noise.

Model year 1974 marked the end of high performance. It had been under serious attack for some time. In December 1970, Congress passed the Clean Air Bill in the National Environmental Policy Act. This established regulations specifying fuel economy and emissions standards. It set targets the big blocks could never meet, giving auto makers less than six years to develop engines that would emit 90 percent less toxic gases. After 1974, there was no 454 and the small blocks lost true dual exhausts to a two-into-one pipe that ran through a catalytic converter before returning to dual-looking exhausts.

Those who thought that the Clean Air Act meant the end of happiness as they knew it were in for a worse shock. In mid-January 1971, members of an 11-year-old group called the Organization of Petroleum Exporting Countries (OPEC) failed to negotiate polite price increases with 17 western oil companies. In frustration, OPEC members agreed to set prices by themselves, ending the previous courtesy of consulting their customers beforehand. Gas prices in the United States climbed

The box-section steel tube frame swings low through the cockpit, making driver changes quick and easy. Ear protection was essential with the 850-horsepower engine exhaust exiting just below the doors through 4-inch pipes. Greenwood preparation was meticulous.

steadily. In mid-March 1974, OPEC, now 13 members strong, settled with its western customers, and crude oil that had sold for $2.11 per barrel in January 1971 went to $14.08 38 months later. Lines formed at gas stations and fuel economy suddenly made a difference. The White House ordered a nationwide 55 mile per hour "energy conservation" speed limit.

Despite all this, Chevrolet sold 30,460 Corvettes in 1973, 25,521 coupes and 4,943 convertibles, with many more buyers preferring the T-topped cars to pure open air motoring. Barely a third purchased an optional engine, yet nearly two-thirds ordered the automatic. The nature of Corvette buyers was changing, and the car kept pace. For 1974, the trend away from convertibles continued. Some 32,028 coupes sold, while only 5,474 convertibles were delivered. Again, however, it set new production and sales records with 37,502 cars sold.

The RPO V54 luggage rack was designed to carry the T-top panels. Some 16,860 buyers paid $73 for the rack, which allowed them to make full use of the luggage area even when the tops were off.

THE L82 BITES THE DUST

On New Year's Day 1975, Zora Arkus-Duntov, Corvette's most devoted engineer (and its chief engineer since December 1967), retired. He was replaced by his heir apparent, Dave McLellan, a GM engineer since 1959. Model year 1975 marked the end of several other Corvette mainstays as well. Chevrolet could no longer offer the L82 engine because of its excessive emissions. James McDonald moved out as general manager and was replaced in December 1974 by Robert Lund, who came from Cadillac but who earlier had been sales manager at Chevrolet. Convertible sales dwindled to only 4,629 cars, less than one-eighth of another record total production of 38,469 cars. Management killed the open cars. This was not just a production decision based on poor showroom performance, but it was also the result of outside pressures. An increasingly intrusive federal government made loud noises about convertible roll-over safety as early as 1970. Congressional hearings and investigations led Detroit carmakers to expect a governmental mandate. That it was no longer an economically viable product made the decision easier, even though the legislation never appeared.

The new fastback introduced in 1978—though definitely not a hatchback—featured styling that nearly doubled rear storage capacity, making the car very useful for long road trips. The pace car replica package included removable glass roof panels and special leather seats.

Initially, Chevrolet planned to assemble just 300 of these replicas. However, demand was so great that by the time they were done, they had produced one for each of the 6,000 Chevy dealers plus a few dozen extras.

(top opposite) Only the Indy Pace Car replica got the rear spoiler. The Silver Anniversary model required only sports mirrors and aluminum wheels. Chevrolet produced 15,283 of these models.

Through 1976 and 1977, Corvette forged ahead, producing two more record sales years and increasing prices. Engineers improved standard engine performance as they got a grip on air pumps and exhaust gas recirculation systems. Base power output returned to 180 horsepower, but this was enough for nearly 85 percent of the Corvette buyers both in 1976 and 1977. By mid-March 1977, Corvette reached a landmark when workers drove the 500,000th car off the assembly line in St. Louis. This was only a precursor to the face-lift that appeared in 1978 to commemorate the 25th anniversary of the Corvette and the 62nd annual running of the Indianapolis 500.

Both cars represented GM's getting the most out of the least. Behind locked doors in engineering R&D and in Mitchell's design studios, dreamers had created mid-engine prototypes using small blocks, big blocks, and even multiple rotary engines clothed in fiberglass, thin sheet steel, and aluminum meant to commemorate 25 years of the car. But cold budgetary realities—and even differing opinions of what was a true Corvette—doomed each of these creations to auto show stands.

For the public, quick and easy changes sufficed. Design replaced Mitchell's sugar scoop rear-window treatment with a large, intricately shaped back window. Plans called for the window to open, giving access to this space, but it was cut due to a tight budget. Under the hood, 1978

(opposite) Another variation available for 1978 was the Silver Anniversary model. This painted the car in light silver above and dark silver below a silver horizontal stripe. The option cost $399.

GM's Corporate Average Fleet Economy requirements limited the 350-cubic-inch displacement L48 base engine to 185 horsepower (except in California where its own emissions standards pulled another 10 horsepower from the engine). The optional L82 offered 220 horsepower. Total production reached 46,776 cars, including the B2Z optional Silver Anniversary and the replica Indy 500 Pace Car, one produced for each Chevrolet dealer.

The 1979 models gained in horsepower due to across-the-board adoption of the twin-snorkel air cleaner from the L82, ingesting cooler outside air. This, plus adoption of the L82's lower back-pressure mufflers, gave the base L48 a 10-horsepower boost to 195 in all 50 states. The L82 also gained a 5 to 225 horsepower boost. Thinner, lighter seats from the pace car were standard for all Corvettes in 1979. The Indy pace car spoilers became a $265 option (D80) for all Corvettes. Base price settled in at $10,220.23, and Chevrolet set a new production record of 53,807 cars. This level of output made GM corporate management question the need to change something that was doing just fine.

Corvette had been enormously profitable for several years. Few people remained in the division who would

It's a distinctive appearance and clearly an acquired taste. John Greenwood produced the first two or three of these Sport Wagons, then turned the operation over to Corvette specialist American Custom Industries in Sylvania, Ohio, who completed perhaps another ten.

The gull-wing design of the rotary engine concept Corvette never made it into production, although this concept was also used in the 1977 Aerovette show car. All photos on this page 2002 General Motors Corporation. Used with permission of GM Media Archives.

buck the status quo. After Duntov left Chevrolet in January, Ed Cole soon followed him out the door, chased by Bill Mitchell, who retired in 1978. Chevrolet's newly named director of engineering, Lloyd Reuss, had no desire to make waves. David McLellan, Duntov's successor, resonated contentment, pronouncing his preference for front-engined Corvettes.

In 1980, buyers got cars with a newly revised, lower drag nose with a standard front chin spoiler. Between this more aerodynamically friendly front end and something like 250 pounds of weight removed from the car, 1980s cars weighed 3,179 pounds, a welcome improvement. One change inside the car was highly unwelcome. Federal standards that lowered national speed limits to 55 miles per hour required all speedometers to provide calibration no higher than 85 miles per hour no matter what the actual top speed of the car might be. In California, only the base 305-cubic-inch displacement engine would pass the state's stringent emissions requirements, so buyers in the Golden State had to be content with this lower-performance engine. Suggested retail price of the base Corvette rose by nearly $3,000, a result of countless federal safety and emissions requirements, to $13,140.24. Still, 40,614 buyers were undeterred by these facts and forked over the down payment or the first lease payment in a form of car financing that had steadily gained in popularity since the mid-1970s.

Improvements continued in fairly undramatic fashion in 1981 and 1982. The 49-state 350 was certified in California, but optional engines disappeared; 190 horsepower was all any buyer could get. Nationwide, under the hood, a new Computer Command Control (CCC) module managed fuel and air mixture in the carburetor and ignition timing to

The rear of the gull-wing followed the angled rear of the Mako Shark II.

The rotary Corvette explored mid-engine mounting for the first time.

(above) Everyone knows Chevrolet did not build a convertible Corvette between model years 1976 and 1986, but if you wanted one, American Custom Industries had just the thing for you. It was even engineered by none other than Zora Duntov. Even better, at Duntov's insistence, it was turbocharged.

(right) Exterior and interior colors respect the 1953 original, another homage to Corvette's history from ACI president Bob Schuller. But Schuller and Duntov moved into the 80s with digital readout instruments, an in-dash computerized telephone and rear stowage cooler. In the end, ACI sold fewer than 100 of these cars.

(right) The new nose and tail pieces, first introduced with the 1980 production models, incorporated fully integrated spoilers. These reduced air drag considerably, improved mileage slightly, and increased radiator air flow by 50 percent.

produce optimum exhaust emission performance and fuel economy, though the latter was a distant second in importance. This system first appeared in 1980 on California-only 305s.

Complaints continued from magazine reviews and buyers alike about the car's fit and finish. Quality control still seemed to be elusive for Chevrolet's most expensive, most visible product. Finally, to control that problem, production began at a new high-tech assembly plant in Bowling Green, Kentucky, on June 1, 1981. Before GM acquired this plant, it had been Chrysler's air-temp division air-condition factory. Corvette assembly overlapped at the old St. Louis facility until model-year production ended on August 1. Bowling Green's new equipment offered not only tighter assembly standards but also new paint. Enamel base colors finished with clear topcoats came from Kentucky, while the remaining St. Louis cars finished up with the old standard lacquer.

Prices jumped another $3,100 as the standard car reached $16,258.52, about $1,660 more than Cadillac's El Dorado. The basic Corvette, however, was highly civilized, and the only remaining options just gilded the lily. Chevrolet sold 40,606 in all.

The existing Corvette body first appeared in 1968, assembled on a chassis that showed up underneath the 1963 Sting Rays. By 1982, Chevrolet certainly had paid off development and improvement costs. Still, mating Alfred Sloan's dictum to make last year's buyer dissatisfied to Ed Cole's philosophy of making a lame duck appealing, Chevrolet chose to make important introductions. Throttle-body fuel injection, which reappeared in a form called "Cross Fire Injection," bumped engine output to 200 horsepower for all 50 states. Engineering replaced the existing three-speed Turbo-Hydra-Matic with a new four-speed overdrive automatic transmission.

Chevrolet offered the final "Shark" for 1982, not only as a well-equipped base model at $18,290.07, but also as a special order Collector Edition. Product planners had watched sales of the 25th Anniversary model and the Indy Pace Car replica and produced a special exterior paint and interior trim option to honor the end of the longest production run and celebrate 30 years of Corvettes. Total production for 1982 was 25,407, anticlimactic after 15 years of production. Still, in 15 years Chevrolet sold more than half a million Sharks, 542,861 in all.

This was all the more remarkable considering the economy. Between 1973 and 1983, the average American salary topped $15,750 as inflation kept up its relentless 10 to 13.5 percent rate. In 1980, this took the prime rate up to 21 percent, making auto loans almost unaffordable at 24 percent. In 1981, GM announced its first loss since 1921, coming up $763 million short for the year. This forced the

It marked the end of the era. The 1982 model body began in 1968, and its chassis first appeared with the 1963 Sting Ray. Corvette enthusiasts expected an all-new car in 1983, so sales of this model year were barely half of those in 1981—25,407 compared to 40,606.

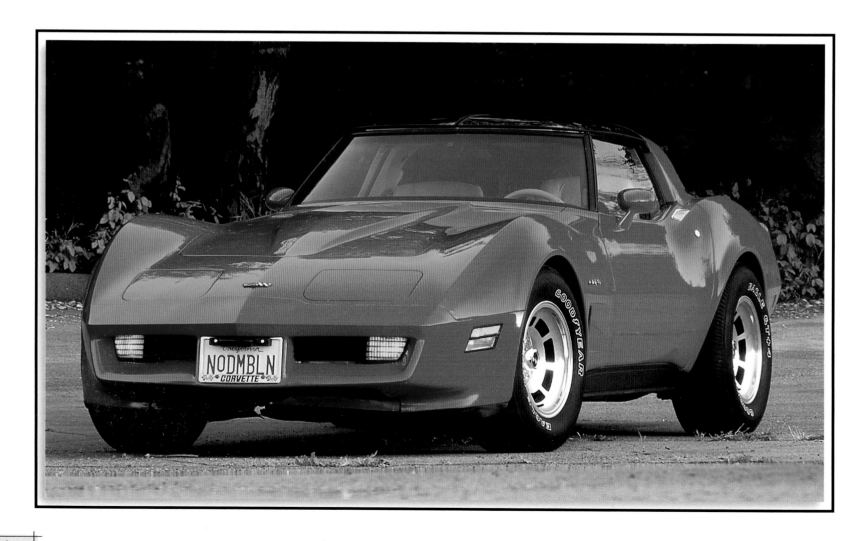

Striving for simplicity between two factories and 50 states, Chevrolet offered only one engine. This 190-horsepower 350-cubic-inch V-8 was all you could get in 1981. The four-speed manual was available nationwide but barely 10 percent of buyers wanted it.

The Cross Fire Injection, twin throttle-body fuel injection (TBI) system was shared by both Corvette and Camaro. The 350-cubic-inch small block was Corvette's first fuel-injected engine since 1965 and developed 200 horsepower.

The TBI engine and new transmission made for the best possible driving combination of performance and fuel economy. The 1982 models even had a cold-air induction system for full-throttle acceleration. The base car retailed for $18,290.07.

board to delay new projects a year or simply cancel them outright. Into this uninviting economy, former Chevrolet general manager John DeLorean introduced his stainless-steel, mid-engined, Irish-built sports car, priced at $25,000. His knowledge of manufacturing steel-bodied automobiles outside the United States would go for nothing, and his car would become a cult footnote once he was arrested for cocaine possession. In 1982, inflation dropped to 6 percent, but this hardly comforted the 9.7 percent of the population that was unemployed when the Shark approached the end of its scheduled life.

1983-1989

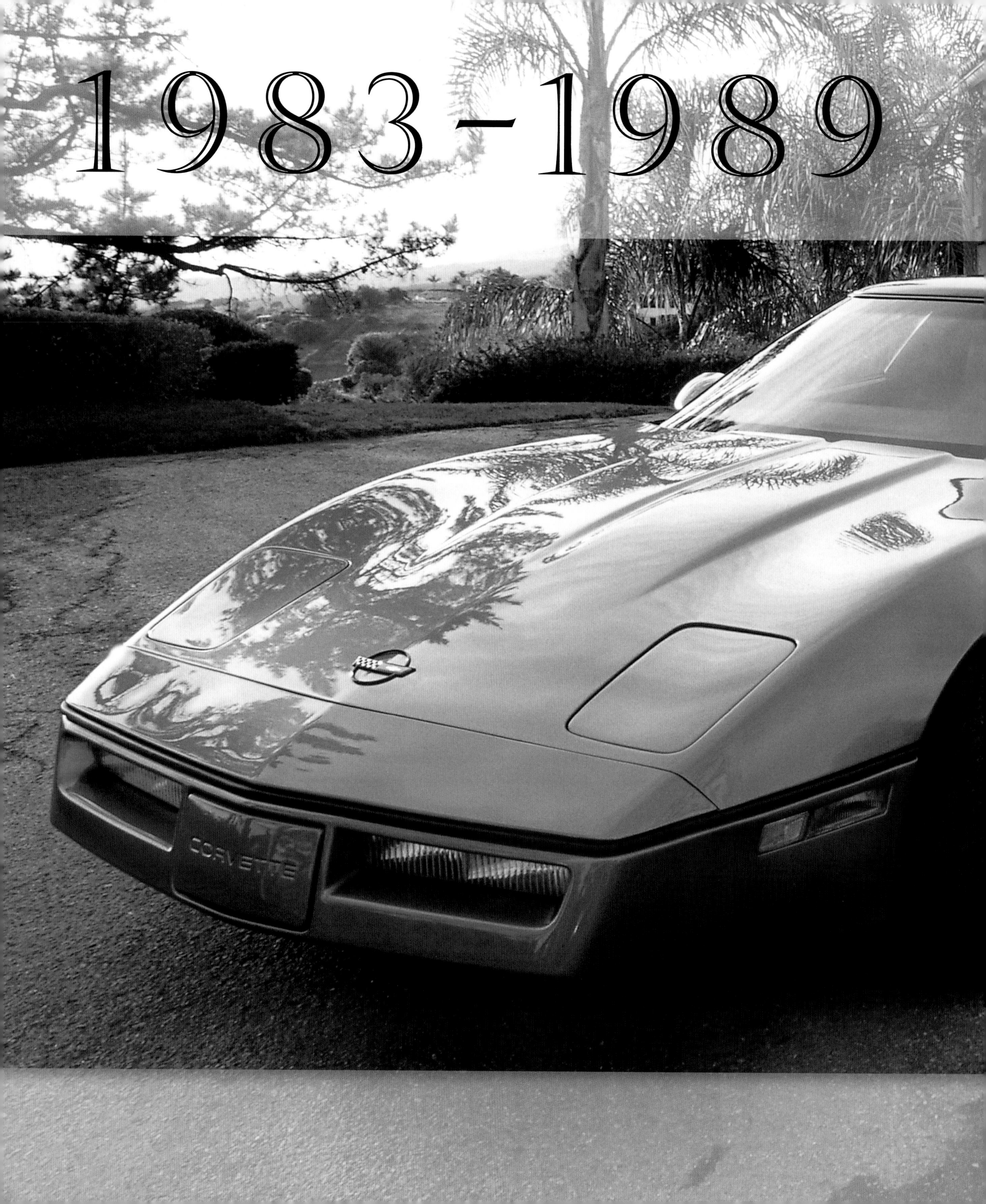

CHAPTER NINE

BETTERING THE BREED FOR THE ROAD AND THE TRACK

here was no 1983 Corvette. At least none were intended for the public. Chevrolet assembled 70 "engineering" cars and probably more than one has slipped out into private hands. But solid reasons led the company to skip the year completely. Historians can trace the decision to skip an entire production year as far back as 1977, when Chevrolet division first imagined the next model, the fourth-generation Corvette.

In 1977, Irwin W. Rybicki became GM's vice president of design when Bill Mitchell retired. Rybicki was very different from Mitchell; he was a conservative, modest man who had directed the Buick-Oldsmobile-Cadillac studios through countless folded-edge designs that sold cars like mad. Rybicki inherited Mitchell's legacy as well as his staff. Mitchell had nurtured Jerry Palmer, who had done Corvette show cars for him in 1969. Palmer began affecting the production cars with the 1973 model. In 1974, Mitchell named him chief designer of Chevrolet Studio 3, the home of the Corvette and Camaro, a job with high visibility and considerable influence.

Over in engineering, Dave McLellan was a veteran of similar training when he was Duntov's protégé. McLellan found himself in a similar position to Palmer in effecting what any new Corvette would become. Both Palmer and McLellan, who had worked well together on the second-generation Camaro in production from mid-1970 through 1980, learned the GM board had decided to replace the long-running and now highly profitable current model (it generated more than $100 million annually). The board authorized a completely new model for 1983 to celebrate the car's 30th anniversary. Significantly, this would be the first Corvette designed, *(previous pages) The 1984 had the flattest-angle windshield to date at 64 degrees. The roof also divided into an openable hatchback—the largest compound surface glass formed until that time—and a removable glass roof panel over the seats.*

Chevrolet carried over the throttle-body, cross-ram induction V-8 introduced with the 1982 Shark, with a few improvements and modifications. It looked perfect under Cafaro's clamshell hood.

developed, and sold without any link to Harley Earl and Ed Cole's 1953 model because Palmer and McLellan joined Chevrolet during the Mitchell/Duntov Sting Ray years.

Ideas emerged quickly. Experiments with Wankel's rotary engines had been disappointing, but engineering and design created the AeroVette with a transversely mounted 400-cubic-inch displacement reciprocating V-8 that restored promise for a new midengine configuration. GM had introduced Chevrolet's Citation X-11 and Pontiac's Phoenix, the X-body cars with transverse V-6 engines driving front axles. McLellan knew this technology was available, but Corvette's 205 horsepower was double what Citation/Phoenix 90- to 110-horsepower drivetrains could handle. It meant instant failure or long, costly development work. But these questions paled in contrast to a government challenge. Federal regulators proposed a gas-guzzler tax punishing fuel inefficiency. GM's fleet average for 1983 had to be 19 miles per gallon, no matter what performance the engineers developed for their Corvette. GM's board would never allow any of *their* cars to suffer that tax.

While John DeLorean had been Chevrolet general manager, he had proposed downsizing the Corvette onto the smaller Camaro/Firebird F-body platform. Corvette could share chassis and development expenses, he argued. Palmer and McLellan both vigorously fought the idea because DeLorean's concept seemed less interested in improving the Corvette than increasing its profit.

Among engineering and design staffs, the debates continued over front-engine versus midplacement. When cast-iron big blocks skewed weight balance heavily to the front, mid engine placement provided better handling but sacrificed load carrying ability. Surveys told marketing that midengine high-performance cars often were the second or third cars in wealthy families. Corvette buyers often had only one car to carry groceries, golf clubs, or vacation luggage.

Heritage was on everyone's mind when McLellan and Palmer started their staffs brainstorming and sketching ideas. Marketing worried that Corvette buyers, generally traditionalists, would balk at anything radically different. The board, still smarting over the entire rear-engine Corvair adventure, had quietly dragged its feet against Zora Duntov's relentless arguments for a midengined Corvette. They knew he would retire in 1975. While he had championed the necessity of 50/50 weight balance, the board knew he had met that target on front-engine models. Despite Duntov's long-held objective of creating a sports car he could proudly drive in Europe, the Corvette was and always would be

The 1984 model was introduced in March 1983, making it the first automobile that complied fully with federal emission and safety regulations. The new design provided higher ground clearance but lower overall height by moving the engine rearward and fitting exhaust and other plumbing into a wide center tunnel. Chevrolet produced 51,547 coupes, its best year since 1979.

a car for American roads and drivers. What's more, McLellan favored the traditional front-engine rear-drive Corvette.

Outside support arrived unexpectedly. Porsche introduced its own Corvette, designed by a former Corvette stylist Tony Lapine, who had created Bill Mitchell's Corvette SS racing car in Studio X. After his promotion to GM's Opel operation in Russelsheim, Germany, Lapine left GM in 1969 to work for Porsche. In 1974, Porsche management feared U.S. regulations might legislate against the handling characteristics of their 911 model. They assigned design chief Lapine to create their first front-engined sports car, the V-8 Type 928. Porsche introduced the car in Germany in the fall of 1977. It was powerful, fast, sleek, and safe, and its arrival encouraged the configuration of the next Corvette.

HIGH-PERFORMANCE TIRES

When Dave McLellan sought performance targets for the 1983 Corvette, everyone agreed they wanted the new model to be the best-handling sports car in the world. To McLellan, that dictated fat low-profile tires on 10-inch-wide wheels. From the time of the Grand Sports, Corvettes introduced the highest performance tires. Furthermore, McLellan accepted Duntov's dictum that Corvette's suspension must remain compliant at full speed over uneven roads. This required vast suspension travel, but it ensured that no driver would be thrown out of control at top speed because the suspension bottomed out.

Design chief Jerry Palmer wanted 16-inch wheels for styling purposes. When McLellan's engineers set the first specifications on paper, they established minimum ground clearance at 5.25 inches, up 0.25 inches from the 1968 to 1982 car. They placed four squat tires at the corners. From there the car's design began, capitalizing on GM's relationship with Goodyear Tire & Rubber. Engineering wanted tires capable of 140 to 145 mile per hour speeds. Yet they also demanded crisp handling, quiet ride, efficient water shedding, an interesting appearance, and at least 10,000-mile tread life even with enthusiastic use. Goodyear based its efforts on its Formula One rain tire development. It developed the VR50 "Gatorback," which met Corvette's parameters with room to spare.

Room to spare was the consideration the tires missed. Fat front tires needed space to clear engine and suspension pieces under full-lock turning. Fitting the Gatorbacks inside the bodywork required McLellan and Palmer to widen the car by 2 inches over the existing model. (Even so, McLellan had to let go of his 10-inch wheel width target, settling for 8.5 inches when wider wheels stuck out beyond the new body.)

Owner surveys had told Chevrolet that the Corvette's Coke-bottle shape pinched shoulder room and created a claustrophobic cockpit. Widening the car helped remedy that. Still, McLellan and Palmer struggled to resolve other concerns. Safety, styling, and engineering improvements over 25 years had added weight and increased size, yet GM's board now ordered divisions to downsize each

(lower left) The large pad facing the passenger seat was part of a passive restraint system mandated by the federal government. It was nicknamed the "breadloaf."

(lower right) Digital readouts and liquid crystal displays filled the instrument panel. "Old-fashioned" analog gauges were not even available, a fact that frustrated magazine reviewers but never seemed to bother buyers.

(above) While the factory quoted 205-horsepower output from the 350-cubic-inch engine, racers knew they had closer to 350 horsepower under competition tune.

In order to lessen factory time spent finishing fiberglass panels, designers created a car body with all the body panel seams hidden under a rub molding that went around the entire car. The line also seemed to stretch the car's length visually.

While Dick Guldstrand drove this one only briefly, the California influence extended not only to the Showroom Stock racing series but to the car itself. Its superb rear suspension was developed from existing successful Guldstrand Corvette racers.

(right) Guldstrand-Morrison-Cook racing won the SSGT championship with Corvette aces such as Ron Grable, John Heinricy, and Don Knowles at the wheel. The power, reliability, and antilock brake system frustrated the Porsche factory greatly.

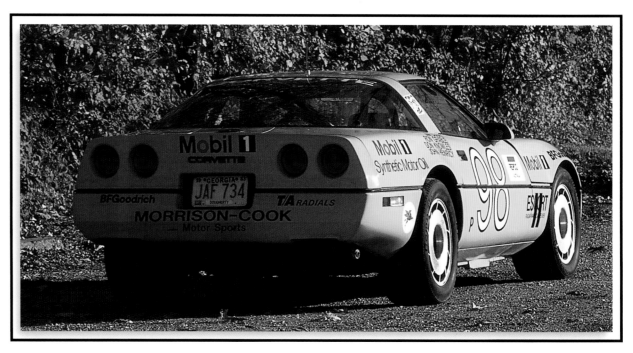

vehicle, yanking away the tightrope's safety net. The Corvette design team forged ahead and filled in the long-standing pinched waist. This added 6.5 inches to interior shoulder room.

Because shoulders are wider than waists, the designers adopted the backbone idea from Lotus car innovator Colin Chapman. He had introduced this central spine into his tiny fiberglass Elan model in 1963. This provided structural rigidity, crucial for a sports car that might go racing. McLellan's engineers widened their center tunnel enough to feed not only the driveshaft but also the exhaust, catalytic converter, plumbing, and wiring between the seats now instead of below them. Maintaining their minimum ground clearance, they still lowered the seating floor 2 inches, to the bottom of the chassis. This increased headroom yet lowered the roofline an inch. This in turn reduced frontal area, decreasing aerodynamic drag and improving fuel economy. With more efficient packaging of the mechanical necessities, McLellan and Palmer shortened overall length 8.4 inches from the existing model. It was wider, yes, but it was lower, shorter, and more fuel-efficient.

With a 350-horsepower engine backbone frame, and Guldstrand-derived rear suspension, the car proved an unbeatable racer.

By early spring 1979, McLellan's engineering staff had a few development mules out testing. Palmer's Studio 3 design staff began creating the new car's look. Randy Wittine, called "Mr. Corvette" because of some 15 years of involvement with the car, worked alongside a new kid on the block, John Cafaro. Cafaro, the studio's youngest designer since Peter Brock, produced a rendering of the new car that incorporated an XK-E Jaguar-type hood that revealed the engine, front tires, suspension, and chassis. The hood opened like a clamshell, split along a seam that ran horizontally around the entire car, a styling element they adopted from Ferrari's midengined 308GTB. In this one drawing, Cafaro created two of the signature styling features. With this mammoth hood, Palmer saw an opportunity to make the engine and mechanical parts appear integrated. McLellan agreed and so both staffs coordinated engine castings, forged suspension pieces, and even spark plug wires for appearance as well as function, and they color coordinated pieces to add visual impact. Cafaro's clamshell seam simplified both molding and joining the fiberglass body panels. His design began to make possible tighter quality control in fit and finish.

Cafaro continued developing his body design. Roger Hughet, Palmer's chief assistant, worked with

Charles Toner and his aerodynamics engineers to improve the body shape in wind tunnels at speeds up to 140 miles per hour. These confirmed that Cafaro's chin spoiler shoveled up enough ground-level air to reach the radiator behind his grille-less front end. High-speed experiments in the wind tunnels led to reintroducing fender-side "gills," the air extractor slots that vented the air-pressure buildup that popped hoods on Duntov's Grand Sports at speed.

As early as 1978, Palmer's interior designers began to mate the instrument panel and interior seating to the sleek, new exterior. The interior staff had other considerations to worry about, however. One was a cluster of federal regulations, Motor Vehicle Safety Standard (MVSS) 208, for driver and passenger safety in a front-end collision. The driver had the collapsible steering column in the event of a head-on crash; the passenger got a padded structure nicknamed the "breadloaf" because of its looks. Congress introduced MVSS 208 in 1977 to go into effect for model year 1982. It became a political issue, postponed eventually for 1985 introduction. Then in October 1981, President Reagan

Sports Car Club of America rules for the Showroom Stock Grand Touring class required a full roll cage and fire-suppression systems in the cockpit. Otherwise the interior had to remain as it came from the dealer.

revoked it altogether, but this was too late for designers to scrap it. The breadloaf was part of the car, and buyers found it where a glove box would have been.

The basic design of the C4 chassis allowed for a convertible version, which Chevrolet introduced during the second year of C4 production. 2002 General Motors Corporation. Used with permission of GM Media Archives.

Chevrolet carried over the throttle-body, cross-ram induction V-8 introduced with the 1982 model year Shark, adding improvements to engine management, a serpentine belt accessory drive, and an electric cooling fan in front of the radiator. It looked perfect under Cafaro's hood.

McLellan's engineers mated the engine to their innovative 4+3-speed manual transmission, a clever variation on the standard Warner Division gearbox re-engineered by Doug Nash. Coupled to the Delco Electronic Control Module (ECM), the Nash transmission provided what were essentially short shifts in second, third, and fourth gears. It was something like an automatic manual transmission, configured specifically to improve mileage for the EPA test. (When introduced, the car's window sticker stated 16 miles per gallon city mileage, 28 highway. The EPA balanced these figures 55/45 percent to arrive at Corvette's 19.8 miles per gallon, exceeding GM's 1984 CAFE number by 0.3 miles per gallon.) Engineering replaced the earlier heavy iron Delco-Moraine disc brakes with Australian Repco aluminum-and-iron versions, saving 70 pounds between the four brakes.

McLellan's people improved the suspension as well. They set out to accomplish 1.0 g of lateral-acceleration cornering power. Their chassis innovations, suspension configuration changes, and Goodyear's Gatorback tires made it possible.

Engineering constructed the chassis from thin sheets of high-strength, low-alloy (HSLA) steel, spot welded into boxes and other shapes to support front and rear suspension, engine, differential, roof, doors, and windshield. Previous Corvette frames involved two separate elements, one chassis/frame and the other a "birdcage" of much smaller members fitted above the chassis/frame to support the body. With the new car, and unlike most other unit-frame cars where the body is a crucial structural element of the car, the fiberglass surface panels merely hid the frame and running gear. Past ladder frames had required cross members to tie outer frame rails together and add structural rigidity to the car, but engineers accomplished this with a single bolted-in cross member used as a front-engine support. The entire frame weighed just 351 pounds, yet it was rigid enough to allow a completely removable roof center section that no longer required the T-roof support.

Onto this chassis, suspension engineers hung all-aluminum forged suspension pieces. The independent rear suspension used a five-link system instead of the previous model's three links. This fixed the rear axle more positively in place, eliminating its tendency to steer the car from the back in certain suspension load-unload transitions. They mounted fiberglass leaf-type springs transversely on both front and rear suspensions. Fiberglass was not only lighter, but it was more resilient and it wouldn't sag after millions of jounce and rebound cycles. Engineers devised another use for the transverse springs, as antisway bars. It worked so well that engineers greatly decreased the diameter of the supplemental antisway bar.

McLellan's engineers raced against time and their perfectionists' desire to get everything right. Magazine stories told consumers a completely new Corvette was coming, and sales of the 1982 model fell off so dramatically that assembly-line engineers began dismantling the production line at Bowling Green in anticipation of the model changeover.

The board faced a dilemma. Engineering hadn't finished with the car. Did engineering and GM release a car that was not ready for production? Two other factors influenced the verdict. If GM waited until early spring, it ensured that Chevrolet had the first 1984 model available rather than the last 1983. It also meant Chevrolet would introduce the first automobile that met 1984 emissions and barrier impact standards. The board slowed engineers enough to conquer the 1984 regulations completely (thereby avoiding re-engineering a hastily completed car). Production fired up on January 3, 1983, and each of the cars bore a vehicle identification number (VIN) identifying it as a 1984 car (although there are reports that 11 cars appeared with 1983 VIN numbers as well).

This made the 1984 model year 17 months long. When it ended and GM completed count, 51,547 buyers drove Corvettes home. (GM kept the first 70 cars or so as continuing engineering development vehicles.) Two years after its introduction, Chevrolet's chief engineer Don Runkle talked to *Road & Track*'s John Lamm about the 1984 and 1985 cars.

"We more or less moved the Corvette away from the classic Corvette customer," Runkle said. "It was deliberate

Midway through 1985, Goodyear began offering $50,000 contingency purses to the SSGT winner. Kim Baker and his team won at Lime Rock and again at Mid-Ohio. $100,000 allowed him to get very serious about racing Corvettes.

With its 205 net horsepower, the Corvettes were a bit below some of the other entries such as Nissan's 300ZX. But the chassis, suspension, and absolutely superior braking brought the car more wins than any other in its class.

The red handle releases the fire extinguisher, a nozzle for which is right beside it. Above that, a black knob controls the heat and ventilation, another knob and several buttons operate the stereo radio, and a set of buttons control the on-board computer.

The production-class rules dictate keeping a stock body. Hood scoops to accommodate engine modifications are permitted, and the roof "rails," the vertical air managers, are required. The parachute is essential.

on our part, primarily because we wanted to make a technical statement with it, but we couldn't figure out how to keep it where it was price-wise and also make that statement.

"We didn't have to make the car cost as much as it does. But if we hadn't put all those features (aluminum front suspension arms, plastic springs, tuned port injection, etc.) into it, the car wouldn't be as good as it is right now. . . . I don't hear many people making fun of the Corvette anymore."

Racers took the car seriously too. As Gregory von Dare wrote in his book *Corvette Racers*, "In the 1980s, ABS brakes allowed Showroom Stock Corvettes to go at racing speeds in the rain where other fine cars such as the Porsche 944 Turbos were spinning all over the track." The factory openly helped teams like Morrison Motorsports, Bakeracing, Rippie Racing, and Powell Motorsports further the development of their racing cars that in turn fed back to the factory important wear and durability information about its chassis, drivetrain, and tires. Racetracks became two-way streets for information and cooperation, benefiting engineers, drivers, and enthusiasts.

"Even though Corvettes were able to beat every car that challenged them in the SCCA's Showroom Stock series," von Dare continued, "they still had to race each other. That's where the fun started."

The "fun" began outside Parkman, Ohio, at an older racetrack called Nelson Ledges, only 100 miles from Detroit. In 1979, the track staged its first 24-hour endurance race for showroom stock cars. They drew 19 entries but much more interest. Each year the entry list grew, and when Chevrolet brought out its new Camaro and Porsche had its first 944 in 1983, the organizers found they had to create a "prototype" class. Porsche's front suspensions proved too fragile for Nelson's city street-like surface. Then the new Corvettes arrived in 1984 and stunned their racing world. They won 19 races in 19 starts. For four years straight, they took every race in the series run first as the Playboy Challenge, then as SCCA Showroom Stock Grand Touring, and finally as the Escort GT Endurance series. Drivers in lesser cars recalled nursing their ailing entries into corners in

If speed gets your attention, than this car should grab you. August 2001: 223.051 miles per hour on the salt flats at Bonneville, Utah. It took Ed and Linda Van Scoy four years to crack the 220 miles per hour barrier.

Ed and Linda Van Scoy had Mike LeFevers of Mitech build their engine. LeFevers gave them a 407-cubic-inch dry-sump V-8 that develops 750 horsepower (and 625 foot-pounds of torque). LeFevers linked it to the six-speed ZF transmission.

the rain, watching a Corvette storm past them implausibly fast, its driver adjusting the radio or the heater, then using the ABS to haul the car through the turn. Kim Baker, owner and co-driver of his yellow #4 Bakeracing Corvette, won the series in 1985 and 1986, and von Dare reported that Porsche bought Corvettes to take apart and study. At the end of 1987, Porsche and others hinted that they might withdraw if the SCCA didn't level the field. The SCCA banned Corvettes from its series beginning in 1988, but Corvette racers were not done.

THE 1985 PRODUCTION CARS

For 1985 production cars, Dave McLellan's engineers addressed complaints about ride harshness, adjusting shock valving on both the base shocks and the Z-51 Bilstein gas shocks and spring rates in the fiberglass transverse leaves. The rear wheels grew to 9.5-inch widths during the 1984 production run; the fronts were upsized as well for 1985.

Under the hood, Chevrolet continued meeting EPA numbers while improving performance. Fuel injection, Tuned Port Injection, replaced Cross Fire Throttle Body injection. The result was engine output up to 230 horsepower, a 0–60 mile per hour time of 6.6 seconds, and top speed nearer the magic 150 miles per hour. Production for the 1985 model year slipped relative to the long 1984 numbers, but the second year of C4 was a 12-month year, and the total reflected more accurately the continuing interest in the car. In all, 39,729 cars sold.

Model year 1986 brought patient enthusiasts a convertible Corvette near the middle of the year. While the chassis had easily accommodated the "Targa" type removable roof, the open car required substantial reinforcement. Engineers enlarged the bolt-in cross member ahead of the engine and the braces connecting that piece to the frame rails. In addition, they fitted a large X-brace below the passenger compartment and added two more crosspieces behind the seats. Convertible buyers could not get the stiff Z51 suspension, but the 9.5-inch wheels were part of the convertible's own dedicated Z52 suspension. Chevrolet introduced the convertible in bright yellow Indianapolis Pace Car replica trim, at a $4,000 premium over the coupes. Base convertible price was $32,507, while the base coupes retailed at $28,502. These "base" cars were nearly fully equipped, and prices reflected the addition of a number of mandatory options. One new standard item was an intelligent ignition key, the PASS-key with an identification sensor, part of an overall Vehicle Anti-Theft System (VATS). Any other key fit into the ignition except for the one coded to the car would fail to start, disabling the

Competing in Bonneville's production class requires a "non-gutted" interior, and of course, a full roll cage. Running with stock interior pieces adds considerable weight, but the rules are intended to create a "true stock" automobile for racing purposes.

Leather sport seats were a $1,025 option that 13,372 buyers selected. Chevrolet produced 7,319 convertibles, selling at a $5,005 premium over sport coupes, $32,032 compared to $27,027.

ignition for any attempt for three minutes. Performance improved once again with Z51-equipped coupes turning 0–60 in 5.8 seconds and registering top speeds of 154. The convertibles were good for nearly 140 miles per hour with the top down, aided in small part by new aluminum cylinder heads made standard for all production body styles when the convertibles appeared. For the 1986 model year, Chevrolet produced 7,315 convertibles and 27,794 coupes.

For 1987, engineering boosted the engine another 10 horsepower to 240 through, among other changes, roller-bearing hydraulic valve-lifters that lessened power lost to friction. In addition, they redesigned the heads to improve burn efficiency by centering the spark plugs in the combustion chamber. Engineering fitted the same stiffening measures used on 1986 convertibles to the 1987 coupes. Chevrolet continued to offer the Z51 suspension on the coupe (with manual transmissions), but the convertible carried over its own Z52 version. The convertible, in magazines tests, scored an impressive 0.87-gram lateral acceleration (the Z51 pulled 0.91 around the 216-feet-diameter circle).

Convertible sales increased to 10,625 (at $33,647), while coupes slipped to 20,007. This was a total of 30,632, down nearly 5,000 cars from 1986.

For 1988, engineers provided a new less-restrictive exhaust system, good for 5 horsepower, taking the performance axle–equipped engine to 245 horsepower. They fitted lower profile Goodyear Z-rated P255/50ZR-16 tires (to allow speeds above 149 miles per hour) on 16-inch "Cuisinart" wheels, nicknamed because they looked like the food processor blades. An optional Z51 (for coupes only) and Z52 Performance Handling Package offered 12-slot "Cuisinart" 17 x 9.5-inch wheels with Goodyear 275/40ZR-17 tires. Engineering changed front disc-brake calipers to dual-piston versions that they wrapped around thicker rotors for more braking power and better brake cooling. They also increased rear-suspension rebound travel and reconfigured front-suspension geometry to improve directional control in severe braking conditions.

Because 1988 was the 35th anniversary, design and product planners created a commemorative edition of 2,000 coupes painted white with a white leather interior. Production for 1988 dipped despite the car's measurable improvements, and Chevrolet sold only 7,407 convertibles and barely twice that many coupes, 15,382, for a total of only 22,789 cars. The coupe base price crept up to $29,955, while the convertible sat at $35,295.

Chevrolet had scheduled the much-anticipated ZR-1 for 1989, but it wasn't quite ready so the division introduced two elements of the long-rumored car. One was its six-speed manual transmission, built

(below) Designer John Cafaro's "clamshell" hood represents a lot of real estate when it's lifted. But the access it provided to the entire front end was unlike anything else in the industry at the time.

(opposite bottom) Chevrolet brought back the Corvette convertible after a ten–model year absence. Because the 1986 model was the Indy 500 Pace Car, all the convertibles were designated as replicas and dealers received decal sets.

Former Corvette racer and current day performance and handling consultant/speed merchant Dick Guldstrand posed alongside his personal GS-80. He was photographed at his famous Thunder Alley shop on Jefferson Avenue in Culver City, California.

in collaboration with Germany's highly regarded Zandfabrik Friedrichshafen (ZF) that was operated by, or more accurately over-ruled by, its own computer, the Computer-Aided Gear Selection (CAGS). This was another engineering effort to satisfy the EPA and the performance lover. A driver, accelerating at one-third throttle or less at speeds below 20 miles per hour with a fully warmed engine, found the CAGS blocking the gates to second and third gear so the shift went straight from first to fourth. At 20 miles per hour in fourth, the engine idled along at 1,050 rpm. It was simpler than the previous much-

(top below) In all, Guldstrand produced about three dozen of these cars. He reacquired his tired warrior when Bridgestone finished its testing and development work.

(bottom below) Magazine reviewers at the time described the 400 horsepower, 400 foot-pounds torque GS-80 engine as a tire shredder. That was good enough for Bridgestone, which bought Dick's personal car from him to use for 200 miles per hour tire testing at Talladega.

Guldstrand was involved in the suspension engineering of the C4, ZR-1, and C5. Chevrolet provided prototype ZR-1 fenders that he fitted to his personal GS-80 to accommodate 17-inch wheels and tires for development testing.

maligned and mostly misunderstood Doug Nash–designed 4+3 speed, yet it accomplished the same kind of EPA numbers *and,* ultimately, the same kind of enthusiast disrespect. It did, however, make very clear the quality and quantity of torque that the 350-cubic-inch displacement L98 engine produced. While cruising at 65 miles per hour in sixth gear, the engine loafed at barely 1,600 rpm. Buyers who ordered the six-speed gearbox also got an engine oil cooler, heavy-duty radiator, and electric radiator cooling fan that were part of the Z51 package.

The other feature Corvette introduced for 1989 was the FX3 Selective Ride Control Delco-Bilstein electronic suspension. Chevrolet offered this only on Z51-equipped six-speed coupes. Drivers could change the four gas-filled Bilstein shock absorbers by a cockpit control that adjusted shock valving from "Touring"

The appearance of these cars was subdued in the first year. Graphics were designed by the series sponsors. In the view of many, this was too subtle.

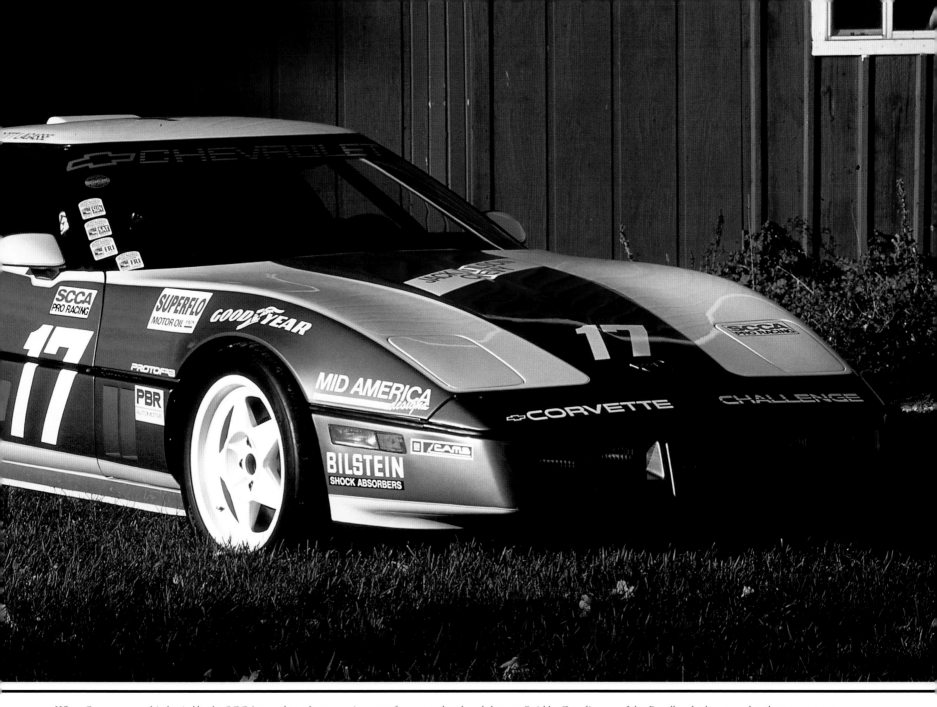

When Corvettes proved indomitable, the SCCA catered to other competitor manufacturers and outlawed the cars. Quickly, Canadian racer John Powell and others created a plan to run a one-marque series, the Corvette Challenge.

The interior remained untouched except for the addition of a full roll cage, a fire-extinguishing system, and a racing seat for the driver. Air-conditioning and stereo radios still worked fine. Chevrolet built 56 of these.

No engine modifications were permitted except for removing the catalytic converters to prevent overheating. The cars were otherwise street legal. The engines, matched as closely as possible, were sealed at the Flint engine plant.

or "Sport" to "Performance" settings that also varied within each shock based on the car's speed at the moment.

If those weren't enough technical marvels, the wheels now contained tire air-pressure monitors that transmitted signals to warning lights on the instrument panel. If pressure fell below desired levels, the lights warned the driver. Engineering intended this system for 1988 introduction, but last-minute problems delayed it to 1989. Base Corvette price, including the Z52 suspension/handling package, was $32,045 for the coupe. Sales reached 26,412 of the coupes and rose again to 9,749 convertibles.

THE CORVETTE CHALLENGE

Once the Sports Car Club of America outlawed Corvettes from its series at the end of the 1987 season, Canadian John Powell, one of those with several victories to his name, reacted quickly. Gathering the support of Baker, Morrison, and others, he proposed to the SCCA a single-marque series, a Corvette Challenge, based on barely modified production cars as he had done in Canada for Camaros and Firebirds with the Player's Cup. The SCCA challenged him to make it work, and Powell quickly got Corvette

The commemorative package was offered for coupes only. All 1988 models got a stronger hood support to better manage the weight of the massive one-piece clamshell.

The Corvette badge evolved over the decades but from the beginning it has incorporated some kind of checkered flag motif to represent the car's dedication to racing.

The 35th Anniversary package also included a striking black and white interior with custom white leather sport seats and white leather–covered steering wheel. The rest of the interior was black, creating a stark contrast.

development manager Doug Robinson's support. Then he enlisted major sponsorship from parts supplier Mid-America Designs and its enthusiast owner Mike Yager, from Goodyear Tire & Rubber and from Exxon. Chevrolet's general manager Robert Berger approved lending the car's name to the series but made it clear GM had no money to fund it.

Within months, Powell had put together a series called the Million Dollar Corvette Challenge, and SCCA put 10 one-hour race dates on the calendar beginning May 1, 1988, at the Grand Prix of Dallas. Powell promoted the series well enough to entice some of the sport's better drivers, including Jeff Andretti, Bobby and Tommy Archer, Kim Baker, John Greenwood, Tommy Kendall, Scott Legase, Johnny Rutherford, Jimmy Vasser, and Desire Wilson. Chevrolet produced 56 matching C4s, removing catalytic converters but remaining otherwise completely stock, retaining air-conditioning and CD audio systems. Nine buyers never raced or converted their cars. For the rest, Powell lined up ProtoFab

Chevrolet built 60 Challenge racers, though only 30 of them ever saw competition.

Engineering in Wixom, Michigan, near Detroit, to add roll cages, on-board fire-extinguishing systems, racing seats, and Bilstein shocks. Racers drove the break-in miles on the way from Detroit to their own shops. Racers paid their dealers for the cars, then an additional $15,000 to Powell for ProtoFab's conversion and their 1988 season entry fee.

By midyear, the series was in serious trouble, coming up about half a million dollars shy of its target. Powell went back to Chevrolet and appealed to Mike Goodman, the division marketing manager who already knew Berger's terms to Powell. Goodman sensed that this series seemed to be selling cars; he not only found the funds but also signed a deal to continue the series through 1989. With that assurance, ESPN agreed to broadcast every Challenge race the second year.

Graphics on the 1988 cars were subtle and the muffled exhausts too quiet to attract attention. The Series and the SCCA modified their rules for 1989, allowing entrants to get their own spon-

(above) Spectators had made it clear to the SCCA that they wanted to hear these cars as well as see them. The rules for 1989, besides allowing modified but matched engines, permitted freer flowing exhaust. The cars began to sound like racers as well as look like them.

Two matched racing seats filled out the interior package, surrounded by a full competition roll cage and cockpit fire suppression system. Still, the cars retained stereo radios, functioning air-conditioning, and power windows.

sorships. This enhanced each car's visual appeal considerably. Engineering changed the exhausts so spectators could hear the cars coming as well as going. Chevrolet constructed 61 of the racers for 1989, although perhaps as many as 31 never got converted to racers.

GM hoped to attract its own co-sponsors for the series, but that never happened. The races provided great drama with entrants often qualifying within hundredths of seconds of each other. ESPN's coverage put viewers inside the cars with full-functioning gauge-readouts on screen. Chevrolet authorized assembly for 1990 even as regular production sales increased through 1989, validating

Goodman's suspicions. Chevy manufactured just 23 cars, coded R9G, before pulling the plug on its sponsorship. Meanwhile, the rest of the racing world had grown envious of the ESPN coverage and had caught up with Corvette's chassis and ABS brakes. The SCCA invited Corvette back into its general series for 1990.

At the end of the second season, Bill Cooper emerged Challenge champion, winning three events in a row and finishing well in most of the others. By late 1989, Porsche and others had mastered ABS systems and increased their horsepower. They let SCCA know they'd be willing to race against Corvettes again.

1990-1996

CHAPTER TEN

IT BECAME PERSONAL
WITH EVERYONE

he very nature of Chevrolet's sports car has always been in question. From Harley Earl's dream to Ed Cole's tool to Zora Duntov's race car, the car has meant something different to each creator. From the beginning up through the two-seat personal luxury car that Dave McLellan and Jerry Palmer created, the decision makers have molded and directed the Corvette. Their goal has always been a vehicle they hoped each board chairman from Alfred Sloan through Roger Smith would bless with a production future.

In early 1986, Don Runkle, Chevrolet's chief engineer, talked with *Road & Track* editors about the future of Corvette. He made clear what he hoped the car might become. He described what in later years enthusiasts know the car became.

"We could obviously build a $100,000 Corvette and blow away the [Ferrari] Testarossa," Runkle said, "but I'm not sure what the point of that exercise is. That just shows that you can do it. Our goal is to do it at 25 percent of the price."

Runkle examined the battles between GM's board and those responsible for the character of the Corvette. Half the decision makers saw Chevrolet as GM's sales volume leader, and every Chevy product must do its part. Others argued that the Corvette is very profitable, and it contributes more than its share of publicity and prestige not only to Chevrolet but to GM as well. Any high-tech development—engine, chassis, suspension—further reinforced Chevrolet's technological stature in the car world. Runkle described a project involving engineering expertise from Lotus and Chevrolet, an engine producing perhaps 400 brake horsepower. This was the car that resurrected the Duntov code name ZR-1 and brought it to a much wider audience. It made Chevrolet division a *(previous spread) There were numerous arguments about how the car should appear. Subtlety won out and only a minor enlargement of the rear bodywork, square taillights, and understated badging marked the car for what it was.*

Once a buyer checked the ZR1 option, there were few choices left. ZR1s got leather everywhere and their own specially laminated windshield.

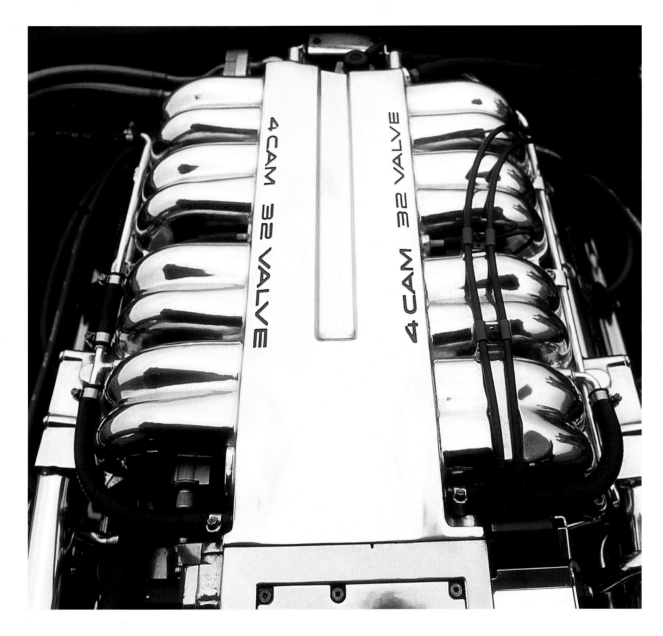

(opposite left) The most obvious difference between regular production models and the ZR1 was the wider rear end (with square tail-lamp lenses). It was enlarged to accommodate Goodyear's P315/35ZR17 rear tires and 11-inch-wide wheels.

Developed at Lotus Engineering in Norwich, England, the dual-overhead camshaft, 4-valve per cylinder V-8 developed 375 horsepower yet operated efficiently enough to avoid paying the gas guzzler tax. Called the LT5, it was hand-assembled at Mercury Marine in Stillwater, Oklahoma.

In 1990, Chevrolet sold 7,630 convertible Corvettes and 16,016 coupes.

lot of money, and it definitely reiterated the high-tech nature of the car.

"It is so expensive," Runkle said at the time. "Some people at Chevrolet don't think the additional volume it would generate would be worth the investment. My position is that this project has nothing to do with volume. This is a different thing. This is to get the Corvette to be an unquestioned leader."

Within weeks of that dinner, Runkle's prediction moved toward reality. At about 2:30 A.M. on May 1, 1986, in Norwich, England, engineers at Lotus fired up the first LT5, Chevrolet's brand-new dual-overhead camshaft, four-valve per cylinder, small-block V-8. They ran it up to 3,000 rpm and held it for 30 minutes. Then they shut it off and uncorked champagne. That half hour culminated 18 months of discussion, design, and development. The LT5 was Chevrolet's first new V-8 for 21 years, since the Mark IV in 1965.

The RPO B2K Callaway Twin Turbo option started out in 1987 as a $19,995 option, and by 1990 the cost had increased to $26,895 plus the price of the car. At this price, it was $121 less than the ZR1. The Callaways raced ZR1s neck-and-neck to 60 miles per hour but outran them at the top end.

The ZR1 was an ideological turning point for Chevrolet. Half the decision makers argued against the car, suggesting its development costs were too high. The other half recognized it as a high-tech status symbol that would enhance not only Chevrolet's but GM's reputation.

The engine developed enough horsepower and torque that 5th gear was a 0.60 overdrive. This was "long" enough gearing to see the car to more than 191 miles per hour.

Getting it done required some unusual alliances, the recognition of values beyond costs, and the identification of who Corvette's next generation of competitors would be and what they would do. Whether anyone went back and read Alfred Sloan and Donaldson Brown, the decision to launch the ZR-1 demanded faith that great ideas need time to pay off.

McLellan's and Palmer's improved Corvette attracted attention from German and Japanese car builders who believed they could build one better. Porsche had used the car as its benchmark for engineering the 944, and if SCCA's Showroom Stock racing series was any indication, Porsche gained respect for Corvette's engineers. Nissan engineers who produced their legendary Z-cars used Corvettes as CAD-CAM computer screen savers. Honda made it clear they produced their high-tech, midengined Acura NSX to show how much technology Japanese engineers had learned from America's automakers.

Anthony Young, an excellent historian on the development of a variety of high-performance engines in recent years, wrote in great detail about the LT5 in his 1994 book *The Heart of the Beast: History of the LT5 V-8 and ZR-1 Corvette.*

This was an official factory option, though it was not factory installed. Called RPO B2K, Chevrolet introduced it for model year 1987. Callaway shipped fully assembled Corvettes from the Bowling Green assembly plant to his facilities in Old Lyme, Connecticut, for modification. By 1990, the Twin-Turbo developed 390 horsepower.

The rear-end styling of the standard 1991 Corvette matched the special ZR-1 model. 2002 General Motors Corporation. Used with permission of GM Media Archives.

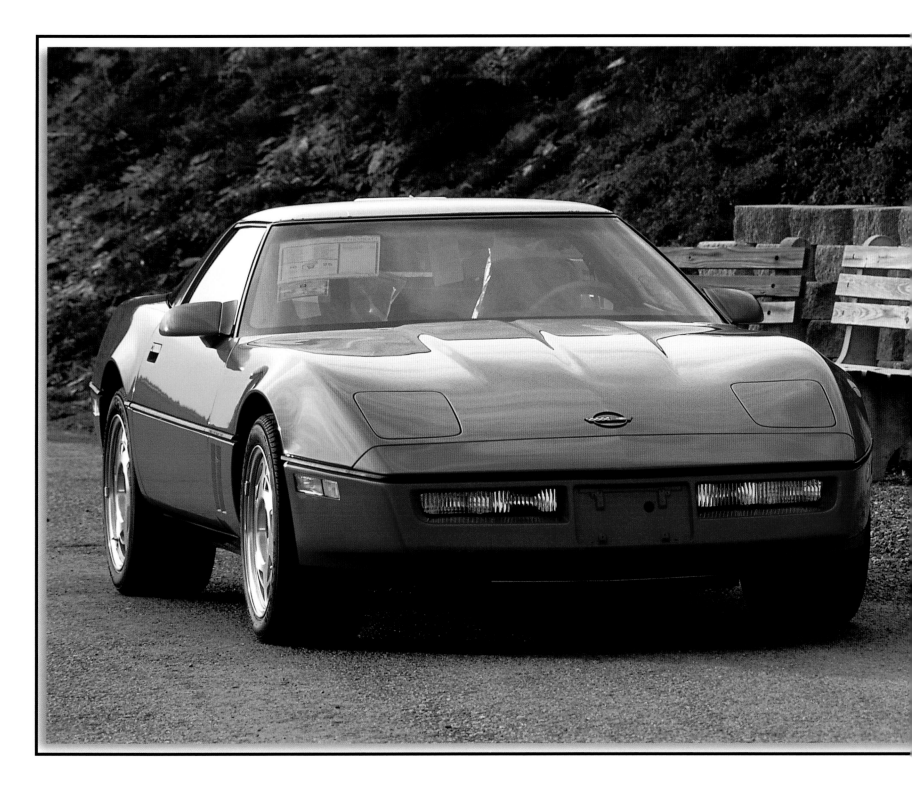

Russ Gee, a director of powertrain engineering at Chevrolet-Pontiac-Canada (CPC) continued alternate powerplant research for the Corvette, following in the footsteps of Wankel developers and others. Inside Chevrolet and out, engineers knew Corvette's engine was its only shortcoming. They had steadily improved the small-block V-8 since its introduction in 1955. Gee tried turbo charging V-6 engines, reconsidering midengine installations. He encountered critical vibration problems and fatal philosophical ones: Corvette owners perceived any engine with fewer than eight cylinders as un-Corvette-like. Early experiments with turbo charging Chevy V-8 engines yielded unacceptable fuel economy (though Reeves Callaway later worked through those).

When the SCCA suspended the Corvette Challenge series at the end of 1989, Chevrolet already had begun creating successor cars for 1990. These "World Challenge" cars, RPO R9G, gave buyers a car with more deletions than additions.

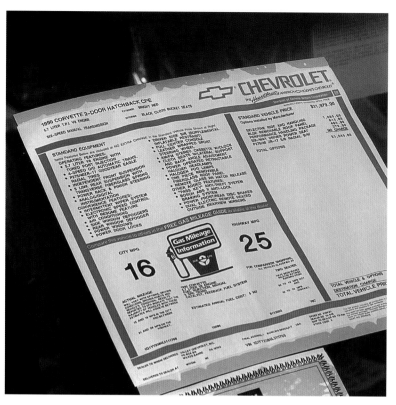

As chief engineer, Lloyd Reuss had overseen the Cosworth four-valve head development for the Vega. He wondered about the V-8. Russ Gee began work in October 1984. In November, Tony Rudd, managing director of Lotus (owned by GM at this time), offered his firm's engineering services. Runkle, Reuss, Gee, and Rudd formed a plan to create four-valve, dual-overhead camshaft heads to fit Chevrolet's small block.

Car assembly realities stopped the design. The Bowling Green assembly line installed L98 engines from the bottom. Any proposed engine had to slip between the frame rails. By April 1985, Rudd and Gee accepted that the taller, wider heads could not fit. Changing the assembly line was enormously expensive; changing the frame rails was unthinkable, since that changed the entire car. Engineers and project managers concluded it made the best sense to create an entire new engine.

The World Challenge cars got stronger springs with the FX3 electronic Selective Ride and Handling Package. With its very few options, this R9G retailed for $35,539.

Lloyd Reuss went before GM Chairman Roger Smith and presented the benefits this engineering offered, over time, to other products throughout GM's entire product line. He emphasized the Japanese threat. The Corvette was significant in Japan because it was the Japanese car manufacturers' target.

Smith agreed. Reuss, Gee, and Roy Midgley, chief engineer of the 90-degree V-type engines at CPC, understood that all days off were canceled, since any change in GM's financial condition or the economy threatened projects. Engine development at GM sometimes took as long as six years. Smith's funding could disappear at any moment. Reuss knew the further the project progressed, however, the more difficult it might be to kill it. Engineering designated the project the LT5; Runkle named it the King of the Hill.

Dave McLellan studied the performance characteristics of every exotic car Corvette owners might consider if they won the lottery. He concluded the LT5 must get the Corvette to 60 miles per hour in four to five seconds. He knew that required at least 360 horsepower, but 400 had a better ring to it. It could not be a gas guzzler. They would design it from scratch, adopting no parts from any existing GM

As with the Corvette Challenge, these cars would have been fitted with full roll cages and on-board fire-suppression systems that sprayed the cockpit and engine compartment with fire-extinguishing materials.

Chevrolet reportedly manufactured just 23 of these coupes in 1990. Chip Miller, of Corvettes of Carlisle fame, fell in love with the Corvette Challenge series, and when he learned of these models, he bought one just to put in mothballs.

Besides appearance, there were numerous engineering improvements that turned Callaway's Twin-Turbo coupes into the Speedster. While the Twin-Turbo option added $33,000 to the price of the Corvette, the Speedsters checked in at $150,000.

engine just as Cole and Harry Barr had done with Cadillac's V-8 more than 30 years before. Then came the tough part: McLellan wanted a prototype engine running by May 1986 and one in a car three months later. CPC made it clear to Lotus that this engine, which might only have a total production run of 6,000 units, would be treated the same as any engine GM expected to go into 6 million automobiles, subject to every test, analysis, and second-guess.

Once Smith approved the LT5, Chevrolet had to find a plant to manufacture it in. It was too small a run for any GM facility, which meant outside vendors. Roy Midgley selected Mercury Marine in Stillwater, Oklahoma. Mercury's sophisticated computer-controlled manufacturing technology could engineer aluminum castings. After months of meetings, Mercury learned in mid-March 1986 that it was the builder.

At this same time in 1986, Lotus began gathering prototype parts from suppliers throughout Europe and the United States with which to build the prototype engine. Jerry Palmer's staff in Chevrolet Studio 3 made sure that if owners raised John Cafaro's large hood, they saw an engine that looked like 400 horsepower. Some features had to be obvious. Lotus engineers concluded that dual-injection intake ports per cylinder were the best way to ensure optimum fuel mix for performance and economy. On partial throttle below 3,000 rpm, each cylinder used one inlet runner, one injector, and one inlet valve. The cam lobe for that valve provided mild timing with little overlap. A heavier foot signaled the electronic control module (ECM) to open the butterflies in the second runners and turn on their injectors. Cam timing for the second intake valves was wilder. Palmer's designers created 16 distinct tubes running from

By his fifth year producing cars under license with Chevrolet, Reeves Callaway let his designer Paul Deutschman have more creative freedom. The result was Callaway's Speedster of which ultimately only 11 were manufactured.

the injection system's main plenum to the cylinders below. They outlined the dual overhead camshafts in sculpted cam covers. The result was an industrial designer's dream: Function dictated form that resulted in something beautiful to see.

By early 1987, Lotus ran brutal durability tests on the development engines. One trial ran alternately at peak horsepower speed for five minutes and then at peak torque speed for five minutes continuously for 200 hours. Cracks appeared in the cast crankshaft that forced an expensive specification change to nitrided forged steel. From there on the LT5 tested flawlessly.

Other problems threatened the LT5. Engineers fretted the details while Reuss fought for its very existence. GM cut budgets throughout CPC, yet Roger Smith let it slip through. On Christmas Eve 1987, Mercury Marine ran the first preproduction prototype LT5 on their dynamometer.

Starting in January 1988, Lotus prepared to assemble an engine with production parts. There was still testing to do. The LT5 would never make a September 1988 introduction. Reuss and Runkle wanted to provide a warranty that demanded they have it right. If the engine broke, GM would replace it. That kind of reliability required some 2,000 design changes. They balanced every moving part within the engine to tolerances common to Formula One racing engines capable of 14,000 rpm, far beyond the LT5's 7,000. At

a press demonstration, Terry Stinson, LT5 project engineer at Mercury Marine, balanced a nickel on its edge on the engine plenum in a completed running car. It remained there, on edge, until he retrieved it.

HANDLING AND ROAD HOLDING

When Dave McLellan matched his vision of this new Corvette to the competition, he recognized the car needed not only exceptional power but also extraordinary handling and road holding. Prior to GM's purchasing Lotus, the small car maker had startled the Formula One world with its active suspension system. With it, drivers Elio de Angelis and others set lap records at circuits that stand to this day. Like Corvettes in Showroom Stock, the FIA, Formula One's sanctioning body, outlawed it. Lotus' system used heavy hydraulic pumps and cylinders, and sometimes the system didn't keep up with the speed of the car, causing unsettling changes. Once it was outlawed, Lotus set it aside.

Active suspension next appeared in Porsche's 959, shown in racing trim as early as 1984 and as a $200,000+ road car in 1986. The electronic system, developed with assistance from Bosch, performed flawlessly. Active suspension intrigued McLellan and others when it was Lotus' project and later when it appeared on a Chevrolet-sponsored racer in the International Motor Sports Association (IMSA) series.

In the early 1980s, rumors circulated that NASCAR would change engine regulations to require V-6s rather than V-8s by the middle of the decade. Indianapolis engine wizard Ryan Falconer worked on Chevy V-6s and routinely pulled nearly 1,200 horsepower from turbocharged versions. That

Both Chevrolet's ZR1 and Callaway's turbos have exercised restraint in design. The integrated ellipsoid rear-view mirror is an example of letting astronomical performance speak louder than outrageous wings and flares.

Acceleration was quoted as less than 4 seconds to 60, and top speeds were above 185 miles per hour. Owners have described the power as "like a rocket-propelled locomotive, smooth and unimaginably fast."

Despite its striking looks and its awe-inspiring power, the Callaway Speedster is a comfortable and user-friendly open car. The glass-enclosed cockpit almost totally eliminates wind buffeting at any speed.

Since the ZR-1s reappeared as press prototypes in 1989, racers like Tommy Morrison wondered how they would hold up as racers. At the end of the 1991 Daytona 24 Hours he knew, with one finishing 12th overall and this one coming in 21st.

Electrical problems and a major impact with another racer slowed the overall progress of this ZR-1. The carbon-fiber bodywork saved nearly 600 pounds. Its teammate, car #92, is on permanent display at the Smithsonian Institution in Washington, D.C.

intrigued NASCAR team owner Rick Hendrick, who looked for another racing series in which to hide his own development efforts. Back in 1980, IMSA had created a grand touring prototype (GTP) class to encourage European teams to compete in their modified 250 mile per hour Group C cars on American circuits. Chevrolet let Hendrick know in late 1985 that it could support his effort. Hendrick hired IMSA GTP veteran Ken Howes to run it. Howes knew of Lotus' suspension and promoted its use. He believed that while the system was troublesome in ultralight F1 cars, the greater room and weight allowance of a GTP car offered the system great potential. As the effort came together, Corvette designer Randy Wittine sketched the body that became the Corvette GTP.

The car first raced in August 1985 at Road America in Wisconsin, with about 800 horsepower in a chassis built for Chevrolet by England's Eric Broadley. The Lotus active suspension used dozens of sensors to register road surface traction and chassis dynamics. It flexed the suspension to eliminate body roll on cornering, rear squat on acceleration, and nosedive on braking. This kept the tires flat on the roadway without transferring unwanted dynamics back to the passenger compartment.

Competition at Daytona usually includes purpose-built prototypes of featherweight and astonishing power. Mercury Marine balanced and blueprinted this engine and parted the cylinder heads. Rumors put its output at 550 horsepower.

Morrison built new cars based on two street-driven models with nearly 10,000 miles on each. Ohio Corvette "tuner" Chuck Mallett fabricated full tube-frame chassis and bumper-to-bumper roll cages. Toledo Pro produced carbon-fiber bodies for car #91 and #92.

Exterior body modifications were minimal. The biggest change for 1992 was under the big clamshell hood, an all new engine. Chevrolet sold 14,604 coupes at a base price of $33,635 and 5,875 convertibles starting at $40,145.

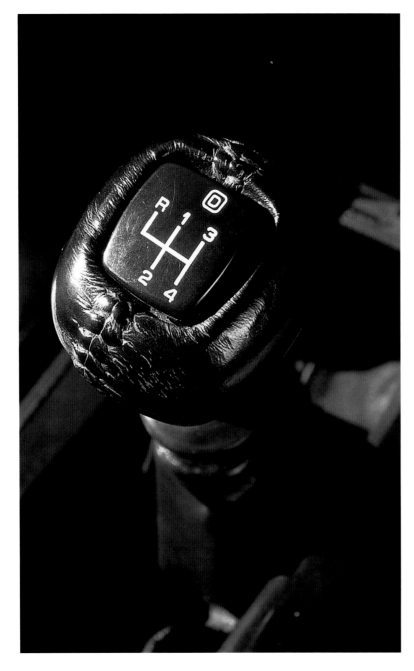

The car proved spectacularly fast, qualifying on the pole for dozens of events between mid-1985 and the end of the program in late 1988. Corvette GTPs won outright at West Palm Beach, Florida, and at Road Atlanta. The highly stressed V-6 failed sometimes, and the suspension challenged engineers. Yet Chevrolet continued its support because the engines offered promise for its Camaro production models and the suspension offered what Dave McLellan envisioned for the ZR1. He built at least one prototype with the GTP system. It fit crab-like over the LT5 engine, its plumbing adding 200 pounds to the car, about 6 inches to the hood height, and immeasurable uncertainty to the reliability the car had to have. The GTP proved that active suspension was worth the effort. McLellan sent his engineers off to work with Bosch on a modified version of Porsche's electronic system.

INTRODUCING THE LT5

The worldwide introduction took place in Geneva, Switzerland, in March 1989. Journalists raced the cars through mountains and praised the crews at Lotus, Mercury Marine, and Corvette. But that was routine compared to the press launch at Riverside Raceway in September 1988, described by Anthony Young. While the project managers spoke during the media introduction, two Mercury engineers, Chris Allen and Ron Opszynski, started assembling an LT5.

"They had been rehearsing this for weeks," Young wrote, "performing like a two-man pit crew. They put their tools down just as Midgley finished his last sentence. Midgley asked Allen and Opszynski if the engine would start. Both gave a thumbs up. Midgley said, 'Gentlemen, start your engine.'

"Ron flipped the switch and the engine turned over. [Chris] pulled the throttle linkage and when those throttle

(top left) In 1989, GM replaced the Doug Nash–designed 4+3-speed transmission shown here with a six-speed Zandfabrik Friedrichshafen (ZF) unit.

(left) The LT2 remained at 350-cubic-inch displacement, yet due to computer optimized ignition timing, a higher compression ratio, new camshafts, redesigned intake manifolds, cylinder heads, and a muiltiport fuel-injection system, Chevrolet boosted power to 300 net horsepower at 5,000 rpm.

plates opened and everyone heard the engine roar to life, that was the moment. In that dark amphitheater camera flashes started going off, people started clapping and whistling—it was amazing."

First production engines built by Mercury employees came off their line on July 13, 1989. The engines developed 380 horsepower. The new Corvettes reached 60 miles per hour in 4.2 seconds and a top speed of 172 miles per hour. They had met McLellan's target.

Midgley and his crew worked to get more power. Subtly modifying and improving air intakes, revising cam timing, and reducing exhaust back pressure helped them reach 405 horsepower for 1993. Even more impressively, they cleared the EPA gas guzzler mark of 22.5 miles per gallon. With 405 horsepower and 180 miles per hour capability, it returned 23.1 miles per gallon on the test cycle.

Option Z25 was the 40th Anniversary package that colored the car Ruby Red inside and out. The commemorative option added $1,455 to the price. Chevrolet produced 6,749 commemorative editions.

A car running 170 to 180 miles per hour needed brakes capable of hauling down this 3,000-pound-plus missile. During early days of development before engines were ready, development mules were still narrow-body Corvettes, not wide versions needed to accommodate Goodyear's new tires. Engineering built a 400-horsepower V-8 with nitrous oxide injection added to it. This would get the car to its top speed in the least distance to allow more runoff in case the brakes failed. Chevrolet hired Corvette Challenge racers Kim Baker and John Powell to do handling and brake testing. In Powell's first test, he targeted a 0.50g deceleration test from maximum speed to get a feel for the car. The calibration was incorrect, however. When Powell got on the brakes, he hauled the car down to a standstill at nearly 1.0g without any problem.

One troubling question Chevrolet faced was whether it should adorn the body with wings, spoilers, or scoops. Reuss wanted visual significance; Palmer disagreed. "The differences should be subtle," he told Anthony Young. "The only ones who really care are the Corvette people. They'll know." Palmer's staff mocked up Reuss' ideas, eventually incorporating many of them in the whole Corvette lineup for 1991. Only Palmer's understated widening of the car's rear end and its squarish taillights distinguished the LT5. The back end enlargement, 1.5 inches on each side, started with new outer door panels feathering in the additional size. It accommodated Goodyear's first 35-series Eagle road tire, P315/35ZR-17 rears, mounted in 11-inch-wide wheels.

Corvettes have often served as pace cars for the Indianapolis 500. 2002 General Motors Corporation. Used with permission of GM Media Archives.

The final question was a name. "King of the Hill" was what it had become, although many insiders knew this would provoke challengers to depose the king. There were other considerations, though. When Doug Robinson, the development manager of Corvette, reviewed McLellan's list of target vehicles, he found Porsche's 928, 968, and 959, Ferrari's Testarossa and F40, and Lamborghini's Countach. For the first time, Chevrolet wanted its car in Europe. Its name had to be easily translatable. ZR1, the small-block racing package introduced in 1970, fit nicely.

Following the media introductions through Switzerland and France afterward, Lloyd Reuss and his colleagues had another production reality to face. They had built only 84 preproduction prototypes for engineering, media preview, and photography with 1989 VINs. Chevrolet sold none of them, and on April 19, 1989, it notified dealers the ZR1 option would not be available until model year 1990.

U.S. buyers had to take normal-production Corvettes for 1989 with their six-speed transmission and FX3 adjustable suspension. This was no slouch, but by midmodel year, the enthusiast magazines had characterized the coming ZR1 as the second coming.

Model year 1990 finally introduced the production ZR1, an option that cost $27,016 on top of the price of the $31,979 coupe. Some 3,049 buyers couldn't resist and paid $58,995 for the car. This was one-third the price of Ferrari's Testarossa and four-fifths the cost of the Porsche 928GT. The ZR1 beat both to 60 miles per hour by 1.5 seconds, however. Due to gas-guzzler burdens, CAFE requirements, and EPA mandates, Chevrolet rated the LT5 at 375 horsepower.

Chevrolet engineers created a "valet switch" protection for ZR1 owners. The owner twisted a key to override the ECM so that no matter what throttle position the parking attendant (or teenage offspring) might try, only the milder injection tube operated.

It took little time before racers saw its potential without the valet. Peter Mills, a West Coast auto journalist, and Corvette racer Stu Hayner approached Corvette's development manager John Heinricy with the idea of using a new ZR1 to go after a 24-hour speed record. Heinricy liked it. Tommy Morrison got involved prepping the cars (Heinricy added an L98-engined coupe as well), and on March 1, 1990, after averaging 173.791 miles per hour for 24 hours to cover 4,221.3 miles on Firestone's Fort Stockton, Texas, test track, they went on another 4 hours and 46 minutes to reach 5,000 miles. This established the speed and durability of Chevrolet's newest ZR1. Morrison then took a look at what the ZR1s might do in long-distance wheel-to-wheel competition.

Design redid the interior for 1990, replacing the instrument panel with a new console (now a combination of LCDs, light shows, and analog dials), door panels, and a driver's side air bag. They gave buyers a real, working glove compartment, replacing the long-lived and unloved breadbox.

Production in 1990 amounted to 16,016 coupes including 3,049 ZR1 buyers, and 7,630 convertibles for a total of 23,646. Production in 1991 decreased to 14,967 coupes; convertible sales also slipped to 5,672. Among the coupes, 2,044 were ZR1s for which Chevrolet increased the price a substantial $4,676 to $31,683, or $64,138 for the second edition of the limited-production coupes.

Chevrolet made what many thought was a mistake in 1991. They adopted for all models the squared taillights first introduced on the 1990 production ZR1s.

The 40th Anniversary package provided Ruby Red leather sport seats; the driver's was power adjusted. All leather seats sold for model year 1993 had a 40th Anniversary logo stitched in, whether or not the commemorative package was ordered.

The pace car replicas used Corvette's 300-horsepower LT2 V-8. The package, RPO Z4Z, sold for $2,816, and Chevrolet ultimately manufactured 527 of the cars.

While the hotter car still wore wider bodywork, 1990 owners had expressed pleasure when others recognized the subtle distinction, and 1991 buyers made their discontent known when that uniqueness was taken away.

Following the land speed record run in March 1990, Tommy Morrison went to Daytona in February 1991 with two freshly converted ZR1s (one completed just hours before practice began; both cars already had at least 9,800 miles on them). Morrison, wary of using Daytona to debut the ZR1 as a race car against some of the world's toughest competitors, was a realist. "The Corvette has an important place as the American flagship car," he said at the time. "What we have to do is outlast the other guys." When the rain-soaked race ended, his car #92 finished 12th overall, 4th in GTO class. Car #91, piloted by Stu Hayner and John Heinricy as well as Scott Legase and Morrison, suffered several delays with electrical problems early and an off-road excursion late at night that damaged front bodywork and broke the oil cooler. Still, it finished 21st overall, 6th in GTO. Morrison

gave both cars bumper-to-bumper roll cages and carbon-fiber bodywork that cut nearly 600 pounds off each car's weight. Car #92 also ran a special Mercury Marine–produced LT5 engine that reportedly developed 520 horsepower. That car then finished 6th in class at Sebring a month later. Because #91 honorably represented American racing efforts and outlasted the others, Morrison retired it to its permanent display at the Smithsonian Institution's National Museum of American History.

More than three decades after the first Grand Sport racing prototypes snuck out of Zora Duntov's shops, Chevrolet commemorated the efforts with these non-racing versions. Offered as a coupe and convertible, Chevrolet produced just 1,000.

CHANGES FOR 1992

Model year 1992 brought numerous changes, including a new LT1 small-block powerplant, an electronic traction control to more successfully get its power to the ground and keep it there, another production offshoot of the GTP racers between 1986 and 1988, and a new Goodyear tire to further aid that task. When the new LT1 reached showrooms 20 years after the original 370-horsepower LT1 disappeared in 1972, it produced 300 net horsepower and provided 0–60 miles per hour times of four seconds, three full seconds faster than the 1972 model. While the old LT1 consumed 12 miles per gallon, the new engine with 50 horsepower more than the L98, returned 17 miles per gallon city and 25 highway.

The Bosch Acceleration Slip Regulation (ASR) performed like its ABS (antilock braking system) in reverse, controlling wheel spin under acceleration, not braking. Meant to limit those "Oh my God!" moments, the ASR worked liked an instantaneously reactive, very intelligent limited-slip differential. Coupled with Goodyear's new Eagle directional, asymmetrical GS-C P275/40Z–17 tires front and rear, Formula One and Indy race car technology for wet and damp and dry racing came to the street.

On July 2, 1992, many of the principals responsible for making the Corvette into what it had become gathered in Bowling Green for a celebration. The one millionth car, a white convertible, drove off the line. It went just a few blocks into storage, where it would await completion of its new home about a quarter-mile from the end of the Bowling Green assembly line.

Board members of the National Corvette Restorers Society voted in November 1988 to establish a national Corvette museum. Setting a budget of $6 million, they raised funds, acquired a site, and selected building architects and exhibit designers. They opened their 68,000-square-foot structure, constructed alongside Interstate 65, in 1994. Now they routinely display as many as 80 Corvettes at a time. The ever-changing exhibits usually include equal numbers of cars on loan from GM's own collection and from private collectors around the world as well as Corvettes the museum owns from generous donations made possible by the museum nonprofit tax-exempt status. The museum hosts numerous events each year, including Pace Car

reunions, and publishes its own monthly magazine, *America's Sports Car,* and it is home to the National Corvette Hall of Fame, a registry for designers, engineers, planners, managers, racers, and owners of significance to the history of the car. One popular feature is the museum's in-house delivery program where buyers of new model Corvettes who select option R8C can pick up their cars under the golden 140-foot-diameter, 100-foot-tall Skydome in the midst of Corvette's history. Following its opening, the National Corvette Museum quickly became a mecca for Corvette enthusiasts.

MORE POWER UNDER THE HOOD

The big news for 1993 was that Midgley's and McLellan's goal of 400+ horsepower under the hood of the ZR1 got to the dealerships. Engineering subtly changed intake valve head shape and the valve seat to improve fuel flow and overall breathing. This micro-tinkering brought output to 405 horsepower. Goodyear's asymmetrical GS-C's improved wet-weather maneuverability over the Gatorbacks at the modest cost of dry-pavement acceleration. Zero-to-60 miles per hour times slipped from 4.2 to 4.5 seconds.

Production was split with 810 coupes and just 190 convertibles. The cars came from the factory with black-painted wheels. Many owners later had them polished or replaced them with brushed or polished chrome.

Outside and inside the car, Chevrolet division celebrated the 40th anniversary with an appearance option, Z25 for $1,455, providing Ruby Red exterior paint and interior leather but no effect on performance. Some 6,749 were produced. Total production crept up slightly to 21,590, with 5,692 convertibles (at $41,195 base) and 15,898 coupes (at $34,595). Only 448 were ZR-1 options, still at $31,683 extra, despite the new engine.

Chevrolet upgraded the PASS-key system introduced in 1986 with the addition of the new Passive Keyless Entry (PKE). Engineering imbedded a tiny transmitter in the key fob that signaled one of two receivers in the car body to open one or both doors and light the interior. As owners walked away with their keys in pocket or purse, the PKE automatically locked their car and set the alarm, confirmed by a brief toot of the horn. With the key fob still in the car while walking away, nothing happened. No horn sounding was a reminder to return for the keys.

For 1994, Corvette engineers replaced the recently reintroduced glove compartment with a passenger-side air bag, and this provided the opportunity for an interior makeover. The interior studio redesigned the seats making them more comfortable to a wider variety of bodies.

Goodyear introduced Extended Mobility Tires (EMTs), essentially run-flat rubber useful at zero air pressure for up to 200 miles as fast as 55 miles per hour. An instrument panel monitor alerted the driver of low—or no—pressure. For a driver alone at night or in foul weather on a freeway in rush hour, there was no longer any risk. Corvettes still carried spare tires, jacks, and tire irons, and the EMT option was available only on about 5,000 of the 1994 model year cars with either the FX3 option (with slightly softer springs) or the base suspension, but not the Z01 or ZR-1.

Engineering and electronics engineers replaced the Engine Control Module (ECM) with a new powertrain control module (PCM) to control not only the transmission but also the new sequential-port fuel injection. In this system, the injectors worked simultaneously with the engine-firing order, offering smoother idle, quicker throttle response, and reduced exhaust emissions.

Production numbers for 1994 inched up again. Total Bowling Green output was 23,330 cars, of which 17,984 were coupes and 5,346 convertibles. Chevrolet sold only 448 ZR1s, though the price of $67,443 dropped a few dollars from the previous year as more equipment on the base car was made standard equipment. The bleed-through of engineering from the ZR-1 to the LT1 had produced a car so good that with few options (the G92 performance axle at only $50 and the FX3 electronic ride and handling option at $1,695), a buyer had as close to a ZR-1 as most customers could measure. The ZR-1's supplemental 105 horsepower made the biggest difference in speed ranges few owners ever saw, and insurance companies began to react to the ZR-1 code as they had to muscle cars in the late 1960s and early 1970s.

The Indianapolis Motor Speedway chose the 1995 Corvette as the 500-mile pace car. Palmer's designers developed a wild dark purple and white scheme and Chevrolet offered replicas to the public. They sold only 527; the two-tone combination put off more people than it attracted. In total, 4,971 convertibles sold, and Chevrolet repeated 1994 ZR-1 production with just 448 cars, making total 1995 coupe sales of 15,771. In anticipation of the C5 introduction, earlier scheduled for 1996, Chevrolet discontinued the ZR-1 package at the end of production of 1995 cars. Even when management

Chevrolet engineers never stopped tinkering with the venerable 350-cubic-inch V-8s. This latest version, LT4, used new aluminum heads, Crane roller rocker arms, revised cams, and other improvements to squeak out 330 net horsepower. It was standard with the Grand Sport Package.

Painted in Admiral Blue and emblazoned with a wide white racing stripe, the other subtle distinction was the pair of red stripes on the left fender.

The new Grand Sport also marked the end of the C4 chassis, fitted with options such as RPO F45 Selective Real-Time Damping. This suspension system read shock absorber loads 75 to 100 times a second and adjusted any one shock to improve handling instantly.

acknowledged that C5 would not be available until 1997, they let the ZR1 disappear. Mercury Marine assembled the last LT5 engine in November 1993. The total ZR1 count was 6,939 from 1990 through 1995.

GOODBYE TO THE C4

Spy photos confirmed that C5 was coming and that 1996 was the final year for C4; once again customers wrestled with waiting for the unknown new car or buying the familiar. To give them something to consider, Chevrolet released its new 330-horsepower LT4. Engineering used a new aluminum-head design, new camshaft, and Crane roller bearing rocker arms.

Externally, designers and product planners created two packages with visual appeal. The first was a silver-painted Collector Edition, the Z15, for $1,250. Besides color and special trim, it used ZR1 wheels (but not the tires), also painted silver. More exciting visually was the Grand Sport Package Z16. Chevrolet produced only 1,000 of these in coupe or convertible form ($2,880 for the convertible option, $3,250 for the coupe). Coupes used the full ZR1 wheel and tire option, including the fat, squat P315/35ZR-

17 rears, barely contained by fender flares (not, however, body panels like the ZR-1). Convertible Grand Sports took advantage of the tire package for the Collector Edition. Chevrolet painted the cars Admiral Blue with twin white racing stripes centered on the car and bright red slashes across the left front fender.

Dick Guldstrand's long racing and engineering relationship with Chevrolet saw him involved with improving the suspension of the C4 during its development. But Chevrolet didn't go far enough, so he took on the project himself with his 6590.

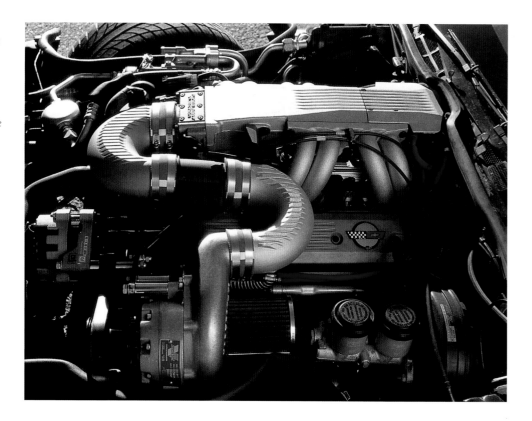

Guldstrand's Nassau Roadsters now boast 400 horsepower out of Chevrolet's LT1 through the use of a Vortech belt-driven supercharger. As always, Guldstrand's work not only performs exceptionally well, it is handsomely done.

This third completed Nassau Roadster carried on the styling cues introduced in Guldstrand's first GS-90 coupe. Huge vents aid in cooling front and rear brakes.

Chevrolet replaced the previous FX3 suspension with F45, "Selective Real Time Damping," a new active system that took road surface and suspension load inputs 60 times per second, revising shock characteristics with equal frequency. Chevrolet produced 21,536 1996 models, including the Grand Sports and 5,412 Collector Editions. The new $1,695 LT4 engine option went into nearly a third of all the cars.

Chevrolet carried on its fourth-edition Corvette for 13 years, another long run for a popular car. It sold 368,180 of them, earning GM nearly $100 million in profit. The car withstood attacks Nissan's 300ZX, Acura's NSX, Mitsubishi's 3000GT VR-4, Porsche's 959, 944, and 968, and from Dodge's 10-cylinder Viper. Lamborghini replaced its Countach with its Diablo, which for all its bravado represented only a slight movement of the benchmark. Only Ferrari, with its racecar-like F40 and F50, and England's Gordon Murray, with his $1 million McLaren three-seat F1, moved off into such rarified space that few could come close. Corvette's competitors came and went. They kept on coming, and to their chagrin, so did Corvette.

Guldstrand's lines put the Coke-bottle taper back into the middle of the car. He flared front and rear wheel houses to allow better brake cooling.

1997-2003

CHAPTER ELEVEN

THE ULTIMATE CORVETTE

t first emerged in the imaginations of a few dedicated individuals as early as August 1988. They hoped it would be released four years later, as a 1993 model, the 40th Anniversary Corvette. Between then and its eventual introduction as a 1997 car, the next generation C5 Corvette endured a Shakespearean saga performed by a cast of characters that included some of the most brilliant and dedicated people in modern automotive history. Like any great story, it also included some characters whose ideas and actions were dubious enough to cause later observers to wonder whose side they really were on. The protagonists broke rules or they rewrote them. They worked and connived to get designs approved, to gather personnel and garner funding, to get prototypes built and development cars to run until they stopped breaking. They produced the C5 seemingly despite diligent efforts by antagonists determined to make new rules, challenge and obstruct the car-building process, and stop this car every chance they found.

The late author James Schefter recorded the dramas that yielded the C5 in his book, *All Corvettes Are Red*. Its title comes from a quote from John Heinricy, Corvette racer, endurance record holder, and supervisor of the C4 until the end of the program. Heinricy maintains that all other colors are just mistakes. (Some Corvette collectors, for example, judge green as suitable only for primer.) Schefter's history takes readers deep inside GM to explain how the C5 came to be.

Titanic egos played roles in this story. Titanic describes their size and, in a few cases, their end. During the car's eight-year gestation—the darkest days of the automobile industry's economy—thousands of employees left the industry. GM lost hundreds of employees, including key engineers. So many engineers had left that during some critical periods of the C5's development, barely enough remained to do the work. Engineering staffs at Ford and *(previous spread) Among the Z06's unique cosmetic touches are the black air scoops for the rear brakes and the split-spoke wheels with a chrome finish.*

The C5's reversed air scoop behind the front wheel echoes Corvette designs of the past, while the car's aerodynamic shape pushes the modern wedge silhouette of recent Corvettes even further into the future.

(top opposite) When Jim Schefter,
historian and author of All Corvettes
Are Red, needed to raise money for
anticipated medical expenses, longtime
friends Bill and Sandie Herron of
Sarasota, Florida, bought his red coupe.

*The partnership between Engineering
and Design resulted in 3 inch lower
doorsills. New seats, produced by Lear,
weighed less, took less interior space,
and were preferred by more drivers.*

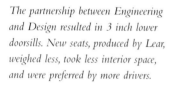

*(bottom opposite) Design and
engineering collaborated on this
Corvette more than any in the past.
The result was more interior space and
storage, better handling, better
performance, and a savings of 80
pounds over the C4.*

Chrysler swelled during this period as these companies took their pick from among hundreds of experienced, qualified individuals who left their jobs because of worries that GM may go bankrupt. As Chevrolet reinvented its Corvette, General Motors, which had reorganized before C5 development started, would reorganize itself a second and then a third time.

Corvette's competition had changed by 1988. Porsche's "affordable" front-engine cars had four-cylinder engines that matched the Corvette's top speed but not its acceleration or, initially, its braking. But Porsche's cars started at $45,000, beyond the price range most Corvette buyers would consider. Japanese cars were Corvette's biggest competition, cars in the Corvette's price range, cars like Mazda's RX-7, Nissan's 300ZX, Mitsubishi's 3000, and its Dodge Stealth twin. Toyota had a new Supra. Acura's NSX, while wildly different from the street-fighter-in-a-suit image of the ZR1, sold for $10,000 less. GM gave Chevrolet division $250 million to develop a car to meet any competition until at least the year 2000. Lloyd Reuss, GM executive vice-president, shared with Corvette Chief Engineer Dave McLellan and Chevrolet Design Studio Chief Jerry Palmer the goal of making a car that would *beat* all comers, in the marketplace or on a race track. Whatever had been good in 1988 must be great in 1993. They would accept only improvements in performance, handling, body design, interior comfort, and baggage space. In 1989, Jim Perkins directed Chevrolet as division general manager and GM vice president. His love for automobiles and the Corvette rivaled Ed Cole's 35 years before him, and few in his business were more enthusiastic.

To the outside world, GM's profit statements looked healthy. Inside, the picture was bleak and drawn in red ink. Worse yet, an offhand remark by GM Chairman Roger Smith, who had previously been something of a friend to the car, wasted a year. Made during a body styling review of

Corvette ideas, Smith's comment set design's development and experimentation chasing after midengine/transaxle configurations.

Worse, Smith's intentional message to the board cost Corvette an additional year. Cost containment realities slipped the 1993 launch back to 1994, and it would be a traditional front-engine, rear-drive Corvette. By midyear, more bad financial news forced the C5 back to 1995.

A SIX-YEAR CAR

Each reschedule led to new design directives. Chuck Jordan, GM's vice president of design since 1986, delivered the messages to his increasingly impatient designers. Jordan rewarded John Cafaro, who had created the C4's basic shape and its signature clamshell hood, with primary design authority for the C5. As each quarter's financial statements brought another year's delay to introduction, however, Jordan beleaguered anyone who'd listen that the Japanese, Corvette's target competitors, were not standing still and they could bring out their cars in three years. The C5 was on the way to being a six-year car.

Everywhere in the world, washing a car in the afternoon guarantees rain in the evening. Historian Jim Shefter's red C5 has found a good home in Sarasota.

Everything about the C5 was new, including its LS1 engine. This freshly designed 346-cubic-inch pushrod V-8 engine produced 345 horsepower at 5,600 rpm. The engine weighed 44 pounds less than the 1996 Grand Sport LT4.

The C5 appeared in convertible form a year after coupe introduction. Design provided the rear deck with a built-in tonneau, operable by a single button, to hide the cloth top.

GM's bean counters voiced their own perspective. Unlike any other GM product, this division sold every Corvette it produced. Congress had ended the car loan interest deduction with a 1986 law effective in 1989. Every U.S.-built model lost sales except Corvette. It continued to bring in profit, something like $4,000 per car, each year after the initial investment was paid off. Production was paid for at 16,500 cars; in 1989 Chevy sold 16,663 coupes, meaning the 163 coupes and all 9,749 convertibles made profits, nearly $40 million worth. Still, when GM's management got a clear view of its financial picture in late fall, it appeared that the Chevrolet-Pontiac-Canada (CPC) group, home of the Corvette, might lose $2.6 billion in 1990. At that point, the new Corvette was not just slipped. It was derailed indefinitely.

The engineering buildings were on the opposite side of the Warren campus from design. Dave McLellan, an imaginative and innovative creator, often led Corvette engineering by leaving his staff alone to make ideas happen. Roger Smith's offhand remark in the design auditorium resurrected midengines and all-wheel-drive ideas dating back as far as the XP-882. Yet bean counters could demonstrate that expensive engineering such as the 1990's ZR1 program had not proven financially beneficial to Chevrolet. Four-wheel-drive was something Corvette would leave to car makers

Corvette again paced the Indy 500 but this time the color scheme was harder for many people to take. Wild graphics adorned a Pace Car Purple finish. The package included bright yellow-painted wheels though these magnesium wheels were a popular option. Chevrolet produced 1,163 replicas (for an extra $5,039) and most owners quickly removed the gaudy exterior graphics decals.

(right) Part of the Pace Car Package was yellow and black leather sport seats. They did not fit everyone's taste.

content to sell cars at prices far above and production levels far below the Corvette.

But the C4 chassis was a problem that did need attention. Setting seats down between the frame rails left a high, broad door threshold that owners had to hurdle to enter the car. Corvettes still rattled and creaked—even the $60,000 ZR1— while other cars selling for less were quiet and felt solid.

Advanced vehicle engineering considered using a "backbone" frame, a variation of a ladder frame in which main rails passed along the outside of the car while cross members tied one side to the other. The tunnel that formed the central backbone fixed these members into place and shrouded the driveshaft between the engine and the rear axle. The C4's modified unibody included the birdcage and its high doorsill along with all the body attachment points that eventually rattled. Comprising 20 separate pieces welded to one another, the unibody always was risky. Any error in measurement, alignment, or welding was magnified when assemblers added the birdcage and attached the body. Now engineering attached the body directly to the frame to eliminate the birdcage. This alone was a significant improvement in chassis integrity and durability.

Thin-walled steel produced under high pressure provided the strength of the old frame with much less weight. Engineering used a technique called hydroforming. They formed the major frame rails for C5, one on each side, from a single piece of rolled, welded steel. The new rails started out as 14-foot-long sheets 2 millimeters thick. The new process rolled these into a 6-inch-diameter tube and then laser welded them shut. The tubes went into a 200-ton press that filled them with water at 7,000 pounds-per-square-inch (psi) pressure. This water pressure expanded the tube like a sausage. The press shaped and bent the steel into the bends and rectangular channels inside of the mold. They came out of the press, 15 an hour, 13 feet long, and perfect.

While $250 million was a sizable sum, it left little allowance for false starts or missteps. Chuck Jordan's designers pursued Roger Smith's front cockpit, midengine, rear-drive idea, even as Dave McLellan's engineers still advocated the front-engine, midcockpit, rear-drive configuration. Still, engineers like the challenges of radical projects and midengines offered designers opportunities to produce a Corvette very different from its past. Palmer and his staff fought hard to keep it alive, but Perkins and Reuss could not afford it.

For the first time since 1962, the Corvette has a trunk with outside access. The efficient body design still allowed 11 cubic feet of storage space in the convertible with the top down and stowed.

Callaway's tweaks to the 346-cubic-inch V-8 yields 440 horsepower at 6300 rpm and a pavement shredding 420 pounds-feet torque at 4800 rpm. The entire package weighs about 3,380 pounds.

(opposite) From the fertile minds that created the Callaway Speedster came this C12 coupe. Its lines—to say nothing of its engine rumble—confuse everyone as to its origin.

(below) Callaway's wizard body designer Paul Deutschman produced something barely resembling the car from which it was derived. He and Callaway composed its body of carbon fiber, Kevlar, and fiberglass.

There are more options for Callaway's C12 interior than Chevrolet offered during the heydays of muscle cars. Carbon fiber peeks out from many panels.

Smith's midengine misdirection forced engineering and design to work side by side for the first time to meet their goal. The two sides created a car with nearly five times as much resistance to twisting and flexing as the C4. This was another benefit to this collaborative working arrangement and to the hydroformed chassis. This backbone chassis encouraged them to use a transaxle, a one-piece transmission-differential they bolted directly to the rear axle. Moving this weight rearward allowed the nearly 50/50 front-to-rear weight balance that midengines offered. With the transmission bulk out of the cockpit foot well, designers and engineers moved the entire compartment forward slightly, opening up rear space for a luggage compartment. Golf was the game of business. Japanese cars accommodated two golf bags. Now so did the Corvette.

In summer 1990, GM's board named Bob Stempel, a former engineer and former general manager of Chevrolet, as its chairman, and Lloyd Reuss became president. While they were longtime

This is the first product of Callaway Cars Europe GmbH though the title registers it as a Corvette. The Borg-Warner six-speed and a switchable traction control give the C12 the versatility to spin rear tires in 1st through 4th gears.

Corvette supporters, they had a corporation to save. GM was in deep trouble. The Corvette took another big hit.

James Schefter reported that instead of a C5 for 1995, the board ordered a thorough reskin for the C4, slipping the C5 back to 1998. Yet all passenger cars sold in the United States for 1997 had to have side-impact protection requiring a structure engineering could not incorporate into the C4. At this point, some directors suggested that the Corvette was superfluous; no other American car maker produced a sports car, and GM could no longer afford the luxury of this exclusive product. Others felt that Chevrolet, GM's car maker for the masses, was the wrong parent for such exclusivity. GM definitely needed it, they argued, but the car ought to be its own division entirely. Jim Perkins protested that making the car its own product line would confuse and destroy customer loyalty. What's more, killing off GM's showcase product would damage its image irrevocably. Corvettes generated more than half the GM-related stories in newspapers or magazines except for disheartening financial analyses at that time. If the board killed the Corvette, writers would dig deeply into how GM foundered so badly that it would kill its profit leader.

Stempel's board gave Perkins a small budget to re–skin the C4, leaving the C5 with a 1998 introduction deadline. Then Lloyd Reuss spoke; recognizing the side-impact requirements, he reinstated the

Testers reached 60 miles per hour in 4.2 seconds, but the real strength of this machine is its long-legged running. A quarter-mile happens in 12.8 seconds at 116 miles per hour. Top speed is better than 188 miles per hour.

This was the third body incarnation that Chevrolet General Manager Jim Perkins conceived when he approved the C5 project. With its fixed hardtop welded in place, it weighed 80 pounds less than the coupe and was 12 percent stiffer.

budget for the C5 for a new body, backbone chassis, and, now, for a 1996 launch. The C5 would be introduced first as a Targa-roof coupe. A full convertible would appear for 1997 as well as an entry-level hardtop, a $25,000 to $30,000 concept close to Perkins' heart, a boy-racer he nicknamed "Billy Bob."

Then profit and loss statements for the corporation arrived. CPC lost $3.3 billion, not the 2.6 predicted. Projections for 1991 hinted that GM could be bankrupt sometime in 1991. Roger Smith had relied on separate plants for separate vehicles much like Billy Durant's uncontrolled product lineup 75 years earlier. Worse, he had replaced low-tech but generally adaptable people with high-tech difficult-to-relocate-and-reprogram robots that now left profitable lines suffering from insufficient capacity. The board cut Corvette's budget and the car slipped to 1997. In 1991, GM lost $4.5 billion; John Smith, GM's new president, relieved Lloyd Reuss of his duties. Bob Stempel, the "car guy" engineer never trained in the financial tricks required to drive a stalled leviathan out of someone else's quagmire, resigned in October 1992. John Smale replaced Stempel as board chairman. Corvette remained in Chevrolet, but the board warned engineering to find a way to retrofit side-impact protection to the C4 as a worst-case 1997 scenario.

Dave McLellan followed Stempel and Reuss out the door, retiring the next August. Dave Hill, Cadillac's chief engineer,

Jim Perkins conceived the body style as a boy racer, a car he lovingly nicknamed "Billy Bob." When accountants realized he was going to remove profit-producing options, they vetoed his idea but approved the bodystyle.

Because this was essentially the convertible's optional hardtop welded on, the new bodystyle kept the convertible's trunk. It provided about 14 cubic feet of storage capacity.

replaced him. Hill had McLellan's brilliance with better management and performance skills. Chuck Jordan retired in October, replaced by European design boss Wayne Cherry as administrative boss and by Chevy design chief Jerry Palmer as director of design for North American operations, now incorporating CPC, Oldsmobile, Buick, and Cadillac divisions.

According to Schefter, the first driveable C5 test vehicle was a $1.2 million mule called CERV-4. Soon after, there was a half-price copy, the CERV-4b. Engineering set 1993 C4 bodies on C5 frames and ran them around Milford and GM's Desert Proving Ground in Mesa, Arizona. They were undistinguishable except that they had a trunk. There was scarcely any money available from the board to create these most necessary first cars, so Jim Perkins discretely funneled other division funds into the Corvette program he'd fought so hard to preserve.

The hardtop got Chevrolet's new LS1 345-horsepower 346-cubic-inch engine and was only available with the manual transmission. Buyers got the Z51 sport suspension as standard equipment.

After the CERVs came "alpha" and then "beta" test cars, each wearing close-to-correct C5 bodies that they heavily disguised, engineering assembled these two, closely matching production specifications. Then came prototypes, nearly perfect from an engineering and design point of view, fabricated from preproduction versions of production parts. As testers devoured these, prepilot cars began to appear, the first ones actually assembled in Bowling Green starting August 1996. Chevrolet command had changed by this time. John Middlebrook took over to replace Perkins, who retired feeling fairly certain the C5 would appear. "Pilot" cars, the first saleable production vehicles, began a month later.

The two CERVs used C4 engines and existed primarily to examine the chassis. They got cobbled-together interiors to test heating, ventilation, and air-conditioning. Engineering created a new powerplant for the C5, known as Gen III. It was an all-new, third-generation version of the decades-old Chevy small block. Responses from thousands of owner and customer surveys reinforced another ZR1 lesson. Corvette owners wanted torque, not turbos or superchargers. They didn't want the added expense of four-valve heads with dual-overhead camshafts. Engineer Dave Hill liked the ZR1 LT5 and Cadillac's 32-valve Northstar, but he was a realist. He knew pushrod engines were not as tall as overhead-cam and multivalve engines. A low hood improved forward visibility, a longtime customer complaint, and this was essential to achieve their aerodynamic drag coefficient targets, which were crucial to meeting fuel-consumption goals.

Black leather seats were the only interior option. Sport seats could not be fitted and other colors were not offered.

John Lingenfelter is as well known a driver as he is an engine builder. Lingenfelter Performance Engineering produced the 1,200-horsepower engine for Reeves Callaway's famous "Sledgehammer" speed record car, and John drove the machine to 254 miles per hour on the 7.5-mile course at East Liberty, Ohio.

Engineering cast the Gen III engine in aluminum to save weight. The aim was to get the car below 3,500 pounds with full tanks, two passengers, and luggage. Every pound of weight increased fuel consumption, and tire, brake, and engine wear. Excess weight decreased shock absorber life, added strain to chassis and driveline, and detracted from performance. Engineering developed research figures equating improved acceleration time with increased sales. Weight became an obsession.

John Cafaro's sleek body had gotten aerodynamic adjustments from engineer Kurt Romberg, who shaved its shape. The C5 measured 0.293-cubic-inch displacement in the wind tunnel, the lowest of any production vehicle made anywhere except for GM's EV1 electric vehicle. With its twin gas tanks straddling the rear axle, and new Goodyear run-flat extended mobility tires requiring no spare (the rears measured 1 inch wider than 1996 C4s), the C5 offered 23.8 cubic feet of trunk space, more than Cadillac's largest full-size sedans. Engineering found ways to eliminate more than 1,400 separate parts from the previous car, each piece costing from fractions of a cent to many dollars. Eliminating these parts also cut 69 pounds from the 1996 C4 weight. The body, formed in plastic, not fiberglass, saved weight as well. The C5 uses sheet-molded compound-plastic (SMC) and reaction injection-molded plastic (RIM). These technologies produced lighter, stronger, and more rigid panels.

In creating the C5, engineering examined not only the cost to buy the car but also ongoing costs of ownership. The huge clamshell hood was removed from the C4 because insurance companies factored in replacement parts and labor charges when establishing premium rates. The large hood with its bonded fenders made the C4 expensive to repair. Engineering bolted the C5 fenders onto the frame.

The rear suspension no longer relied on the half-axles to perform suspension duties. Upper control arms locked the rear wheels into place much more accurately. As a by-product of the C5's stiffer backbone frame, engineers softened the transverse fiberglass springs technology adapted from the C4. This allowed a better ride and kept the tires in contact despite road surface changes.

The GEN III LS1 engine produced 345 horsepower, 15 more than the C4 LT4. This moved the car from 0–60 miles per hour in 4.7 seconds with the six-speed manual gearbox. Yet EPA fuel economy numbers were published as 18 city/29 highway miles per gallon. Chevy quoted top speed at 172 miles per hour.

While magazine reviewers loved the car, buyers barely sauntered to dealerships. With only a fastback coupe available, Chevrolet produced just 9,752 of the coupes, at a base price of $37,495. But the pace accelerated throughout model year 1998 when Jim Perkins' convertible appeared. While it weighed 114 pounds less than the 1996 convertible, it was four times stiffer. While its trunk, the first in a Corvette since 1962, measured 13.8 cubic feet (just over half the coupe's capacity), it still held two full golf bags. And while it sold for $44,425, Chevrolet produced more of them than it had 1997 coupes, 11,849 in all, as well as 19,235 coupes. Of the 31,084 Corvettes manufactured, 5,356 featured the optional active handling system, a $500 version of the earlier racing GTP's immensely complicated suspension. Fewer buyers selected the $5,408 Indy Pace Car replica option. Its vivid purple

(lower left) John Lingenfelter offers modification packages for the C3, C4, and C5. Most impressive is this 500TT twin-turbocharged model with 500 horsepower and 500 foot-pounds of torque. He mounts the turbos low, flanking the oil pan.

(lower right) For those to whom information is important, LPE pays attention. A small, lighted boost gauge mounted on the driver's A-pillar is an optional part of the package for an additional $339.

After interviewing other "tuners," the owners went to Chuck Mallett of Berea, Ohio, looking for a 50-state legal, street-drivable car that could run 200 miles per hour in order to win a Nevada open road race. Only Mallett could deliver a car that could also pass California's stringent smog tests.

exterior, wild graphics, yellow wheels, and yellow and black leather interior spoke to only 1,163 souls. The Corvette itself, however, spoke clearly again to the automotive media, which named the 1998 model the North American Car of the Year during the North American International Auto Show in Detroit.

GOING RACING

On November 4, 1998, Chevrolet division's general manager John Middlebrook made a startling announcement. Chevrolet was going sports car racing, and not just in some clandestine Zora Duntov manner in which various engineers coincidentally took vacations during race weekends at Daytona, Sebring, or Le Mans. This was a full-on and very public effort. The program would be overseen by

Mallett's options include lowering the car 1.5 inches, fitting Fikse three-piece forged alloy wheels, and a catalog full of other things. Basic conversion to the Mallett 435 cost $34,650, though nothing about the result is basic.

That's not low altitude flight velocity. That's all four wheels on the ground during the Silver State 100, an unlimited speed open road race over Nevada highways. This car won the 2001 event by 2 seconds.

GM's motorsports manager, Herb Fischel, and racing program manager, Doug Fehan. They intended to compete internationally in FIA's category GT2, where the racer car's chassis must be production-based, engines production-derived, and bodies only slightly modified. The Corvette would race head-to head against twin-turbo Porsche 911 GTs and V-10 Vipers among others. Their C5-R would debut at the January 30 to 31, 1999, 24 Hours of Daytona, then move on to the Sebring 12 Hours and through several of the Petit Le Mans series events in preparation to attempt the full 24-hour French race in June 2000.

Fischel and Fehan tagged Ken Brown, the engineer who had designed the C5's chassis and suspension for Corvette chief engineer Dave Hill, to design the C5-R. Corvette brand manager Jim Campbell told them their "primary focus was to improve the breed," and "to squeeze valuable engineering information from each lap Corvette turns on the racetrack." They reduced the weight from the production car's 3,245 pounds to 2,510 pounds. John Cafaro's production body, reproduced in carbon fiber, helped save weight. It needed only minor attention from aerodynamicist Brian Miller, who developed front underbody ducting to assist with engine cooling, down force, and drag. He also added a rear wing and

Before trials and tribulation, before dirt, and before victory, the GTS class-winning C5-R Corvette pitted for tires, fuel, and a driver change. Hyper-efficient pit stops helped hold its lead, even after a spin put it into the gravel traps. Photo copyright Peter Brock

Mallett's technicians offer a "four-point chassis stiffener," and created this eight-point roll cage and other required safety equipment to meet race rules. The owners added the navigation and timing devices.

(below) Moments from sweet victory, both team cars had spent most of an exceptionally wet race running on rain tires, avoiding disasters on the track, and making up time from frustrating parts failures. At the end of 24 hours, none of it mattered. Photo copyright Peter Brock

From its introduction at Road Atlanta in mid-December 1998, through the 1999 racing season, the C5-R ran silver and black Mr. Goodwrench colors before going to all yellow. Here, in late afternoon during the American LeMans Series, called Petit LeMans, its headlights announce a fast qualifying run was underway. Photo copyright Peter Brock

The 2nd place finisher at Sebring 2001 sits beside a spare engine before the start of the 12-hour race. Mechanics tie-wrapped a spare oil-pump drive belt to an engine mount, a preparation that saved the entry during the 24 Hours of Le Mans four months later. Photo copyright Peter Brock

rear diffusers. FIA rules strictly prescribed horsepower output based on vehicle weight, increasing the technical challenges. To meet the formula, Joe Negri, GM's motorsports engine director, revised engine dimensions from the production Gen III LS1's 346-cubic-inch displacement to 365-cubic-inch displacement. Chevrolet published output as 600 horsepower at 7,200 rpm. By the end of the 24-hour Daytona race, drivers Ron Fellows, John Paul Jr., and Chris Kniefel had nursed their silver and black C5-R #2 through a time-consuming and position-sacrificing morning oil leak to finish 3rd in GT2 and 18th overall, having climbed as high as 5th overall through much of the night. The second car, #4, finished well back after breaking a rear suspension upright. While everyone had hoped for better results, racing is an alchemist's blend of preparation and luck. By season end, Fehan and his crew had learned lessons about parts and tracks. They committed to run at least four events in 2000.

Production numbers for 1999 road-going cars were strong, with a total of 33,270 produced, including 4,031 of the new hardtop that Jim

Perkins first envisioned. His plan was to provide privateer racers an "option deleted" fixed-roof version, with cloth seats, no air-conditioning, power steering, brakes, windows, door locks, no radio, and rubber mats in place of interior carpeting. Weekend hobbyists could trailer these to parking lot Auto Cross or SCCA Solo I events. When cost accountants examined Perkins' first proposal, they revised the description because losing the profitable options would cost the division too much. When the hardtop arrived it was well equipped.

CORVETTE HITS LE MANS

Model year 2000 was one of refinements, improvements, revisions, increases, and continuing healthy sales. While the hardtop production dipped almost in half to just 2,090, overall figures totaled 33,682, and Corvette's racing effort officially reached Le Mans. Following a February second-place overall finish behind a French-entered Viper GTS-R, Chevrolet prepared to go abroad. Already plans were floating to promote and sell the C5 in Europe and in Great Britain. European journalists told *Corvette Quarterly* editor John Stein that they considered the Corvette more a touring car than a sports car. That was before the race. When it ended on June 18, one of the Corvettes, #63, having had its racing transmission replaced in 16 minutes, set the quickest laps in GTS class, ahead of every Porsche and faster than the Vipers. With two hours to go, the #64 car lost its starter in the pits, consuming another 12 minutes for the replacement. Then the checkered flag fell. The Corvettes finished 10th and 11th overall, 3rd and 4th in GTS class. Dave Hill, who admitted Le Mans was always in his plans for the C5, told John Stein that he was "very glad we came."

The Corvette has a long served as a platform for the introduction of new technologies, and the C5 is no exception. A heads-up instrument display, drive-by-wire throttle, and a stability control system are all part of the leading-edge C5.

Only the hardtop body was stiff enough to handle the potential of the new LS6 engine and Z06 package. Both numbers harkened back to higher performance times (the LS6 was Chevrolet's monstrous 454-cubic-inch muscle engine in the early 1970s.)

In the fall of 2000, Chevrolet resurrected the Z06 racing model designation that brought wide grins and wild eyes even to Corvette buyers who only wanted to grand tour. Available only in the hardtop body, the 2001 model car reminded historians and racers alike of the ZR-1 models from 1990 and even Duntov's first production racers from 1963. With 385 horsepower in a 3,115-pound car, the Z06 achieved 0–60 miles per hour in 4.0 seconds flat, half a second quicker than the ZR-1s. The car's interior was slightly less refined than the convertibles or coupes, but its nature was performance at the expense of grand touring. Stronger valve springs allowed its LS6 engine to reach 6,500 rpm where the standard LS1 was limited to 6,000 rpm. Under the hood, design and engineering fitted red engine

The Z06 got its own suspension designation for 2002 in the FE45 system. It included a stiffer rear leaf monospring, a larger diameter front stabilizer bar, and revised front camber settings to improve cornering.

The original LS6 Z06 option provided buyers with 385 horsepower. Several internal modifications brought that output up to 405 horsepower for this 2002 model. The original Z06 was a racer's package available in 1963.

covers, while red-disc brake calipers peeked through the wheels and functional ventilation cooled the rear brake rotors. It arrived as Corvette's highest priced variant, at $47,500, just $500 more than the convertible. Production finished at 5,773 copies for its first year.

On February 1, at Daytona International Speedway, Ron Fellows, Chris Kniefel, Frank Freon, and Johnny O'Connell brought their C5-R home in first place, first overall, and first in class. They were soon followed by the late Dale Earnhardt, his son Dale Jr., Andy Pilgrim, and Kelly Collins, who finished in fourth overall, second in GTS class. The two Corvettes were split by a pair of GT1 Porsches, identical to models that had won Le Mans in 1998. Fellow's car covered 2,335.4 miles averaging 97.3 miles per hour. The results humbled project manager Doug Fehan, who told *Corvette Quarterly* editorial director Jerry Burton, "The fact that we can compete with them at all is testimony to how far we've come and how great a car the Corvette is." Just four-and-a-half months later, Corvettes proved Daytona was no fluke, finishing first and second in GTS class at the 24 Hours of Le Mans and establishing the car's reputation worldwide.

For model year 2002, Chevrolet continued to improve its production Corvettes, boosting Z06 output to a muscle car–era 405 horsepower by fitting slightly softer piston rings, using a well-known NASCAR engine–builder's trick that allows even higher engine speeds. Chevrolet designers and engineers in Detroit and assemblers in Bowling Green did such a good job refining the car that J. D. Power named it the best premium sports car in their Initial Quality Study. Yet the future and time wait for no one.

In a design studio in Pasadena, clay modelers fashion concepts of the C6. Conceived at one time to be the 50th Anniversary model, it has been slipped back like many before it. Those who have been privileged to see the shapes have struggled for words, and then finally, haltingly, concluded that "if they build that one, they'll blow everybody else off the road. Everybody!"

Whether Chevrolet will select one of the Pasadena designs or one of the Warren versions is a question perhaps best left to Las Vegas odds makers, or certainly to GM's new chief executive officer Bob Lutz. The visual lineage of the car has evolved more subtly through the C4 into the C5, while changes from the C1 through the C2 to the C3 were more radical. But these design and engineering decisions are based on money and courage and faith and optimism. The Europeans say that winning at Le Mans is not a one-time thing. They rebuke Audi, which won outright in 1999 but then went into Formula 1. Yet racing is staggeringly expensive and no corporation will continue when

Both the 50th Anniversary logo and the wheel were distinctive and different. The wheel had a unique warmer, more golden color than stock wheels and was only available for the commemorative package. 2002 General Motors Corporation. Used with permission of GM Media Archives.

In a striking departure from the past, the Anniversary models were delivered with a shale—khaki—interior rather than the traditional all-black Corvette interior.

money gets tight or priorities change or other products need massive infusions. Before year-end 2001, Chevrolet announced it will not sell Corvettes directly in England in 2002. Yet the car has made money and it has made converts. The C4 brought us the ZR1 and world distance records, and the C5 brought us the Z06 and world-class, headline-making racing victories. It is tantalizing to slip into a new Corvette, squint past the heads-up information display, and try to imagine the road ahead for America's sports car.

Getting a jump on its anniversary, the 50th Anniversary Package debuted at the 2002 Indy 500 as the official pace car. Chevrolet had no plans to offer replicas (though it considered offering a pace car graphics package as a dealer option) and only three pace cars were built.

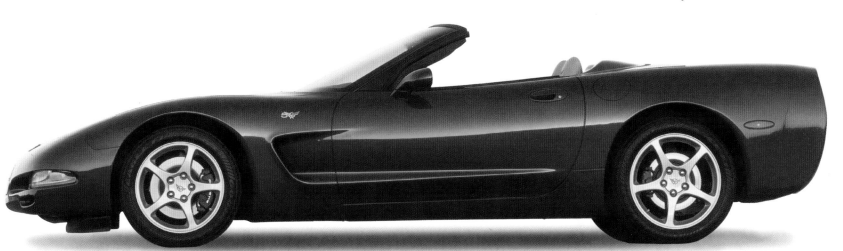

INDEX